Francis A. Drexel
LIBRARY

Books For College Libraries
Third Edition

Core Collection

HARVARD HISTORICAL STUDIES

Published under the direction
of The Department of History
From the income of
The Henry Warren Torrey Fund

VOLUME LXXX

FARM POLICIES AND POLITICS

IN THE TRUMAN YEARS

BY ALLEN J. MATUSOW

HARVARD UNIVERSITY PRESS

CAMBRIDGE, MASSACHUSETTS · 1967

For my mother and father

PREFACE

During the presidency of Harry S. Truman, food, farmers, and farm policies had a large, sometimes even critically important part to play in both foreign and domestic affairs. It was grain, for instance, from American farms that saved Europe after World War II and votes from the farm belt that helped elect Truman in 1948. In addition, policy-makers of that era met the threat of surpluses with creative answers that have had lasting effects on the debate over the farm problem. The story of farmers and public policy during the Truman years seems, therefore, worth telling, but no effort has been made in this study to tell it all. I hope the subjects selected here will illuminate the larger character of the Truman Administration and chart the course of farm politics in a crucial transition period.

I should like to express my sincere thanks to Professor Frank Freidel of Harvard for his unfailing kindness and good advice during the preparation of this monograph. I thank, too, the Truman Foundation and Rice University for their generous grants in support of my research. Mr. Wayne Rasmussen and Miss Gladys Baker of the United States Department of Agriculture contributed many hours of conversation, information, and criticism that were an invaluable aid. To Miss Helen Finneran of the National Archives and Mr. Jerry Hess of the Truman Library, I owe the debt felt by all scholars to the conscientious archivist. To Mrs. Betty Griffin and to my mother, I offer my gratitude for their able secretarial assistance. And finally, I thank my father for his careful and intelligent criticism of this manuscript and for his encouragement at every stage in its preparation.

Allen J. Matusow

Cambridge, Massachusetts
Summer 1966

CONTENTS

FARM POLICIES AND POLITICS
IN THE TRUMAN YEARS

ABBREVIATIONS

Ag. Hist. Br.	Agricultural History Branch
BAE	Bureau of Agricultural Economics
ERS	Economic Research Service
ESA	Economic and Statistical Analysis
FU	Farmers Union
FUL	Farmers Union Library, Denver, Colorado
Gen'l Cor.	General Correspondence
N.A.	National Archives, Washington
OF	Official Files
OFAR	Office of Foreign Agricultural Relations
OPA	Office of Price Administration
Sec. of Ag.	Secretary of Agriculture
TL	Truman Library, Independence
TP	Truman Papers, Independence
USDA	United States Department of Agriculture

1 A SEASON OF DRIFT

✦ Harry S. Truman was the first president since Ulysses S. Grant to work part of his adult life as a dirt farmer. "That boy," his mother once said of him, "could plow the straightest row of corn in the whole county."[1] Though Truman did not actually take to the plow until he was twenty-two, he had never really been far from the land. Some of the happiest years of his childhood were the three that he spent on the farm of his maternal grandfather in Grandview, Missouri. There he lived the rural idyll so celebrated by poets and politicians, playing in mudholes, going to county fairs, eating apple butter, and riding his own Shetland pony.[2] When he was six, his father moved to the nearby town of Independence to raise his family and to make his fortune. But in 1902, less than a year after Harry graduated from high school, John Truman went broke speculating on grain futures, and his son had to give up hope of going to college. In the next few years, Harry Truman worked for the Santa Fe Railroad as a timekeeper, for the *Kansas City Star* in the mailing room, and finally as a bank clerk in Kansas City. In 1904 his father, still down on his luck, moved back to the 600-acre farm in Grandview to take over management for his mother-in-law.

---

[1] Cyril Clemens, *The Man from Missouri* (New York: International Mark Twain Society, 1945), p. 15.

[2] Harry S. Truman, *Memoirs,* I (Garden City, N.Y.: Doubleday and Company, Inc., 1955), 113–117.

1

Two years later Harry Truman quit the bank to share in the labor and for the next eleven years, mixed his sweat with the soil.[3] According to one enthusiastic biography, he soon "learned to bang the No. 12 scoop against the corn-crib door and yell 'whoo-e-e' to call the hogs from a quarter of a mile away, and to bellow 'so-o boss' until the cows over the hill came galloping awkwardly to the barn . . . He learned to 'juice' a cow in a matter of minutes, and listened for the first streams of milk to rattle into the tin pail . . ." [4] He also saved his money and in 1916, the same year that he fell heir to a part ownership in the Grandview farm, he invested in zinc mining and became an officer and stockholder in an oil venture. But it was World War I rather than the oil business that was to rescue him from the oblivion of the plow. As Truman himself later recognized, the network of friendships that he made as an officer in Battery D of the 129th Field Artillery Regiment made possible his success when in 1922, at the age of thirty-eight, he entered local politics. (Jim Pendergast, for instance, nephew of the infamous Tom Pendergast, boss of Kansas City, served as a lieutenant in the 129th.) In the years that followed, a series of astounding accidents took this sometime farmer from county commissioner of Jackson County to the presidency of the United States.[5]

Unprepared for the awesome responsibilities that suddenly became his, the new president struggled to accustom himself to the power that he now possessed but claimed he never desired. At first unsure of his powers, Truman in his first

[3] Jonathan Daniels, *The Man of Independence* (New York: J. B. Lippincott Company, 1950), pp. 46, 49, 54, 59, 72; Alfred Steinberg, *The Man from Missouri* (New York: G. P. Putnam's Sons, 1962), pp. 29–32.

[4] Frank McNaughton and Walter Hehmeyer, *This Man Truman* (New York: McGraw-Hill Book Company, Inc., 1945), p. 27.

[5] Daniels, *Man from Independence*, pp. 80–83, 90, 98–99; Steinberg, *Man from Missouri*, pp. 59–60; Truman, *Memoirs*, I, 136.

term tended to rely on his subordinates to perform the real tasks of policy-making. Even in farm matters where he might have legitimately claimed special interest or knowledge, Truman was a minor figure who intruded only infrequently into the realm of policy. Because some of the most urgent problems of his early presidency were farm problems, his abdication of executive authority was no mere historical curiosity, for it aggravated the serious food crises that the nation faced as it began the postwar period.

The farm problems that almost overwhelmed Truman's early presidency had their origin in the war. "Food will win the war and write the peace," said the Department of Agriculture, but the Department was often reluctant to believe its own slogan. Conditioned by the long trauma of the Depression, many food officials labored through the war years more fearful of returning surpluses than of the world food shortages that were mounting yearly. Nevertheless, by the war's end, in spite of hesitancy and foreboding, American agriculture had expanded production by 33 percent above the prewar (1935–1939) average, an achievement that kept allied armies reasonably well supplied and gave pride to farmers and the Government.[6] Critics have noted, however, that this expansion was considerably less than the Department's own studies showed possible.[7] Moreover, the government's management of the food supply often seemed wanting in courage. The insistent demand of American consumers for more food found a better reception in Washington than pleas from liberated areas abroad or from the allied governments. Suddenly in possession of large income, Americans ate better

[6] On expectation of returning surpluses, see for instance Walter W. Wilcox, *Farmers in the Second World War* (Ames, Iowa: Iowa State College Press, 1947), pp. 278–280.

[7] For a critical discussion of the government's food policies, see Bela Gold, *Wartime Economic Planning in Agriculture* (New York: Columbia University Press, 1949), *passim*. For Gold's discussion of gap between potential and actual production, pp. 69–77.

in World War II than in any previous era of their history, per capita consumption rising 12 percent above the prewar average by 1945. (Between 1909 and 1939, the per capita increase was only 6 percent.) After 1943, while consumption at home was reaching new records, America repeatedly failed to meet the commitments that it had made to help feed the liberated areas.[8]

In 1943 impatience with the Department's performance led Roosevelt to create a War Food Administration (WFA) composed of most of the action agencies of the Department and part of the War Production Board to handle food problems. Claude R. Wickard, Secretary of Agriculture since 1940, was thereby permitted to hold his title, but the real power went to the Food Administrator, who, for most of the rest of the war, was former Congressman Marvin Jones. Since the Department of Agriculture staffed the War Food Administration, this Rooseveltian improvisation proved inadequate. If anything, matters got worse.[9]

In the last half of 1944, when fears of possible postwar surpluses became intense, the government made its most serious mistakes. The WFA had been listening to military prophecies that victory was only months away. It had observed with relief an easing of the domestic shortages that had plagued the nation in 1943. And most important, it had examined a few shreds of doubtful evidence and concluded that the famine long expected to descend on Europe at the end of the war would never occur. Decreasing exports, cutbacks in military needs, perhaps even domestic depression would soon produce "the greatest surplus of food and fibers ever known in the history of the world," to quote one food official. The emphatic dissents of Herbert H. Lehman of the

[8] Gold, *Wartime Economic Planning*, p. 328 and pp. 297–319.
[9] Dean Albertson, *Roosevelt's Farmer* (New York: Columbia University Press, 1961), *passim*.

4

United Nations Relief and Rehabilitation Administration (UNRRA) and Howard R. Tolley, chief of the Bureau of Agricultural Economics, went unhooded, and the Government proceeded to take steps to protect itself from overproduction. It relaxed rationing controls so that American civilians could eat up the food stocks that now seemed a threat to future markets. It set production goals for 1945 that retreated far from a policy of expanding farm production. Worst of all, stockpiling for relief came to a complete halt. One observer defined this "bare-shelves" policy as an effort "to come as close as possible to seeing that the last GI potato, the last GI pat of butter and the last GI slice of bread was eaten just as the last shot was fired." [10]

Not until March, 1945, did the great danger of these policies become evident. By then the military had stopped boasting of quick victory, serious shortages, especially in meats, had reappeared in the big cities, and somber reports from abroad reawakened the vision of a starving Europe. As meat, especially pork, began to disappear from American butcher shops, an outraged public and a critical Congress besieged the Administration with complaints. In the first months of Truman's presidency, few other issues aroused such public anger. [11]

One feature of the renewal of the food crisis was the rekindling of the debate over relief. In the spring of 1945, an ever growing legion of experts began pointing in alarm to the specter of famine that again seemed ready to stalk through Europe. "It is now 11:59 on the clock of starvation," said former President Herbert Hoover, himself an old hand at famine problems. Herbert Lehman, onetime governor of New York and now Director General of UNRRA, supported Hoov-

[10] Gold, *Wartime Economic Planning*, pp. 427–436; many of the same points are covered in Wilcox, *Farmers in the Second World War*, pp. 275–284.
[11] Gold, *Wartime Economic Planning*, pp. 432–435; on pork shortage, see Wilcox, *Farmers in the Second World War*, p. 273.

5

er's warning with facts, figures, and tireless pleas for more help. Appalled by the failure of his country to meet even the small commitments that it had previously made, Lehman assumed the thankless role of rebuker of the public conscience. The American Government itself, however, supplied him a supporting chorus. Late in April, 1945, Judge Samuel I. Rosenman returned from a food survey mission for F.D.R. and, reporting to a new chief, described the pitiful condition of the European continent, recommended an enlarged role for UNRRA, and warned that unless the nation were willing to share its food and coal, democracy abroad faced a doubtful future. To help prevent worldwide "unrest, chaos, revolution," another high official told the President that Americans would have to suffer "a necessary reduction in our own consumption" to increase exports. Belated confirmation that all was not well came too from the Department of Agriculture. In the year that lay ahead, said the Department, Europe would need twelve million tons of imported food, but unfortunately, except for wheat, world supplies of farm commodities would be seriously inadequate. Late in May, 1945, President Truman took cognizance of the impending crisis and issued an order that made known his good intentions but soon got lost in the bureaucratic maze that surrounded him. "As a matter of national policy," Truman wrote to all relevant officials, ". . . I request your agency to grant the priority necessary to meet the minimum civilian requirements of those of our allies who have been ravaged by the enemy." [12]

[12] For the Hoover quotation, see *New York Times*, May 9, 1945, p. 16; for an example of Lehman's rhetoric, see *New York Times*, May 21, 1945, p. 11; for Rosenman's report, White House press release, April 30, 1945, OF 426, TP, TL; Leo T. Crowley, Foreign Economic Administrator, to the President, April 30, 1945, OF 174, TP, TL; USDA press release, May 7, 1945, Releases 5–2 file, Records of Office of Information, USDA, N.A.; *Public Papers of the Presidents: Harry S. Truman, 1945* (Washington: United States Government Printing Office, 1961), pp. 61–62.

Less than a week after Truman gave his order, the Department of Agriculture announced that, since supplies at home were scarce, shipments of meat to the Allies and to the liberated countries would be halted for July, August, and September. "The decision," noted the *New York Times*, ". . . apparently startled some observers, who felt that the food needs of war-stricken and devastated Europe were particularly acute at this time." By mid-June, Lehman was so distressed at the Department's continued failure to supply UNRRA even what had already been promised that he wrote a letter directly to President Truman asking him to intercede on UNRRA's behalf. Truman replied that while it would be impossible to do "as much as we should like for the liberated area, nevertheless, ways and means must be found to meet irreducible minimum needs and to prevent starvation." The President forwarded Lehman's letter to the proper officials with a request that it be considered "with special care." UNRRA, however, remained a neglected if petulant stepchild.[13]

In the Congress, anxiety over food shortages was born of concern for the hungry and unhappy American consumer rather than the distressed of Europe. Both houses created committees to investigate the crisis of supply and to recommend remedial action. The special House committee, chaired by Representative Clinton P. Anderson of New Mexico, traveled to a dozen cities on both coasts from mid-April to June, 1945, assembling an indictment of bureaucratic mismanagement and making of its chairman a public figure of some note. The lucid reports of Anderson's committee explained that the scarcity of pork was the result of the Government's failure to support hogs at the guaranteed minimum in 1944, of decreases in the Government's production goals

[13] *New York Times*, June 2, 1945, p. 1; Herbert Lehman to the President, June 15, 1945, OF 550, TP, TL; the President to Lehman, June 23, 1945, OF 423, TP, TL.

for 1945, and of a cut of $1.00 in the support price for 1945 hogs. In the committee's view, the shortage of choice cuts of beef was no less the fault of the Government, especially those of its policies that discouraged cattle feeders from fattening animals to heavy weights. In its analysis of the sugar shortage, the committee admitted that disruption of usual supply sources accounted for most of the problem, but offered a prescription that could only disturb the supporters of European relief. In case of continuing shortages, said the committee, allocations for foreign claimants should be reduced. Though demanding an end to the WFA's bare-shelves policy, the committee obviously expected the American public to be the chief beneficiary of future full-production policies.[14]

These policy suggestions were of more than passing interest. Before the last of the committee's reports was written, Truman accepted the resignations of both Wickard and Marvin Jones and was in search of a man to head a reunited Department of Agriculture. For a time, rumors circulated that he was considering Chester Davis, once head of the Agricultural Adjustment Agency, and J. B. Hutson, former president of the Commodity Credit Corporation.[15] Finally in mid-May, Truman called Anderson to the White House and offered the secretaryship to him. Anderson's committee, after all, had attracted much favorable publicity and Anderson himself had emerged as a champion of abundance for the American consumer. What better way to divert the public outcry against the Government than to transform the chief critic of food policy into its chief administrator?

[14] For committee's view on meat problems, see "Preliminary Report of the Special Committee . . . to Investigate Food Shortages," May 1, 1945, House Report No. 504, *House Reports,* II, 79th Cong., 1st sess.; on sugar, "The Sugar Situation," May 21, 1945, House Report No. 602, *House Reports,* III, same Congress.

[15] *Wallace's Farmer and Iowa Homestead,* Des Moines, April 21, 1945, p. 14.

Forty-nine years old when he took the oath of office on July 1, 1945, Anderson had lived the American dream. Constantly plagued by diseases, particularly tuberculosis and diabetes, he nevertheless had risen by skill and energy to riches and a measure of fame. Tuberculosis had driven him in 1917 from Michigan Law School to New Mexico where he tried his hand at journalism for a few years. Then he turned to the insurance business and quickly made his fortune. In the 1930's, his great energy led him into Government service, first as holder of several appointive offices in his adopted state, and in 1940 as a member of the United States House of Representatives. When the food investigations offered him his chance, this restless and ambitious man let the world know who he was.[16]

The search for Anderson's public identity is by no means easy. A glib, quick-witted, and intelligent politician, Anderson did not fit the neat labels of liberal or conservative, but instead responded to events with cautious pragmatism. His career and his character were marked by paradox. He could be both past president of Rotary International and a supporter of Roosevelt and the New Deal. He possessed great ambition and energy but was often immobilized by indecision and vacillation. In him resided both a capacity for petty acts and an abiding sense of history. Sometimes ruthless, sometimes high-minded, he was always wary, always fearful of entrapment in error, always hesitant to commit himself too early. Anderson's term as Secretary of Agriculture provided him ample scope to display these ambiguities.

Nothing cast greater suspicion on Truman's sincerity on the subject of relief than his appointment of Anderson, who

[16] Biographical information on Anderson can be found in USDA press release, May 26, 1945, Releases 5–2 file, Records of Office of Information, USDA, N.A., and press release, Dec. 21, 1945, same file; Clinton Anderson to Lincoln Library, June 14, 1946, Records 7–3 file, Records of Office of Sec. of Ag., Gen'l Cor., N.A.

was widely expected to put American consumers first in allocating scarce supplies. In truth, Anderson, who came to the Department as an outsider with few connections to past policies and little experience to equip him for his new job, did not really know what his relief policies would be. He lost no time, however, in giving expression to that brutal candor that occasionally marked his public utterances. "America," he said, "cannot feed the world." When the Office of War Information (OWI) issued a statement late in July saying that the country could supply one third to one half of all relief requirements, Anderson told OWI, "I would be tempted to question and to question very severely the statement . . . It seems to me that the (estimate) is extremely high." Significantly, the Secretary offered no estimates of his own.[17]

Anderson began referring to himself publicly as "the apostle of abundant production"—for the American consumer, of course[18]—and he quickly turned his attention to that most complicated of problems, the meat shortage. Partly in response to the recommendations of the Anderson committee, the Government had already begun to take remedial measures. The Office of Price Administration (OPA) promised that the Government would not alter the favorable price ceilings on live animals until September, 1946, while subsidy payments to feeders of cattle were increased in order to make their valuable contribution to the meat supply more profitable. Anderson for his part assured farmers that even if surpluses accumulated, the Government would not retreat from its promise to support farm prices at high levels for the two years after the end of the war. Dutifully taking up the

[17] On Anderson's supposed preference for American consumers, see *New York Times*, July 15, p. 5E; address by Anderson to Advertising Federation of America, July 11, 1945, file IX B5, WW II Records, ERS, ESA, Ag. Hist. Br., USDA; Anderson to Maury Hanson, July 30, 1945, Reports file, Records of Office of Sec. of Ag., Gen'l Cor. N.A.

[18] Anderson's address to Advertising Federation.

cant of the farm bloc, Anderson also argued that to encourage production, the subsidies that OPA paid to certain farmers to keep prices down should be gradually terminated and prices raised accordingly.[19] For a time, the Department of Agriculture was tempted to have the Government pay subsidies on wheat sold as feed for cattle, so that more wheat would be diverted from human to animal use. Caution dictated against a wheat feed subsidy, however. If Europeans should really fall victim to famine in the coming winter, they would need all the wheat they could get for bread. In announcing that it would not pay a wheat feed subsidy, the Department noted that farmers were free, as before, to feed as much wheat as they wished to their animals to supplement the usual corn diet. Indeed, though no one said so at the time, an obvious side effect of the drive to increase the meat supply might well be a sizable increase in animal consumption of all grains. If the dark prophecies of Lehman and Rosenman came true and a real famine befell Europe, the policy of increasing the meat supply might be disastrous.[20]

The unexpected surrender of Japan in early August, 1945, stilled for a time the raging public debate over relief. The sudden triumph of American arms, however, left Anderson and the Department of Agriculture in confusion. The in-

[19] For OPA's promise, see *Wallace's Farmer and Iowa Homestead,* April 21, 1945, p. 21; for announcement on subsidies to cattle feeders, see USDA press release, May 21, 1945, Records of Office of Information, USDA, N.A.; for Anderson on Government's intention to keep its price support promise, see USDA press release, July 1, 1945, same file; for Anderson's attack on subsidies, see his speech to Advertising Federation.

[20] On possibly paying subsidies on wheat, see interdepartmental memo from C. C. Farrington to Anderson, July 25, 1945, Grain 3 file, Records of Office of the Sec. of Ag., Gen'l Cor., N.A.; for announcement that no wheat subsidy would be paid, see USDA press release, July 28, 1945, Releases 5–2 file, Records of Office of Information, USDA, N.A.

scrutable future held two distressing possibilities: either slackening demand and re-emerging surpluses or world famine and catastrophic shortages. The crucial policy decisions of the next months would be shaped by which of these alternatives the Department decided to anticipate.[21]

It soon was evident that Anderson stood in fear of overproduction and surplus. The crusade for more production was over. Impressed by the sharp cutbacks in military requirements, Anderson became convinced that America possessed more than adequate supplies for both sides of the Atlantic. Two weeks after Japan's surrender, Anderson told the press that meat would be in ample supply and could soon be removed from rationing. Chester Bowles, Price Administrator, whose job it was to police rationing, told Anderson that he was "naturally very disturbed at the statements on meat rationing," that it was premature and would weaken public support of the program.[22] As the summer waned and reports of a huge spring wheat crop came into the Department, Anderson raised the export goal for wheat from 250 million bushels for the crop year 1945–1946 to 325 million and still later to 400. At the same time, he eased restrictions on the use of grain by bakers, brewers, and distillers. By September, it seemed even to Chester Bowles that the meat famine was over. True, autumn is the time when hog marketings are heaviest; still, there were few signs that demand for pork might later exceed supply. Caught up in the general rush to abandon wartime regulations, Bowles even concurred in Anderson's proposal for an end of slaughtering controls, that is, regulations designed to ensure equitable meat distribu-

[21] On uncertainty in the government, see *Wallace's Farmer and Iowa Homestead,* Sept. 1, 1945, pp. 14 and 15.

[22] *New York Times,* Aug. 18, 1945, pp. 1 and 24; Chester Bowles to Clinton Anderson, Aug. 18, 1945, file VI B b(2), WW II Records, ERS, ESA, Ag. Hist. Br., USDA.

tion. Perhaps, Anderson suggested publicly, production in 1946 should actually be reduced.[23]

In mid-September President Truman told the nation that in view of abundant supplies, the only remaining food problem was one of finance. Shortly after V-J Day, the American Government had stunned and angered the Allies by terminating lend-lease at the very moment that European food, coal, and currency reserves had reached their lowest level of the war. At the same time UNRRA, sole provider for the liberated nations, was approaching insolvency. The United States had promised 1.35 billion dollars to UNRRA to be paid in full by the end of 1946, but having appropriated merely 800 million dollars and owing 550 million more for 1945, Congress was only leisurely addressing itself to the task of providing more funds. (The Administration, however, authorized new expenditures for food exports in the expectation that Congress would eventually fulfill its obligation, as in due course it did.) The President assured the country that if the financial problem were solved, even the approaching end of rationing would not diminish the flow of food that was nourishing Europe.[24]

Then in the early autumn, new reports from abroad cast suspicion on the optimism of recent months. The Office of

[23] Clinton Anderson, Report to the President on 1945–1946 Famine Relief Food Shipments, July 8, 1946, Reports file, Records of Office of Sec. of Ag., Gen'l Cor., N.A.; for order discontinuing slaughtering controls, *Federal Register,* vol. 10, pt. 9 (Sept. 11, 1945), 11578; USDA press release, Sept. 25, 1945, Releases 5–2 file, Records of Office of Information, USDA, N.A.

[24] *Public Papers of the Presidents: Harry S. Truman, 1945,* pp. 321–324; on UNRRA appropriations, see William Adams Brown, Jr. and Redevers Opie, *American Foreign Assistance* (Washington, D.C.: The Brookings Institution, 1953), pp. 77, 109; on Administration's decision to spend emergency funds for relief, J. B. Hutson to John W. Snyder, Sept. 1, 1945, War 5 file, Records of Office of Sec. of Ag., Gen'l Cor., N.A.; and Snyder to Anderson, Sept. 8, 1945, same file.

13

Foreign Agricultural Relations (OFAR) in the Department of Agriculture assembled the latest data and published some shocking conclusions. Continental Europe was actually in need of 18 million tons of food imports during the year July 1945–June 1946, and of this, 15 to 16 million tons would be wheat. The experts had previously assumed Europe's food needs to be 12 million tons and were now both surprised and alarmed by the new estimates. When the OFAR added the needs of other food deficit areas to the needs of Europe, world import requirements stood at the staggering figure of 35 million tons. Only mention of the bountiful American wheat crop relieved the gloom of this statistical survey. But Maurice I. Hutton, head of the British Food Mission to America, noting that world wheat needs might exceed supply from all sources by six million tons, raised a solitary and quickly forgotten warning that animal consumption of American wheat might menace even American stocks. His terse memorandum to Clinton Anderson suggesting conservation of American wheat was ignored.[25]

Reports from Europe during the fall of 1945 steadily worsened. By mid-November, the *New York Times* correspondent was writing, "Europe faces one of the bleakest, saddest winters since the chaos of the Thirty Years War . . . The resistance of Europe is down. Tuberculosis is rife. The very young and the very old are beginning to die in droves as the Autumn leaves fall." The same day that the *Times* published this dispatch, the Department of Agriculture reported that American civilians were eating 11 percent better than before the war. Meat consumption in 1946 would actually be fifteen to twenty pounds more per capita than in

---

[25] Office of Foreign Agriculture Relations, *World Food Situation in 1945*, Oct. 1, 1945, Reports file, Records of Office of Sec. of Ag., Gen'l Cor., N.A.; Maurice I. Hutton to Anderson, Oct. 24, 1945, Grain 3 file, Records of Office of Sec. of Ag., Gen'l Cor., N.A.

1945. On November 18, Anderson went on the radio to assure the nation that all was well on the food front.[26]

The man who emerged to challenge the policy of drift was Chester Bowles, once a successful advertising executive and since 1943 head of OPA. Bowles had made a brilliant record in the war years and was currently enjoying high popularity. One of the few liberals of influence still in the Government, Bowles now attempted to become the conscience of the Administration. On the second day of November, 1945, he wrote an unusual letter to the President, admitting that he had no special information on European conditions but pointing out that if press reports were accurate, Europe was nearing tragedy. Bowles recommended that the Government cut American rations of meat, sugar, and fats and oils by 10 percent so that more food could be shipped abroad. These commodities and dairy products were the only foods still under rationing and thus under Government control. Bowles said that if the President decided against a cut in domestic rations, he (Bowles) would favor an end of all rationing. Only if the government significantly increased food exports for relief would domestic supplies become scarce enough to justify continued maintenance of rationing machinery.[27]

Bowles's letter was Truman's opportunity. At Potsdam the President had promised that he would do his utmost to prevent European starvation. There was only one way to redeem this promise and that was to reduce domestic rations. Truman sent Bowles's letter to Anderson for comment, for it was Anderson who had legal authority, subject to presidential approval, to determine the need for rationing and the alloca-

[26] *New York Times*, Nov. 13, 1945, pp. 1 and 13; Nov. 19, 1945, p. 18.
[27] Chester Bowles to the President, Nov. 2, 1945, OF 174, TP, TL.

tion of rationed commodities. In commenting on Bowles's letter, Anderson ignored most of the issues that it raised. Rather he took the opportunity to inform the President that in view of ample supplies, it might soon even be possible to abandon meat rationing, and in that way made it clear that he opposed Bowles's policy suggestions. Privately Anderson believed that the time to increase relief exports would be during the anticipated depression in the spring of 1946. Then, of course, we could "have the very predominantly selfish reason of trying to protect the American producer of meats." Why unnecessarily antagonize the American public by cutting consumption while demand was still high? As for fats and oils, the Department was actually soon to increase the amount flowing to American consumers. Truman chose not to interfere with the autonomy of his subordinates. Food was Anderson's province, and so rations would remain as they were—Chester Bowles notwithstanding.[28]

True to his word, Bowles moved now to end the rationing machinery that seemed to have no further use. Bowles told Agriculture that his rationing boards were disintegrating and asked for a review of the meat situation. Anderson needed little coaxing, for he had publicly been forecasting the end of meat rationing since September. Agriculture accordingly found that meat was now in ample supply and agreed that meat rationing should end. When, in late November, 1945, representatives of Agriculture and OPA gathered in the office of John Snyder, head of the Office of War Mobilization and Reconversion, to talk over rationing, they quickly convinced

[28] Anderson to the President, undated, Termination of Rationing file, Senator Anderson's Office, Washington. (Shortly after the author examined Senator Anderson's personal files on his tenure as secretary, the Senator gave these papers to the Truman Library, and they were moved from Washington to Independence, Missouri, where they may now be consulted); Anderson to John Bird, Asst. to the Sec., Nov. 5, 1945, Public Relations 11–5 file, Records of Office of Sec. of Ag., Gen'l Cor., N.A.

Snyder that meat rationing was no longer needed. Agriculture was about to leave the meeting when OPA asked about fats and oils. The Department replied that these commodities would undoubtedly remain scarce through the early months of 1946, and that not until the middle of the year could the question of ending fats and oils rationing even be considered. OPA thereupon reminded Agriculture that by the peculiar mechanics of the system, to end meat rationing meant also to end rationing for fats and oils, for both kinds of commodities were tied together in red points. "We insisted," Anderson recalled a few months later, "that OPA might be able to issue some new type of ration evidence [to] put its boards to work, and it again pointed out to us that the boards were quitting rapidly." OPA consequently insisted on the simultaneous end of rationing for both meats and fats and oils. Agriculture reluctantly gave in. Thus, under the prodding of the champion of economic stabilization, the machinery of food rationing was dismantled. Chester Bowles was one of the most sagacious members of the Administration, but he would one day regret the haste with which he destroyed the mechanism that had for so long made price control possible.[29]

It was not until late December, when winter transformed probability into irrefutable fact, that the American Government faced the truth about Europe. Suddenly torrents of bad news flooded Washington. For the first time, food officials perceived the full consequences of drought on the Mediterranean harvest, assessed the shortage of seed, fertilizer, and manpower on the 1945 European crop, and recognized the critical shortage of transportation that threatened to keep even available supplies from the peoples of Europe. All

[29] For Anderson's personal recollection of how rationing was abandoned, Anderson to Walter Winchell (unsent letter), April 22, 1946, Termination of Rationing file, Senator Anderson's office, Washington.

at once, foreign governments gauged the full seriousness of their plight and rushed pleas to America for more food. The world wheat shortage forecast in September became a grim reality, and Clinton Anderson now admitted that Europe would need 25 to 30 percent more wheat than could be shipped from all sources in the first six months of 1946.[30]

As the new year began, the news got worse. A grain crisis of unimaginable severity was rapidly taking shape. Instead of combined exports of 6.7 million tons of wheat, poor harvests in Australia and Argentina forced those countries to scale down their commitments to 3.2 million tons. The Danube Basin, a traditional heavy supplier of Europe's wheat needs, would actually require imports. Reports drifted in from Asia that the East as well as the West faced mass starvation. China and Japan were in the clutches of drought, and a tidal wave had damaged thousands of acres of rice land in India. On January 5, 1946, Secretary of State James Byrnes urged the President to mobilize the Government for a great effort "to export during this crucial period every bushel of wheat we can." Almost overnight, wheat had become the central concern of the world. When storage bins seemed near to overflowing a few months before, America had pledged six million tons of wheat for shipment between January and June, 1946. These bushels, the Government finally realized, were critically important. Europeans could live without the meats, sugar, and fats and oils that Bowles wanted to send in November, but they would die without bread.[31]

[30] For the summary of the factors that led officials to underrate the famine, "Statement by Andrew Cairns on the World Food Situation," June 24, 1946, FAO Conference file, Records of BAE, International Organizations, Committees, and Conferences, N.A.; Anderson to J. M. Johnson, Jan. 7, 1946, Public Relations 5–11 file, Records of Office of Sec. of Ag., Gen'l Cor., N.A.

[31] Famine developments in early 1946 summarized in *New York Times*, Feb. 10, 1946, p. 21; James F. Byrnes to the President, Jan. 5, 1946, OF 426, TP, TL.

Reflecting general unconcern with the problem of relief, the Department of Agriculture had been procuring wheat for its export program only half-heartedly and had made no attempt to stockpile in case of emergency. So it was that the Government awaited the January report on wheat disappearance in the United States with more than ordinary curiosity. Completed on January 25, the report showed a total wheat disappearance of 19 million tons from June to December, 1945, a figure so huge and unexpected that it shattered what little complacency still remained in the Department of Agriculture. More wheat had disappeared in the last quarter of 1945 than in any comparable period in history, and disappearance for the entire six months exceeded that of the last half of 1944 by 4.3 million tons. The great campaign to end the meat shortage had led farmers to divert record quantities of wheat to their animals. While America still owed Europe six million tons for the first six months of 1946, only 16.9 million remained from the 1945 crop for all purposes. Those who dared translate these figures into the loaves of bread that might never reach Europe could feel only deep dread. Whether or not America could still meet her wheat commitment was a question on which the fate of nations literally depended.[32]

[32] *New York Times*, Feb 9, 1946, p. 1; wheat disappearance is also discussed in speech by Clinton Anderson, Digest of Proceedings of Food Conservation Conference, March 7, 1946, Committees file, Records of Office of Sec. of Ag., Gen'l Cor., N.A.; and J. B. Hutson to Emanuel Celler, March 21, 1946, Grain 3 file, same records.

2 "THE WHEAT CRUSADE"

On February 8, 1946, alarmed at the chaos and confusion that, to him, had immobilized the Administration from its beginning, Budget Director Harold Smith determined to use his weekly conference with the President to deliver "an audacious lecture." "There is disorder all around you," Smith told his chief, "and it is becoming worse . . . You need good, continuous, organized staff work and you are not getting it." The current bad example was the Department of Agriculture. "Not more than three or four weeks ago the top people in Agriculture were making speeches which indicated their worry about possible food surpluses in this country. Now you are issuing a statement about black bread . . . If this sort of thing continues, Mr. President, the people of the country will think that the Administration has gone completely crazy. It was entirely possible to know precisely the situation months ago rather than weeks ago . . . Frankly I don't know who does what around here." (The President nodded sad acquiescence to this indictment of his Administration.) Quipped Smith, "The top people in the Government are solving problems in a vacuum and the vacuum is chiefly in their heads."[1]

But for Clinton Anderson, the period of drift had already ended. The report of January 25 on the disappearance of

[1] Harold Smith Conference Record (diary of conversations with Truman), entry for Feb. 8, 1946, Harold Smith papers, Bureau of the Budget, Washington.

wheat finally convinced him to act. The Secretary promptly informed the Cabinet that a food crisis was indeed at hand and that the Government would have to take measures to curtail domestic consumption of wheat. The President then designated the Secretaries of State, Commerce, and Agriculture as a committee to devise suitable conservation measures. In a matter of days the committee completed the report, and the fight against famine finally began.[2]

During the first week of February, the American citizen was beginning to learn the truth about food. Eager to cast off the discipline of wartime and encouraged by the optimistic pronouncements of his government, he had happily interpreted the abandonment of rationing to mean the end of all food problems. He was shocked, therefore, to read in his newspaper in early February that the British people had just suffered an unexpected cut in food rations to a level below that of even the darkest war year,[3] and that, in the words of the President, the world stood on the brink of the worst famine in modern history.[4] In the next months export statistics and reports from Europe would not let him forget that while he was waiting impatiently for new cars and beefsteak, millions of human beings were nearing tragedy. If all too often in the spring of 1946 he was to prefer self-indulgence to sacrifice, the blame rested partly with a government that had not only been slow to warn him but had destroyed the rationing machinery that alone could make sacrifice effective.

On February 6, 1946, Truman informed the public of the facts of the food crisis and spelled out the Government's

[2] For Anderson's personal recollection of those hectic days, letter from Anderson to Walter Winchell, April 22, 1946 (unsent), Termination of Rationing file, Senator Anderson's office, Washington.

[3] New York Times, Feb. 6, 1946, p. 1.

[4] Papers of the Presidents: Harry S. Truman, 1946, (Washington: United States Government Printing Office, 1962), pp. 108–115.

remedial program. The President asked the public to conserve food, announced limitations of grain going to industrial users, and gave assurances that the Department of Agriculture would find ways to curtail animal consumption of wheat. He reaffirmed the six-million-ton (225 million-bushel) wheat export commitment for the January to June period and promised in addition that by June 30, 1946, the United States would ship overseas 375,000 tons of fats and oils, 1.6 billion pounds of meat, and unspecified amounts of dairy products.

Actually Truman's program, while promising much, offered few specific measures to save grain. He invoked his war powers to forbid brewers of beer and distillers of whiskey to use wheat, and he raised the wheat flour extraction rate (the quantity of floor produced from each bushel of wheat) from seventy percent to eighty percent for the duration of the crisis. These measures, Truman said, would save 1.2 million tons of wheat.[5] Some experts outside the Government estimated the savings at only 0.7 million tons, and events proved even this figure optimistic. Critics soon spotted another weakness: millers customarily sell that part of their wheat not converted into flour as feed for animals; by raising the extraction rate, the Government was actually reducing the total quantity of animal feed and thereby adding to the pressure on existing supplies. The affected industries, of course, bitterly protested the Government's program.[6]

The brewers and bakers were not the real problem. As the

[5] *Papers of the Presidents: Harry S. Truman, 1946,* pp. 106–108.

[6] For a criticism of the conservation program, see "The Food Scandal," *Fortune,* 33: 89–95 (May 1946); for figures on failure of program to save grain, Clinton Anderson to the President, April 5, 1946, Famine Emergency Committee Material file, Senator Anderson's office, Washington; and *New York Times,* April 3, 1946, p. 6; on reaction of processing industries, transcript of press conference, Office of the Secretary, Feb. 8, 1946, unmarked file, Senator Anderson's Office, Washington; and *New York Times,* Feb. 8, 1946, p. 8.

Government pieced together the grain story, it was clear that the enemies of the relief program were the hogs and chickens and cattle that were devouring millions of bushels of precious grain every week. The corn crop harvested in the early autumn of 1945 had been of record size, and feed grains seemed in ample supply. But the crop proved high in moisture content and therefore low in feed value. As hog farmers and cattle feeders responded to the Government's program for heavy feeding, the pressure on feed supplies became intense. Hog farmers grow most of the corn in America, and eighty percent of the crop is usually consumed on the farm where it is produced, with the remaining twenty percent finding its way into commercial markets. But as the 1945–46 season advanced, poultrymen and dairy farmers in deficit feed areas outside the Corn Belt found little corn for sale to feed their greatly expanded stock, and they turned to wheat to save their flocks and herds. As long as a farmer in the Middle West could get the equivalent of $1.40 a bushel for corn by feeding it to his hogs, he would be reluctant to sell corn commercially at the legal ceiling of $1.18. This was the real cause of the large wheat disappearance in the last quarter of 1945. Corn was so scarce that even industrial users, who take only four percent of the corn crop in normal years, had to curtail their operations, though corn syrups were needed to combat the sugar shortage. The problem was complicated by the persistent hope of the farmers that the Government would raise the ceiling prices of grains. Holding grain on the farm was simply shrewd business. Soon even wheat, suddenly in demand as feed, was moving to market slowly, and stock men on the East and West coasts faced the prospect of forced liquidation of their milking cows and chickens. Somehow the Government had to induce the hog farmer to sell his corn instead of feeding it; only in this way

23

would the animal consumption of wheat diminish and reckless slaughter of needed animals be averted.[7]

In his press conference on February 8, 1946, Secretary Anderson explained the Government's dilemma. Superficially the corn problem seemed easy to solve; either the ceiling price of corn would have to be raised to the point where it was worth more sold as grain than as pork, or the ceiling on hogs of heavy weights would have to be lowered to make excessive feeding unprofitable. But the old policy of encouraging meat production tied the Government's hands. OPA had promised in April, 1945, not to change hog ceilings until September, 1946, and had given its word to farmers in December, 1945, that corn prices would not be changed during that crop year. But, said Anderson, the Government had a third commitment; it had promised that Europe would not starve. This commitment had priority. The only question was, which of the other two would have to be broken. Anderson was unwilling to raise corn prices since this would be unfair to those farmers who had responded to the Government's pleas to market their corn early. Thus Anderson's solution was to adjust hog ceilings to discourage feeding to heavy weights.[8]

In mid-February Anderson flew to Des Moines, Iowa, the heart of the Corn Belt, to explain why the Government might have to break its promise on hog ceilings. He tentatively proposed a reduction of fifty cents in heavy hog ceilings and an increase of fifty cents in the ceiling for lightweight hogs. Anderson made this speech over the strong protest of OPA, which was anxious to find alternatives to any policy

[7] For best explanations of grain shortage, Anderson's press conference, Feb. 8; and J. B. Hutson to Rep. Joseph W. Martin, March 15, 1946, Grain 1 file, Records of Office of Sec. of Ag., Gen'l Cor., N.A.; see also *New York Times*, Feb. 10, 1946, p. 21; and Blair Carlton to Rep. Reid F. Murray, undated, Grain 1 file, Records of Office of Sec. of Ag., Gen'l Cor., N.A.

[8] Anderson's press conference, Feb. 8, 1946.

that meant breaking a promise of the Government. This opposition and the lack of enthusiasm among farmers led Anderson to drop the plan.[9]

By March, with grain more scarce than ever and no other solution apparent, sentiment in the Department of Agriculture began to favor a sizable rise in grain ceilings and an outright repudiation of OPA's December promise.[10] The longer the Government debated what to do, the more determined farmers became to hold their grain and wait for higher ceilings. At one point Anderson tried to blame lack of transport for the slow movement of grains into the nation's ports, but as the Office of Defense Transportation easily demonstrated, the problem was not box cars but profit-minded farmers in the Corn Belt. Government procurement statistics told the story. In February, the Government was able to acquire for export only 750,000 tons of its promised one million tons for the month. In March, procurement fell 100,000 tons below the commitment. For the January–March quarter, only 2,687,000 tons of the 3,000,000-ton goal actually was shipped.[11] Two months after Truman promised that ways to curtail animal consumption of grain would be found, no effective measure had been taken.

On April 5, 1946, Anderson informed the President that the nation's relief program had "encountered great difficulties."

[9] USDA press release, Feb. 18, 1946, Releases 5–2 file, Records of Office of Sec. of Ag., Gen'l Cor., N.A.; on OPA's opposition, James F. Brownlee's undated memo, Meat–Livestock file, Records of Office of Sec. of Ag., Gen'l Cor., N.A.; *Wallace's Farmer and Iowa Homestead*, March 2, 1946, p. 12; March 16, 1946, p. 24.

[10] Mordecai Ezekiel to the Secretary, March 8, 1946, Committees file, Records of Office of Sec. of Ag., Gen'l Cor., N.A.

[11] Anderson to John W. Snyder, March 13, 1946, Grain 3 file, Records of Office of Sec. of Ag., Gen'l Cor., N.A.; J. M. Johnson, Director of Office of Defense Transportation, to Snyder, March 14, 1946, same file; for export statistics, Anderson to the President, April 5, 1946, Famine Emergency Committee Material file, Senator Anderson's office, Washington; and *New York Times*, April 7, 1948, p. 8E.

Livestock was consuming corn and wheat at reduced but still excessive rates. Unless the Government soon took effective measures, it would fail to meet its grain commitment by perhaps one million tons. Supported by most of the interested agencies in the Government, Anderson proposed an immediate twenty-five-cent increase in the ceiling price of corn to induce farmers to bring corn to market.[12]

Powerful dissenters mobilized against the Anderson proposal. Chester Bowles, now Stabilization Director, and Paul A. Porter, the new Price Administrator, viewed it as inflationary. Strangely, they were now ready to support Anderson's February plea for alteration of hog ceilings, probably because the new proposal seemed far more dangerous than the old. On April 10, Chester Bowles wrote a memorandum to the President. He argued that Anderson really was proposing a rise in feed costs, which would result in higher retail prices for meat and dairy products, both of critical importance in the battle for price stabilization. Furthermore, higher feed costs would cause an increase in the parity index and a consequent rise in all food price ceilings. "In my opinion," wrote Bowles, "the 25 cent corn increase is dangerously inflationary and totally unnecessary." As an alternative, Bowles suggested that the Government "offer to buy 50 million bushels of corn . . . at 20 cents per bushel over the present ceiling price. This offer would apply only to the first 50 million bushels which are made available and it would be clearly stated that the ceiling price would be held firmly on the remainder." The Government would then sell this corn in deficit feed areas at ceiling prices to relieve demand for wheat. This twenty-cent bonus combined with adjustments in hog ceilings would ease the feed problem. As for food grains for export (that is, wheat), he recommended that a ten-cent bonus over the ceiling be paid to procure maximum

[12] Anderson's letter to the President, April 5, 1946.

quantities. Bowles could not resist reminding the President that had his advice been heeded in November, 1945, much of the present crisis could have been averted. "I must make it clear," he lectured the President, "that . . . we simply must live up completely and fully to our responsibilities overseas." [13]

Bowles temporarily prevented a rise in the corn ceiling. But Truman was not ready to employ the Bowles's alternative of a cash bonus for wheat and corn. The hope of the Government rested instead on a measure favored by Anderson, accepted without enthusiasm by Bowles and recently adopted by the Administration: the certificate plan. Under its provisions, the wheat farmer holding his crop in expectation of higher prices or for sale at some later date for income tax reasons could offer his wheat now and accept payment at the market price on any date designated by the farmer between the time of delivery and April 1, 1947. While many in the Government hailed the certificate plan as the solution to the relief problem, the ever skeptical Chester Bowles made known his reservations.[14]

At the same time that the Government was battling to divert grain from the animal population, it waged a campaign for Americans to eat less. On February 27, President Truman had appointed a Famine Emergency Committee, composed of twelve prominent citizens, including Henry Luce and George Gallup, with Herbert Hoover as honorary chairman and Chester Davis as actual head. The Committee was to formulate a program for the voluntary reduction of food consumption and to sell it to the public.[15] During the

[13] Paul Porter to Chester Bowles, April 9, 1946, Famine Emergency Committee Material file, Senator Anderson's office, Washington; Chester Bowles to the President, April 10, 1946, same file.

[14] On the certificate plan, Anderson's letter to the President, April 5, 1946; for Bowles's skepticism, see Bowles's memo to the President, April 10, 1946.

[15] Press Release, Feb. 27, 1946, OF 950, TP, TL.

first week of March the Committee asked a 25 percent reduction in the national consumption of wheat products and called for an increase in the wheat export goal from six to eight million tons. After two weeks the Committee, in a frenzy of enthusiasm, demanded even greater consumer sacrifice: Americans were now to eat 50 percent less wheat and 20 percent less fats. To assure implementation of this goal, the Committee furnished a list of thirty-nine ways to conserve needed foods.[16]

Almost immediately the policy of reliance on voluntary conservation faced opposition. Having resigned from UNRRA in mid-March, 1946, Herbert Lehman now devoted all his energy to a campaign for re-establishment of the mandatory rationing abandoned by the Government in November, 1945. (Lehman, Truman privately growled, had "sat on his fanny" for years, botched up UNRRA, and now was merely angling for a seat in the Senate.) Many other liberals, like the editors of the *New Republic*, joined Lehman's crusade, and the moderate *New York Times* gave rationing its reluctant support. The President heard dissident voices even inside the Administration. Budget Director Harold Smith used one of his weekly conferences with the President in May to warn him against Anderson's supposed incompetence and plead for a return to food rationing. Smith told the President that he was "convinced that our international relations depended more on what we did about the food situation than on all the negotiations of the State Department put together." Smith emphasized that he had "no confidence whatever in a voluntary effort." But the forces of voluntaryism were strong indeed. Predictably, Herbert Hoover threw his influence behind the voluntary program. Clinton Anderson, while never enthusiastic about voluntary conservation, took the view that re-establishment of rationing boards would require four

[16] *New York Times,* March 3, 1946, pp. 1E and 2E; March 12, 1946, p. 1.

months and by that time the crisis would be over. While Lehman warned that the winter of 1946–47 would be worse than the present one, Anderson, with President Truman following his lead, held that the next harvest would end the crisis.[17]

On March 30, 1946, Lehman gained a formidable ally. Fiorello La Guardia, recently retired as mayor of New York City, assumed command of UNRRA. Master of the wisecrack and unmatched at making headlines, La Guardia wasted no time in jumping into the growing debate on relief. "Ticker-tape ain't spaghetti," he said, and he began a one-man war against official delay and indecision. After six days on the job, he announced that UNRRA "is being kicked around," and it was clear that in his view America, by its failure to meet commitments, was doing the kicking. La Guardia called on President Truman to take whatever measures were necessary to relieve famine.[18]

In spite of its great efforts and high hopes, the Famine Emergency Committee accomplished little. After six weeks of well-publicized preaching, it admitted that its voluntary program was inadequate and that its meager savings had been offset by increased feeding of wheat to livestock. Its eight-million-ton export goal now looked ridiculous. While the Committee did not favor rationing, it called for new administrative measures to get grain off the farm.[19]

Though the critics of voluntary conservation had been

[17] On Lehman's view of voluntary conservation, see *New York Times,* March 18, 1946, p. 11; on Truman's view of Lehman, Harold Smith Conference Record, entry for May 15, 1946, Harold Smith Papers, Bureau of Budget; "Famine: America's Duty," *New Republic,* 114: 595–597 (April 29, 1946); *New York Times,* March 19, 1946, p. 26; Smith's remarks to the President are recorded in his diary entry for May 15; on disagreements between Anderson and Hoover on one hand and Lehman on the other, see *New York Times,* March 23, 1946, p. 1; for example of Truman's optimism, transcript of President's press conference, March 28, 1946, Records of White House Reporter, TP, TL.
[18] *New York Times,* March 30, 1946, pp. 1 and 5; April 7, 1946, p. 8.
[19] *New York Times,* April 18, 1946, p. 10.

right, it is doubtful whether rationing, which was their solution to the relief crisis, was a workable alternative. As Anderson had said, since it would take months to set up rationing machinery, rationing could have no effect on the famine of the spring of 1946. Anderson was wrong when he predicted the end of the crisis by June 30, but no one could accurately estimate shortages until the world wheat harvest began in June. If famine then threatened, there would be time enough to begin rationing before the onset of winter. But the most important fact in the debate on rationing went unmentioned: The American public, without whose support any rationing program would fail, was in no mood to accept a return to austerity. Anderson was a man who molded policy to fit such facts.

As April waned, Europe and parts of Asia gravely watched their reserve stocks diminish and their rations fall to dangerously low levels. Fifteen hundred calories per day will sustain the life but not the health of an adult human being. In Austria and Poland daily per capita consumption was now averaging 1,250 calories; in Germany and Japan, it was near 1,000. Daily consumption in Italy, Greece, and China also had fallen below 1,500. The European harvest was six months away, and the American winter wheat crop would not be ready until July 1. In April, May, and June, only United States exports from the remainder of the 1945 crop could keep alive the millions who dwelled in Europe's cities. In some parts of the continent, the infant mortality rate had begun to exceed 20 percent, evidence that slow famine was beginning to take its toll. According to one estimate, at least twenty million children in the spring of 1946 were badly undernourished and developing tuberculosis, rickets, and anemia. On April 1st, nine million tons of American wheat remained for all purposes, and more than half of this was still on farms. If farmers decided to retain their grain rather than sell it, the result could be catastrophic. As April entered its third week, new facts darkened American hopes of meeting the commitment. The certificate plan was not working. The United States had fallen nearly 200,000 tons below the goal for the first twenty days of the month and was now 512,000 tons behind its goal for the period that began on January 1.[20]

The Government could no longer delay stronger measures. On April 19, it announced a bonus of thirty cents per bushel for wheat delivered to it by May 25, and a bonus of thirty cents for the first 1.3 million tons of corn offered before May 11. These were essentially the measures that Chester Bowles had proposed two weeks before as an alternative to higher grain prices. In addition the Government limited flour production to 75 percent of the quantity distributed in corresponding months of 1945 and curtailed grain inventories of millers to a twenty-one-day supply. The program, it was estimated, would draw four million tons of all grains from the farm and effectively limit consumption of bread and baked goods. "There will be a springtime flood of wheat to the elevators," said Clinton Anderson, and to hasten the deluge, he went into the Wheat Belt to plead with farmers to market their grain. With him went Fiorella La Guardia, who, by a minor irony, found himself making speeches at crossroad towns in North Dakota.[21]

[20] For a report on European caloric consumption, see article by Cabell Phillips, *New York Times*, April 28, 1946, p. 5E; on infant mortality rate and condition of children, see USDA press release (speech by Herbert Hoover in London), April 5, 1946, file XII B1, WW II Records, ERS, ESA, Ag. Hist. Br., USDA; on wheat disappearance, see *New York Times*, April 11, 1946, p. 1; on export failure for first twenty days of April, USDA press release, April 25, 1946, Releases 5–2 file, Records of Office of Information, USDA.

[21] On the bonus offer and new conservation measures, *Federal Register*, vol. 11, pt. 4 (April 24, 1946), 4542–4543, and (April 23, 1946), 4445; for the Anderson quotation, see *New York Times*, April 28, 1946, p. 1; on La Guardia see *New York Times*, April 27, 1946, pp. 1 and 8.

But the flood did not come. On May 8, some two weeks after the bonus offer, Under Secretary of State Dean Acheson noted that although Americans had a quarter-million-ton export goal for the first week in May, only 0.1 million tons had been sent. "We are not doing so well," he said. He publicly demanded that the Government requisition wheat off the farm, a measure which the Department of Agriculture, resentful of Acheson's interference, dismissed as impractical.[22]

The Government had tried the certificate plan, and it tried bonuses, but farmers resisted these inducements, and grain stayed where it was. Throughout the month of April, Bowles had successfully resisted efforts to raise grain price ceilings, but in May, with the crisis still unresolved, Bowles's objections were finally swept aside, and farmers got what they had wanted all along. On May 10, the day the corn bonus expired, the Government announced a twenty-five-cent rise in the price ceiling of corn and a fifteen-cent rise in the wheat ceiling and assured farmers that no further price increases would be made that season. The wheat bonus, with two more weeks to run, combined with the higher ceiling, presented wheat farmers with a real inducement to market quickly. Thus in the end the Government had to follow Anderson rather than Bowles. The rise in price ceilings was indeed inflationary, but there are worse things than inflation. Wheat soon began flowing from American farms into ships and finally to the hungry peoples abroad.[23]

Even if America attained its goal, the estimated world wheat deficit for January–June was six million tons. The Allied Combined Food Board, composed of food officials from the United States, Britain, and Canada, placed the world deficit from May 1 until the European harvest in September at

[22] *New York Times*, May 8, 1946, p. 1.
[23] For new grain ceilings, see *Federal Register*, vol. 11, pt. 5 (May 14, 1946), 5218 and 5223.

eleven million tons. To assess these figures and report on the general food situation, President Truman sent Herbert Hoover abroad in April, 1946, as his personal food ambassador. President Truman had recalled Hoover to public service in February to exploit his reputation as an expert on relief. But Hoover had not been content merely to perform his ceremonial role as exhorter of the public conscience, and he soon assumed leadership of the conservative side of the food debate.

Now Hoover found himself traveling through three continents as arbiter of the diet of one third of the human race. With claimant nations usually concurring, Hoover recalculated their import requirements on the basis of a per capita diet of 1,500 to 1,800 calories per day. As he explained on May 13 in his report to the President, he thereby succeeded in lowering import needs for May through September from 18.5 to 14.5 million tons. The hungry nations had not previously presented inflated claims but had based their requests on a barely adequate rather than a subsistence diet. Hoover claimed further that his survey had uncovered a possible worldwide total of 10.9 million tons of wheat for export in the same period. Thus, said Hoover, as a result of his mission, the world wheat deficit had fallen from 11 million to 3.6 million tons.[24]

D. A. FitzGerald, once Anderson's chief adviser on relief matters, accompanied Hoover on his mission and was the real author of the report. A cautious bureaucrat, FitzGerald nevertheless proved a poor statistician. Harold Weston, Director of Food for Freedom, an organization interested in famine relief, demonstrated in a little-publicized speech that Hoover's estimate of grain exports rested on a miscalculation. In one place Hoover or FitzGerald counted April shipments as hav-

[24] Herbert Hoover, Report to the President, May 13, 1946, OF 950, TP, TL.

33

ing been completed by May 1, and in another as part of the supplies exported after May 1, thus counting the April shipment twice. Rather than a deficit of 3.5 million, Hoover's own figures, properly used, indicated one of nearly six million tons. Before Weston delivered his speech, he went to Hoover and pointed out the error, but Hoover refused to admit the mistake. Another curiosity in the report, however, gave Hoover's conclusion an accidental validity. Ever solicitous of the Agriculture Department's reputation and fearful of putting embarrassing demands on it, FitzGerald estimated the American contribution at about 1.3 million tons below the actual commitment for April, May, and June. When Fitz-Gerald prepared the report, he did not know that America would keep its promise. This miscalculation partly canceled out the other one, and Hoover was correct when he said that the supply gap had been significantly narrowed.[25]

The confusion in Hoover's report exemplified the ambiguity of his contribution to the relief program. Sometimes he pleaded with the public to make sacrifices for the hungry; sometimes he said that the crisis was not really so serious after all. Liberals like James G. Patton of the Farmers Union and the editors of the New Republic felt that the total effect of Hoover's efforts was to lull the sense of national urgency. Moreover, his ideological predilections crept into the food debate with frequently unhappy results. Thus voluntary measures would solve this crisis. Normal commerce would be the best relief distributor. "The world must quit charity as a basis of widespread food distribution," he said. Though he called for an end of the activities of UNRRA by September 1, 1946, he also played a key role in obtaining larger grain

[25] Harold Weston, "The Inside Story of the Hoover Report" (a speech), May 22, 1946, file XII B1, WW II Records, ERS, ESA, Ag. Hist. Br., USDA; for the error in the Hoover report, see Tables II and V of his Report to the President, May 13, 1946.

supplies from Argentina, some of which went to UNRRA.[26]
As wheat continued to flow to the grain elevators, the
high tension of the past few months diminished. After the
rise in the ceiling of wheat, the bonus offer lured five million
bushels (more than 130,000 tons) a day into the hands of
the Government. The bonus program yielded 2.2 million tons
of wheat and almost a million tons of corn. The scarcity of
wheat led the Government to change its wheat commitment
to a grain commitment and to include most of the bonus
corn in the promised six million tons, though corn was less
suitable than wheat as a bread grain. Partly as a result of
the Government's measures, bread lines formed in American
cities and the corn processing industry had to curtail its
operations.[27]

By June 30th, the Government had shipped 5,160,000 tons of
wheat and 396,000 tons of corn. Enough grain was at ports
on July 1 to bring the total grain procurement for relief to
six million tons for the first half of 1946. Thanks to its desperate measures of April and May 1946, the Government had
performed a remarkable achievement. From July 1, 1945, to
June 30, 1946, the United States had gathered for export 16.5
million tons of foodstuffs, of which 10.3 million tons were

[26] For Hoover in a grim mood, USDA press release (speech in
Chicago), May 17, 1946, Famine Emergency Committee Material file,
Senator Anderson's Office, Washington; FU press release, April 5, 1946,
Press Release file, FUL; "Statistics of Death," New Republic, 114:
750–751 (May 27, 1946); on Hoover's views on best methods of food
distribution, speech by Herbert Hoover, Proceedings of the First Plenary
Session of the FAO, May 20–28, FAO conferences file, Records of
BAE, International Organizations Committees and Conferences, N.A.; on
Hoover's success in Argentina, see statement by Mr. Hoover on Latin
American Food Situation, June 19, 1946, material sent to Mr. Hoover
file, Office of D. A. FitzGerald, U. S. State Dept.

[27] On results of the bonus program, see C. C. Farrington to the
Secretary of Agriculture, May 31, 1946, Reports file, Records of Office
of Sec. of Ag., Gen'l Cor., N.A.; on bread lines, see New York Times,
June 5, 1946, pp. 1 and 2.

wheat and 1.4 million were other grains. Although the United States had failed to redeem the President's pledges on exports of meat, fats, and oils, it could take pride in the fact that one out of every six pounds of its food supply had been shipped abroad. In terms of grains alone, these exports represented some 35.1 trillion calories, enough to provide 300 million people with approximately 320 calories every day for a year. Counting all food exports, the number of calories per person approached 400. It is no exaggeration to say that American relief shipments in 1945–46 were the salvation of Europe.[28]

The man who deserved much of the praise for overcoming the famine was the same man who helped create it: Clinton P. Anderson. By his failure aggressively to procure grains in the fall of 1945, by his decision not to cut United States rations in November, which brought an end to rationing, and by his early complacency in the face of mounting evidence that famine was imminent, Anderson bore a measure of responsibility for the crisis. But from February, 1946, he had performed well. OPA finally had to admit that his proposal for lowering hog ceilings was right. Only when the Government followed his advice on raising grain price ceilings was it able to fulfill its commitment. Usually fearful of antagonizing the public, Anderson had boldly risked a bread famine in America when he ordered millers to curtail production of flour. But many interested in relief, including most liberals, turned against Anderson at the very time he was moving so vigorously. One cause for this hostility was Anderson's

[28] On grain export figures, see Granville Conway to John R. Steelman, July 3, 1946, Records of Office of Sec. of Ag., Gen'l Cor., N.A.; Clinton P. Anderson, "Report to the President on 1945–46 Famine Relief Food Shipments," July 8, 1946, Reports file, Records of Office of Sec. of Ag., Gen'l Cor., N.A.; estimates of caloric value of foods are based on data in USDA, *Composition of Foods*, Agricultural Handbook No. 8, revised ed. (Washington: Government Printing Office, 1963).

opposition, on good grounds, to rationing. The other cause was less easy to define, but just as significant. What the liberals and their allies really wanted was a man to lead a moral crusade against hunger, to raise an earnest and eloquent voice on behalf of national sacrifice. Anderson was constitutionally unfitted to play such a role. His habitual caution made him fearful to ask too much or raise expectations too high. Thoughtless comments, like his remark that America was in the position of a man who would have to choose which of his puppies to drown, enraged the moralists. In his public statements on relief matters, Anderson vacillated too often between optimism and pessimism, sometimes giving the impression that he was resigned to failure. La Guardia, Lehman, James Patton of the Farmers Union, and journals like the *New Republic* and *Commonweal*, opposed him with varying degrees of passion. Years later, Patton admitted that Anderson, though aroused only with difficulty, had gone on a "wheat crusade" and paid tribute to his achievement. In the spring of 1946, Patton had not been so charitable.[29]

[29] For examples of liberal journals opposing Anderson, see "Famine: America's Duty," *New Republic*, 144: 595–597 (April 29, 1946); "Mr. Anderson Should Bow Himself Out," *Commonweal*, 44:157 (May 31, 1946); on Farmers Union attitude, FU press release, May 14, 1946, Press Release file, FUL; Patton paid his tribute to Anderson in an interview with the author, August 1, 1961.

3 AGRICULTURE AND
THE DEATH OF OPA

✥ The two great issues facing America, said the *New Republic* in the spring of 1946, were food for Europe and survival of price control. Following the disintegration of the wartime bureaucracy soon after the Japanese surrender, the Office of Price Administration stood as a lonely fortress against the hosts of inflation. Special interests, their congressional allies, and powerful forces in the Administration itself joined to undermine OPA's ramparts. Farmers, the farm bloc in Congress, and Clinton Anderson did much to achieve its final destruction.[1]

A few days after Anderson became Secretary, Chester Bowles, Price Administrator, wrote a colleague in OPA, "We can accomplish a great deal with Anderson if we give him the maximum possible attention during the next two or three weeks. He is probably watching suspiciously to see how we work with him, and I believe we have a real chance to win his confidence." But affability could not overcome the inherent conflict between OPA and the Department of Agriculture. OPA regarded itself as the consumer's defense against rising prices. The Department frankly existed to safeguard the interest of the farmer, which meant higher prices for food. Throughout the war, in spite of determined opposition from

[1] *New Republic*, 114:599 (April 29, 1946).

the Department, OPA's views generally prevailed. Should OPA ever fail to restrain farm prices, however, labor would demand higher wages; business, higher prices; and the stabilization program would be destroyed. No wonder, then, that Bowles hoped to befriend Clinton Anderson.[2]

Even before Anderson took office, the farm bloc tried to use him to free the farmers of OPA. On June 23, 1945, while waiting to take over the Agriculture Department, Anderson watched his fellow congressmen pass an amendment to the Price Control Act transferring to the Secretary all important controls over food, including control over price, but excepting rationing. Anderson viewed such a gift of power with mixed emotions, for OPA's duties included enforcement of its regulations, a thankless task that meant unpopularity. To satisfy Anderson the House replaced the amendment with one more acceptable to the Secretary-to-be. Henceforth, the Secretary's prior written approval of all food regulation would be required, and he could cancel existing OPA regulations at will. In their losing fight to retain this amendment in the House-Senate conference committee, supporters freely admitted that Anderson favored it. Thus even before taking office, Anderson gave comfort and assistance to the enemies of OPA.[3]

Almost immediately after taking the oath of office, Anderson challenged OPA on the crucial issue of special wartime subsidies for farmers. In April, 1943, after a year of failure to restrain the upward march of prices, President Roosevelt had issued an order to hold the price line. In the next month,

[2] Chester Bowles to James Brownlee, July 4, 1945, Agricultural Relations file, Records of OPA, N.A.; for background of antagonism between the agencies, see Dean Albertson, *Roosevelt's Farmer* (New York: Columbia University Press, 1961), pp. 256–263.

[3] *Congressional Record*, 79th Cong., 1st sess., vol. 91, pt. 5, 6570–6579, 6605–6609, 6623–6626; on Anderson's view of first version of the amendment, see *New York Times*, June 23, 1945, p. 1.

FARM POLICIES AND POLITICS

besieged by labor demands for relief from high food costs, the Administration rolled back meat and butter prices by 10 percent and paid subsidies of 500 to 700 million dollars a year to producers and processors to cover the loss. By the war's end, the Government was paying subsidies of 1.6 billion dollars on eighteen farm products, partly to increase returns without raising prices and partly to compensate for the roll-back of 1943. Though the program achieved remarkable success in ending the rise of food prices, it incurred the hatred of the organized farmers. They argued that subsidies led the consumer to expect artificially low prices and made farmers dependent on the whim of Congress. Opposition to the wartime subsidies became part of the religion of American agriculture.[4]

Early in July, 1945, Anderson announced that subsidies were a hindrance to production (a questionable accusation) and that he had begun discussion with the proper agencies to bring about their termination at times favorable to the farmer. A few days later Anderson showed casual disregard for the Government's stabilization program by remarking to the press that since consumers had enough money to pay for higher prices for food, subsidies should be ended and prices raised. OPA was not happy with Anderson's comments. Hoping to maintain over-all stability in the food price index, OPA intended to lift subsidies (and therefore prices) of foods in the subsidy program only when the cost of nonsubsidized foods declined. By the end of Anderson's first month in office, Bowles must have regarded his early hopes for harmoney as somewhat naive.[5]

[4] On wartime subsidies, see Walter W. Wilcox, *Farmers in the Second World War* (Ames, Iowa: Iowa State College Press, 1947), pp. 254–260; for views of organized farmers on subsidies, R. T. Smith, president of Washington Farm Bureau, to Secretary of Agriculture, Prices 2–6 file, Aug. 3, 1945, Records of Office of Sec. of Ag., Gen'l Cor., N.A.

[5] USDA press release, address by Sec. Anderson, July 11, 1945, file

After V–J Day, sparring between the two agencies continued. Bowles, whose job it was to police rationing, resented Anderson's premature remarks on the possibility of rationing's early end, and minor disputes on price ceilings continued to mar agency relations. Peace, however, had brought a radical change of climate. OPA was now on the defensive. As long as fear of ascending prices persisted, OPA was impregnable. But demobilization was expected to bring slackening demand, unemployment, and price deflation. The War Manpower Commission forecast that three months after the end of the war, five million unemployed workers would walk the streets. Labor leader Sidney Hillman voiced a common belief when he predicted unemployment of ten million. Even in November, 1945, Clinton Anderson was basing his policies on the expectation that six to eight million workers would lack jobs in the spring. In farm circles pessimism fed on the memory of the collapse of farm prices after World War I, and the American Farm Bureau Federation talked ominously of a return to production restriction. By autumn, in spite of growing evidence that Europe needed food, Anderson was considering a call for reduced output, and he foresaw food surpluses and price supports rather than shortages and price control as his real problem. Was it not obvious that controls fashioned in war were irrelevant to an economy facing depression? Against this background, the next phase of the subsidy struggle unfolded.[6]

IX B5, WW II Records, ERS, ESA, Ag. Hist. Br., USDA; on OPA's reactions to Anderson's remarks, Geoffrey Baker to James F. Brownlee, July 16, 1945, Subsidies–1945 file, Records of OPA, N.A.

[6] Bowles to Anderson, Aug. 18, 1945, file IV B6 b, WW II Records, ERS, ESA, Ag. Hist. Br., USDA; on interagency sparring, Anderson to Rep. Clarence F. Lea, Aug. 9, 1945, Prices 1 file, Records of Office of Sec. of Ag. Gen'l Cor., N.A.; views of War Manpower Commission and Sidney Hillman cited in Sumner H. Slichter, "Seven Surprises in Our Economic Picture," *New York Times Magazine,* Nov. 25, 1945, p. 5; for Anderson's forecast, Anderson to John Bird, Nov. 5, 1945, Public Relations 5–11 file, Records of Office of Sec. of Ag., Gen'l Cor., N.A.;

One uncertain voice challenged the prophets of depression. The day after the surrender of Japan, Chester Bowles wrote that inflation was still a threat and that subsidies would be needed until mid-1946. Not until nonsubsidized foods fell in price would OPA consider ending payments on subsidized foods, and any consequent rise in price ceilings would compensate farmers only in part for the subsidy loss. At first it seemed likely that this policy would lead to war with Agriculture.[7] But at the interagency committee meetings in September, called at Anderson's insistence to discuss subsidy termination, both Agriculture and OPA gave ground, and the issue seemed resolvable.

At the interagency meetings, both agencies accepted the principle that consumer and producer would have to share the burdens of termination. Agriculture was now willing to time the end of subsidies with expected declines in other food prices, and OPA consented to adoption of a tentative schedule for removal of individual subsidies. Economists in both agencies foresaw a deflation in the food price index during the next twelve months of 7.5 to 8.5 percent. Thus subsidy termination would cause no net increase in the food price index. The interagency committee recommended the end of the rollback subsidy on butter by October, the end of the hog subsidy by November, cheese by December, sugar by January, and cattle, sheep, dairy products, and flour by June 30, 1946. In the case of some of these products, ceiling prices would not be raised to cover the entire loss of the

---

for Farm Bureau views, see for instance, *New York Times,* Sept. 19, 1945, p. 17; for Anderson's public comments on reducing production, see *New York Times,* Sept. 25, 1945, p. 1.

[7] For differing views of the two agencies on subsidy termination, Chester Bowles to John Snyder, Aug. 6, 1945, Termination of Food Subsidies file, Senator Anderson's office, Washington; H. B. Boyd to the Secretary of Agriculture, Aug. 21, 1945, Prices 2 file, Records of Office of Sec. of Ag., Gen'l Cor., N.A.

subsidy, and producers and processors would lose 700 million dollars.[8]

On October 1, the Advisory Board of the Office of War Mobilization and Reconversion met and approved the interagency report on subsidies. Anderson seemingly had overcome the last obstacles in his campaign. Then Chester Bowles began to have second thoughts. For some days, while Anderson fumed, Bowles prevented publication of the Government's schedule. Finally Anderson asked Truman to call a high council to settle the issue once and for all, and sometime near mid-October, the interested parties met in John Snyder's office for a showdown.

Bowles and Anderson met head-on. It soon became apparent that Bowles had shifted his ground since September. Then he had agreed that declines in the food price index were sufficient to justify termination of subsidies. Now he argued that no terminations should take place until they could be offset by declines in the whole cost of living index. Anderson answered "that food had to be treated separately and not jointly with anything else." In Anderson's view, it was unjust that farmers be made to endure continuing subsidies merely because, for example, landlords raised their rents. After a long debate in which he stood alone, Bowles finally agreed that the announcement of the tentative schedule ending subsidies should be made on October 22. On

[8] For Anderson's own account of these events, see "1946 Extension of the Emergency Price Control and Stabilization Acts of 1942, As Amended," Hearings before the Committee on Banking and Currency, U. S. Senate, 79th Cong., 2nd sess., pp. 333–339; "Proposal of the Department of Agriculture for the Removal of Food Subsidies," undated, Termination of Food Subsidies file, Senator Anderson's Office, Washington; Interagency Staff Committee to Economic Stabilization Director, Secretary of Agriculture, and the Price Administrator, "Proposed Policy and Program for Terminating Food Subsidies," Sept. 8, 1945, Termination of Subsidies file, Senator Anderson's office, Washington; on the expectation of both agencies of price deflation, "Review of Food Subsidies Removal Program," Jan. 8, 1946, Records of OPA, N.A.

that day the cost of living index would be published, and it was expected to show a minor decline. But soon after the meeting, Bowles won yet another postponement. Finally, after constant prodding from Anderson, John C. Collet, Economic Stabilizer, in whose hands the final decision lay, announced on November 9, 1945, a new schedule for termination of most subsidies by June 30, 1946. While Collet's schedule differed in some respects from that desired by Agriculture, the new program, like its aborted predecessor, was a major victory for Clinton Anderson.[9]

Bowles's hesitation on the subsidy issue rested on his renewed conviction that price deflation was not inevitable. Should inflation emerge as the real postwar problem, subsidies would once more be needed. By the end of November, the economists began to observe inflationary tendencies. Sumner H. Slichter, economist from Harvard, pointed to several unexpected developments: consumer buying had not declined substantially; shortages were greater than anticipated; wages had been moving upward; the high speed of conversion had meant less dislocation of production and employment than predicted. Slichter called, among other things, for the extension of the life of OPA.[10]

Meanwhile food subsidies quietly began to expire. First to go was the rollback subsidy on butter, and the butter ceiling rose five cents a pound. OPA hoped that fruits and vegetables would begin their descent to balance this and other price rises. On November 9, supported by the Department of Agriculture, Bowles reported that the supply of citrus

[9] This account of the debate on subsidy termination is based on a memo from Anderson to Keith Himsbaugh, Nov. 8, 1945, Termination of Rationing file, Senator Anderson's office, Washington; for the announcement of the tentative schedule, OWMR press release, Nov. 9, 1945, same file.

[10] Sumner H. Slichter, "Seven Surprises," New York Times Magazine, Nov. 25, 1945, p. 5.

fruit was ample and in anticipation of a price decrease, recommended suspension of their price ceilings. On November 19, the Government freed citrus fruits from its control. The next day prices in wholesale markets almost doubled. By mid-December retail citrus prices remained substantially above the old ceiling, and OPA admitted that decontrol had been a mistake. For a time, Agriculture fought to keep citrus fruit free, but early in January, 1946, the Government returned them to the iron hand of OPA. By that time the hasty assumptions of September had been discarded. Bad news from Europe and from the grain belt meant that there would be no decline in food prices. The great supply of money and the wild desire of Americans for goods in short supply ended any hope for unenforced stability in other parts of the cost of living. Suddenly these pressures seemed ready to destroy the stabilization program. Subsidy termination, wrote Chester Bowles late in December, was a policy in need of reappraisal.[11]

Though Anderson at first promised to keep an open mind on the subsidy question, he soon dashed any hope of peaceful cooperation. On January 2, 1946, Anderson released his dairy program to the other agencies of the Government. The heart of the program was a proposal for termination of dairy subsidies by May 1. Contrary to OPA expectations, the consumer, according to Anderson's program, would bear the full burden of the removal by paying prices equal to the old ceiling plus the full subsidy. In addition, Anderson asked an immediate additional five-cent rise in the price of butter, to be followed, of course, by still another increase of 13 cents

[11] On citrus fruit and price control, the following documents: Bowles to John C. Collet, Nov. 9, 1945, OWMR file, Records of OPA, N.A.; J. B. Hutson to J. C. Collet, Nov. 13, 1945, same file; E. C. Walsh to Geoffrey Baker, Nov. 20, 1945, Fruits and Vegetables file, Records of OPA, N.A.; John Gaskie to Bowles, Dec. 17, 1945, Prices 1–4 file, Records of Office of Sec. of Ag., Gen'l Cor., N.A.; Bowles to J. C. Collet, same file; on Bowles's reconsideration of subsidy termination, Bowles to Collet, Dec. 21, OWMR file, Records of OPA, N.A.

when subsidies ended. Milk at retail would go up one and one-half cents instead of the original one-half cent announced in November.[12]

The rise in the price of butter, according to Anderson, would help to overcome the severe butter shortage then plaguing the country. For years butter had been a problem, and in OPA's last months it became a subject of major public concern. In September, 1945, anticipating a recession that would end the unsatisfied demand for dairy products, the Government had suspended regulations on the use of butter-fat. Producers immediately began to divert butterfat from butter production to the manufacture of table cream, cheeses, and ice cream, whose price ceilings were more favorable than those for butter. When unexpected persistence of heavy demands placed diminishing butter supplies into the hands of black marketeers, OPA acknowledged that something had to be done. Raise the price of butter, said Anderson. Increase the butter subsidy, said Bowles. Whether there would be any subsidies at all after June 30 was a question still under consideration at the highest levels of the Government.[13]

By this time Chester Bowles had come to regard himself as a "lone wolf" (to use his own phrase) in an Administration dominated by opponents of his stabilization program. According to him, neither business nor labor was doing so much as John Snyder and Clinton Anderson to undermine public

[12] On Anderson's initial pledge to keep an open mind on the subsidy question, Anderson to Bowles, Dec. 27, 1945, Food–Subsidies file, Records of OPA, N.A.; Anderson to Collet, Jan. 2, 1946, OWMR file, Records of OPA, N.A.; on difference between Anderson's dairy program and November schedule, Review of Food Subsidy Removal Program, Jan. 8, Records of OPA, N.A.

[13] On wartime background of dairy problem and effects of suspending butterfat regulations, see Wilcox, *Farmers in the Second World War*, pp. 142–151; also on effects of suspending butterfat regulations, USDA press release, Oct. 30, 1945, Geoffrey Baker–Food Price Revision file, Records of OPA, N.A.; for a public expression by Bowles of opposition to a rise in butter prices, see *New York Times,* Jan. 10, 1946, p. 1; for extended statement of OPA's position, Colin S. Gordon to James G. Rogers and Geoffrey Baker, Jan. 10, 1946, Records of OPA, N.A.

confidence in the OPA. Their actions consistently belied the anti-inflation rhetoric of the Administration. Giving vent to his frustration and depression in one of his periodic letters of resignation, Bowles told the President, "We find ourselves in our present situation because members of your official family working on this program have lacked teamwork and unity of purpose; because government has failed to maintain a consistent policy; because too often it has succumbed to pressure rather than facts." Anderson's position on dairy subsidies raised questions of the highest moment for the future of OPA, and Bowles determined at last to have his way.[14]

Changes in price assumptions since the autumn, OPA argued, altered the old calculations. Now removal of all subsidies would cause a 6.45 percent rise in the food index and a 2.61 percent rise in the cost of living, rather than the 5 percent and 2 percent previously estimated. Given the unrest in the labor movement and mounting pressures in other quarters, OPA felt that the economy could ill afford such a jolt. On January 21, 1946, President Truman transmitted his State of the Union Message to the Congress. "In September," he said, "we were hopeful that the inflationary pressures would by this time have begun to diminish," but they had not. Truman asked an extension of the life of OPA for one year beyond June 30, 1946, and a continuation of food subsidies after that date. "If prices of food were allowed to increase . . ." said the President, "I must make it clear that, in my opinion, it would become extremely difficult for us to control the forces of inflation." The schedule for subsidy termination agreed on in November was now discarded,[15] and so, of course, was Anderson's dairy program.

[14] Chester Bowles to the President, Dec. 17, 1945, Chester Bowles Papers, Coombs file, Washington; Bowles to the President, Jan. 24, 1946, same file; Bowles to the President, Feb. 6, 1946, same file.
[15] "Review of Subsidies Removal Program," Jan. 8, 1946, Records of OPA, N.A.; *Public Papers of the Presidents: Harry S. Truman, 1946* (Washington: U.S. Government Printing Office, 1962), pp. 54–55.

Anderson had lost. It was by now public knowledge that he had argued against the positions so firmly expressed in the President's message. Only with reluctance did he accept the President's decision. His hope now was for termination of subsidies by December 31, 1946, but OPA soon let it be known that subsidies would probably continue through the spring of 1947. The month of January seemed to mark the beginning of a renaissance for OPA. For Anderson, defeated by OPA and suddenly faced with famine in Europe, January was the nadir of his tenure.[16]

The dairy problem grew worse in February and March. By this time, however, the difficulty was not merely butter. Rising labor and feed costs had cut the profits of the dairy farmers, and they had begun to reduce the size of their herds. The Department asked farmers to produce 120.8 billion pounds of milk for 1946, a figure 12 billion pounds below what could be consumed. It appeared now that farmers would produce only 117.5 billion pounds. Somehow the Government would have to increase returns to dairy farmers. The stage was set for a repetition of January's battle. Only now Chester Bowles was head of the Office of Economic Stabilization, one step above Anderson in matters of price and subsidy.[17]

On April 1, 1946, Anderson wrote Bowles proposing a series of price increases sufficient not only to increase returns but to make possible a gradual reduction of dairy subsidies. Bowles countered, as was by now his custom, that rather than increase prices the Government should increase sub-

[16] On Anderson's persisting hope in subsidy termination, Anderson to Victor Tresank, April 22, 1946, Prices 2 file, Records of Office of Sec. of Ag., Gen'l Cor., N.A.; for OPA's view on subsidy extension, Colin Gordon to Geoffrey Baker, Feb. 20, 1946, Subsidies–1945 file, Records of OPA, N.A.

[17] On problems of dairy farmers, Harry C. Trelogan of Dairy Branch, Production and Marketing Administration (PMA), to T. C. Stitts, March 22, 1946, OF 223, TP, TL.

48

sidies immediately and assure the farmer of still further gains on July 1, either through subsidies or price increases, depending on what Congress should decide. On April 15, having been rebuffed by Bowles, Anderson appealed directly to the President for higher dairy prices. That same day, the Government announced a program for increased returns for dairy farmers in accord with Bowles's proposals and took steps to reimpose restrictions on the use of butterfat in products other than butter. Only a few days before, the Administration had rejected Anderson's proposal to raise the ceiling price for corn and chose instead to offer bonus payments.[18]

Time, however, was on Anderson's side. April 15 was also the day on which the Government issued orders to control the slaughter of meat animals. If the problem of milk was difficult, the problem of meat was insoluble. Sprawling and complex, the great American meat industry posed baffling technical problems for the OPA. But more serious even than these were the practices of producers, slaughterers, processors, and distributors, who had made the black market in meat one of the worst scandals of the war. It was at the slaughtering level that most leakage into the black market occurred. At the beginning of the war, a few hundred federally inspected meat plants slaughtered 68 percent of the nation's meat animals. Only federally inspected meat can cross state lines and consequently these plants, which were easily regulated, supplied all the needs of the armed forces and most of the needs of the big cities. Because of their numbers and their lack of contact with the federal government, the thousands of small, nonfederally inspected slaughterers found it a simple matter to evade OPA regulations, to bid above the ceiling for live animals, and to sell their meat to black market distributors.

[18] Anderson to Bowles, April 1, 1946, Records of OPA, N.A.; letter from Bowles to Paul Porter and Anderson, April 11, 1946, same records; Anderson to the President, April 15, 1946, same records; *Federal Register*, vol. 11, pt. 4 (April 17, 1946), 4240.

During the war the number of nonfederally inspected slaughterers increased alarmingly, and the amount of meat going to federally inspected plants and thence into legitimate channels in the cities decreased. Rationing by itself proved only partly effective in achieving fair distribution.[19]

By the spring of 1945, with meat supplies critically low and nonfederally inspected slaughterers handling ever more of what little existed, a serious meat shortage descended on the cities. OPA decided to take strong measures. No nonfederally inspected slaughterer, it decreed, could kill more animals than the number that it slaughtered in 1944. All slaughterers were required to ship meat in proportionately the same quantities and to the same areas as in early 1944, a period when meat was flowing at a reasonable rate into the cities. OPA also decided to increase its enforcement staff. According to an official history, these controls achieved "fair distribution of slaughter between federally inspected and non-federally inspected [slaughterers], and provided means for securing a reasonably equitable distribution of the civilian meat supply." In September, 1945, fear of a possible meat surplus led Anderson to recommend suspension of all controls over slaughter and distribution. OPA agreed, and they were accordingly lifted. In November, the Government also ended rationing, the last of the machinery that had once supported the effort to control meat prices.[20]

In January, 1946, slaughter in federally inspected plants again began to decline and soon beef at the legal ceiling grew scarce in the cities. By April, 1946, nonfederally inspected slaughterers were killing twice as many cows as in April, 1944, and their slaughter now actually exceeded that

[19] Marshall B. Clinard, *The Black Market* (New York: Rinehart and Company, Inc., 1952), pp. 115–153.
[20] Judith Russell and Renee Fantin, *Studies in Food Rationing* (General Pub. No. 13, Historical Reports on War Administration: OPA, 1947), pp. 337–363.

50

in federally inspected plants.[21] The American Meat Institute, a formidable producers' group, declared war on the OPA. Legitimate slaughterers, it said, were unable to buy their share of cattle and stay in compliance with OPA regulations. Privately, Paul Porter, Price Administrator, had to agree. "We are faced with the possibility of a breakdown of the cattle regulations," he said. Since November OPA had struggled to hold the price line on foods without the aid of rationing. Now it appeared that the attempt had failed. As beef and butter became more scarce, public support for OPA grew weaker, and Congress threatened it with enfeeblement.[22]

OPA was at first reluctant to consider reimposing the slaughtering quotas that had worked so well one year before. But by March, it recognized the necessity of action, and after some hesitation, Agriculture went along. On April 15, 1946, the government announced that beginning April 27, each federally inspected and nonfederally inspected slaughterer would be permitted to kill no more animals than in 1944, a year of approximately normal distribution. If effective, this order would restore a fair supply of animals to inspected slaughterers. But without area distribution controls similar to those established in the spring of 1945 and without rationing, the new program faced an uncertain future.[23]

On May 1, 1946, Anderson committed an indiscretion that considerably dimmed the prospects of the new controls. Testifying before a Senate committee, he said that if the new

[21] "Changes in Livestock Slaughter, 1944–1946," undated, Price Control and Decontrol Material file, Senator Anderson's office, Washington.

[22] Paul Porter to Bowles, March 21, 1946, Prices 1 file, Records of Office of Sec. of Ag., Gen'l Cor., N.A.

[23] For the decision to invoke slaughtering controls and difficulties they faced, see Russell and Fantin, *Studies in Food Rationing*, pp. 366–370, 387–388; for the order on slaughtering, USDA press release, April 15, 1946, file V b 1, WW II Records, ERS, ESA, Ag. Hist. Br., USDA.

meat program failed to end the black market in ninety days, he would favor "abandonment of these controls." Though ambiguous, Anderson's remark in context seemed to mean that if supply continued tight, price controls on meat should be lifted, and he was so interpreted by the press and throughout the meat industry. If this were indeed his meaning, Anderson was issuing an invitation to cattlemen to withhold their animals from market and kill forever the controls they hated so much. To make matters worse, no less an Administration stalwart than Speaker Sam Rayburn publicly admitted two days later, "I have spoken to people in high places and told them that I think that cattle ought to be removed from control." Even as Rayburn was speaking, the White House was preparing an announcement to explain that Anderson had intended to refer only to possible abandonment of slaughtering controls, not price control. Regardless of the black market in meat, said the White House, price controls would remain. But the damage was already done. On May 4, three days after Anderson's comment, marketing of cattle in Chicago dropped to one of the lowest levels since the early 1930's, a development which observers attributed to farmer uncertainty about the future of controls. For the next two months, the movement of cattle remained slow. Without cattle, slaughtering controls were useless.[24]

In the meantime, the focus of attention shifted to Congress. Three months after the President had asked for an extension of OPA, the price control bill still languished in committee. On April 17, it finally reached the floor of the House, where it was mutilated by amendment in an angry twelve-hour

[24] "Extension of Emergency Price and Stabilization Acts," Hearings before Banking and Currency Committee, U.S. Senate, 79th Cong., 2nd sess., pp. 1075–1076; *New York Times*, May 2, 1946, p. 1; for Rayburn's statement, see *Congressional Record*, 79th Cong., 2nd session, vol. 92, pt. 4, 4418; *Public Papers of Harry S. Truman, 1946*, p. 231; on cattle movement into markets, see New York Times, May 5, 1946, p. 35.

session. The House bill granted OPA only nine more months of life. It ended meat subsidies on June 30, 1946, and all other subsidies by the end of the year. Any agricultural or industrial product attaining production levels equal to 1941 would automatically be freed of controls, a provision that would kill most controls on food immediately. To the businessman, the bill granted ceilings equal to the cost of every product plus a reasonable profit at every level through which it passed, including producer, processor, wholesaler, and retailer. Only the most optimistic friend of OPA could expect kinder treatment in the Senate.[25]

By May the shortage of meat and the hostility of Congress threw OPA on the defensive. On the tenth day of the month, faced with the failure of the bonus plan, Bowles had to grant higher ceilings on corn and wheat to save the relief program. When higher grain prices again placed dairy farmers in a cost squeeze, OPA finally surrendered on the subsidy issue and on May 29 announced increases in retail prices of one cent for a quart of milk, ten cents a pound for butter, and five cents a pound for cheddar cheese. The days of OPA's agony had begun.[26]

On June 11, three weeks before the expiration of the old price control law, the Senate Banking and Currency Committee reported out a price control bill that was the handiwork of Senator Robert A. Taft of Ohio. The Committee's bill cut down but continued food subsidies until May 1, 1947. However, livestock, dairy products, and poultry and eggs would be free of all controls on June 30, 1946. The Secretary of Agriculture could raise price ceilings on food whenever he felt that this would stimulate production. The full Senate continued the hatchet work by approving one amendment

[25] *Congressional Record,* 79th Cong., 2nd sess., vol. 92, pt. 3, 3872–3942.

[26] For new price regulations for dairy products, see *Federal Register,* vol. 11, pt. 6 (June 1, 1946), 5954–5955.

sponsored by Senator Taft and another by Senator Kenneth Wherry of Nebraska. The first required prices of manufactured and processed products to reflect 1941 prices plus all subsequent cost increases; the second granted to distributors, wholesalers, and retailers prices equal to current cost of acquisition plus the 1941 mark-up. Since OPA commanded wide public support, its congressional opponents chose to strangle it slowly by amendment rather than kill it at a stroke.[27]

A House-Senate conference committee reported a compromise price control bill superior to either of its predecessors. Livestock, dairy products, poultry, and eggs would remain under control. Money was appropriated for payment of subsidies, provided these were progressively lifted and finally ended by April 1, 1947. Though wide powers over decontrol would still reside in the Secretary of Agriculture, those provisions leading to immediate decontrol of most farm products were deleted. But the conference report retained both the Taft and Wherry amendments. On June 28, two days before OPA was to expire, the bill passed the Congress and went to the President.[28]

The last days of June were marked by confusion and discord. Aware that price control as it had operated during the war would soon be gone forever, businessmen and farmers withheld their goods from market in anticipation of higher ceilings or no ceilings at all. Bread, butter, suits, and shirts almost disappeared from store counters. Marketing of meat animals, continuing its decline, fell to record low levels, and half the nation's butchers closed their doors. In the last hours of the month, the White House pondered the bill sent over by Congress. Senate Majority Leader Alben W. Barkley and

[27] *Congressional Record,* 79th Cong., 2nd sess., vol. 92, pt. 5, 6621–6624, 6708, 6729, and pt. 6, 6812–6813, 6841.

[28] *Congressional Record,* 79th Cong., 2nd sess., vol. 92, pt. 6, 7499–7509, 7871.

other congressional Democrats told the President that no better bill would come from this Congress and advised him to sign it. But Chester Bowles, warning the President that the bill merely legalized inflation, recommended a veto. Tired after years of struggle and harassed by a growing legion of enemies, Bowles resigned from the Government on June 28. No one yet knew what Truman would do.[29]

On June 29, the President defied all predictions and vetoed the bill. In a veto message that contained some economics and much politics, Truman centered his fire on the Taft and Wherry amendments, pointing out that mark-ups were higher in 1941 than any year in the last ten, and that while profit per unit had indeed declined since 1941, volume and correspondingly total profits had increased. These amendments, conveniently bearing the names of leading Republicans, would mean thousands of unneeded price increases costing billions of dollars. Truman asked Congress for a one-year's extension of OPA without crippling amendments and a subsidy appropriation sufficient to hold the line on food prices for the next six months. On July 1, the House passed an emergency extension of OPA for twenty days, but the Senate failed to act. The nation had itself a holiday from price control.[30]

The resulting inflation was spectacular. In three days wholesale food prices rose to the highest levels since 1920. By July 15, retail food prices had gone up 13.8 percent over the June 15 level. Food increased more rapidly than other commodities, with retail meat prices rising 30 percent and butter, 32 percent. Live steers were bringing as much as $23

[29] For description of days before expiration of old OPA act, see "OPA Death Watch," *Life,* 21: 26–27 (July 1, 1946); on Barkley's advice to sign the bill and Bowles's appeal for a veto, see *New York Times,* June 29, 1946, p. 1.

[30] *Public Papers of the Presidents: Harry S. Truman, 1946,* pp. 322–329; *Congressional Record,* 79th Cong., 2nd sess., vol. 92, pt. 6, 8059–8088.

per hundred pounds, six dollars over the OPA price. Fear of revived controls induced livestock farmers to rush their animals to market, and in a single day in July, 12,000 cows and 14,000 hogs entered the nation's stockyards, more than three times the number marketed on that day one year before. In Omaha, cattle and hogs died from the heat as trucks lined up for miles waiting to unload. The consumer paid dearly for it, but at last there was meat.[31]

In the month ending July 15, the cost of living index rose 5.5 percent over June 15, the highest jump ever recorded by the Bureau of Labor Statistics. Public pressures for a new OPA kept pace with the rise in prices, and Congress began the painful task of drafting another bill. After some rancorous sessions, a House–Senate conference committee finally hammered out a compromise measure, which Congress passed late in July. Though the new bill contained a chastened Taft amendment and other crippling features, Truman signed it into law. In truth the long price holiday had done irreparable damage to the stabilization program. As OPA prepared to use its now feeble powers to halt the price stampede, it could look forward only to the pale satisfactions of a martyr's end.[32]

Among the many peculiarities of the new price control law was this significant provision: Livestock, milk, grain, and a few other agricultural products were exempt from price control until August 20. On that day either they would automatically return to control or a price decontrol board, created by the act, would declare them still free. Thus livestock

[31] On wholesale food price rise, see *New York Times*, July 4, 1946, p. 1; on retail food price rise, see *New York Times*, Aug. 11, 1946, p. 2E; on price of live steers, see *New York Times*, July 11, 1946, p. 1; on rush to market livestock, *New York Times*, July 21, 1946, p. 1.

[32] U.S. Dept. of Labor, Bureau of Labor Statistics, *Consumers Price Index*, Aug. 15, 1946, p. 1; *Congressional Record*, 79th Cong., 2nd sess., vol. 92, pt. 8, 9754–9764, 9777, 9875–9876.

growers had at least three more weeks to rush their animals to market and gather in the returns from peak prices. By mid-August hogs were $8.40 per hundred pounds above the old ceiling, and cattle had risen from $17.00 on June 28 to $20.75. As August 20 approached, both the harried consumer and the hopeful farmer turned their attention to the Decontrol Board.[33]

On the three-man Decontrol Board appointed by President Truman sat Roy L. Thompson, president of the Federal Land Bank of New Orleans; George H. Mead, paper and pulp manufacturer; and Daniel W. Bell, former Under Secretary of the Treasury. Throughout the month of August these men listened to scores of witnesses and read countless documents, but twenty-four hours from the deadline, they still had made no decision. On the morning of the 20th, they finally reached agreement. That night the country learned that dairy products and grains would remain free of control. But meat, the product on which public concern centered, would once more come under price ceilings. The board put meat under control to insure a proper diet to low income workers and thus speed up industrial production. On September 1, the Government would announce the new ceilings, and the happiest two months in the history of the meat industry would come to an end.[34]

Meat control would be the test of whether OPA still had any effectiveness, and the agency girded itself for one last fight. OPA had authority to determine meat ceilings, though the Secretary of Agriculture could raise them later. Paul Porter intended to pay most of the old subsidies and restore the ceilings on livestock to near their June level. For hogs

[33] On hog and cattle prices, see New York Times, Aug. 18, 1946, p. 2E.

[34] "Prices: Meat Muddle," Newsweek, 28:15-17 (Sept. 2, 1946); press release, Determinations of the Price Decontrol Board, Aug. 20, 1946, OF 20–B, TP, TL.

this meant $15.50 per hundred pounds; for cattle $19.25. While the new price lists were being printed, Anderson informed OPA that these ceilings were too low and that he would soon raise them in accord with his powers under the law. OPA delayed its announcement and went to John R. Steelman in the Office of War Mobilization and Reconversion to resolve the controversy. But on the very day Steelman's ruling was expected, Anderson chose to act alone. He took the extraordinary step of announcing his own ceilings, which for cattle were $20.25 and for hogs $16.25. Faced with a fait accompli, the rest of the Government gave in.[35]

If Anderson expected his intervention to placate the livestock industry, he was soon disappointed. In September as in June the marketing of meat animals dropped sharply. But this time farmers were withholding their products not out of hope that Congress would destroy OPA. This time they were going to wreck price control by themselves. During the first week under the new ceilings, cattle marketings declined from 300,000 to 70,000, and hog marketings from 656,000 to 166,000. The Government bravely claimed that this decline resulted from excess marketings during the price holiday and that by October, the usual run of grass-fed cattle would relieve supply problems. The truth was that animals were already on farms in record numbers. The reason that they stayed there, as a spokesman of the meat industry said, was that the producers were in a mood to take their time. In other words, livestock farmers had declared a producers' strike.[36]

---

[35] For a good account of the conflict between the agencies, see "Anderson Lifts the Lid," New Republic, 115:277–278 (Sept. 9, 1946); for Anderson's price ceilings, USDA press release, Aug. 28, 1946, Releases 5–2 file, Records of Office of Information, USDA, N.A.

[36] On livestock marketings, H. E. Reed, Director of Livestock Branch, PMA, to Secretary of Agriculture, Sept. 23, 1946, Agricultural Commodities 4 file, Records of Office of Sec. of Ag., Gen'l Cor., N.A.; for official view of the shortage, see Public Papers of the Presidents: Harry S. Truman, 1946, pp. 433–435.

By the last week in September the country was deep in a meat famine. In Chicago, then meat packing center of America, 90 percent of the retail butchers were forced to close. The Democratic Governor of Massachusetts, Maurice J. Tobin, wired the President that hospitals in his state were without meat and that either packing plants should be seized or controls ended. Like many others outside the Government, Tobin refused to admit that livestock farmers could be the cause of the shortage and instead blamed the meat packers. But there was little meat in the packing houses; it was still on the hoof in the feed pens and cattle ranges of the West.[37]

OPA believed that it could defeat the strike. Beyond a certain point, ran its argument, feeding of livestock would become unprofitable, and farmers would have to surrender. While this was true, it overlooked two factors of the greatest importance: the public wanted meat now, and the congressional election of 1946 was only weeks away. For the first time OPA had become a political liability. Throughout the war and afterward, it had commanded the support of the nation's housewives, workers, and organized consumers. But the meat shortages of September radically altered OPA's place in the affections of the urban public. In July and August there was meat and no OPA. Now there was OPA and no meat. Wrote a *New York Times* reporter, "all the zeal and passion that had gone into the crusade to save OPA was suddenly turned with equal vehemence on killing it." [38]

Democratic politicians anxiously watched their best issue turn into the unhappy target of public frustration. On September 25, House Majority Leader John W. McCormack urged suspension of meat controls for ninety days—that is, until

[37] *New York Times,* Sept. 29, 1946, p. 1; Maurice J. Tobin to the President, Sept. 25, 1946, OF 795, TP, TL; on meat packer inventories, Preston Richards to Nathan Koenig, Oct. 3, 1946, Prices 1–6 file, Records of Office of Sec. of Ag., Gen'l Cor., N.A.

[38] On OPA's strategy, Goeffrey Baker to John R. Steelman, Oct. 2, 1946, Records of OPA; for quotation on political liability of OPA, see *New York Times,* Nov. 3, 1946, p. 9E.

after the elections. The next day the Democratic Executive Committee met with National Chairman Robert E. Hannegan in panicked consultation on the meat crisis. Big city bosses Edward J. Kelly, Mayor of Chicago, and Edward J. Flynn of the Bronx warned their fellow members of impending political disaster. The Committee instructed Hannegan to consult with the Decontrol Board to find "ways and means of increasing the meat supply." The real sentiment of the meeting apparently favored a sixty-day suspension of controls. The Committee telephoned the White House and reported its views.[39]

One hour later, President Truman called a press conference. OPA was guiltless of the meat shortage, he said. The price holiday was the real cause, and October marketings would vindicate the meat policies of his Administration. Against the advice of the politicians, Truman informed the country that meat controls were on to stay.[40]

During the last week of September marketings increased somewhat but shortages continued. Rumors were abroad that Anderson planned to requisition animals from the farm to relieve the shortage. The New York City Council asked President Truman to seize all the meat in the country and distribute it fairly. Congressmen and senators feared that the shortage was threatening the health of their constituents. Through it all, Paul Porter insisted that the Government would hold firm.[41]

[39] For McCormack's suggestion, see *New York Times*, Sept. 26, 1946, p. 1; for an account of the meeting of the Democratic Executive Committee, see "Meat: Political Slaughter," *Newsweek*, 28:29–30 (Oct. 7, 1946); for another account of the same meeting, "The Politics of Meat," *Time Magazine*, 48:21–22 (Oct. 7, 1946).

[40] *Public Papers of the Presidents: Harry S. Truman, 1946*, pp. 433–435.

[41] On marketing increase, see Geoffrey Baker to John R. Steelman, Oct. 2, 1946, Records of OPA; on rumors of requisitioning animals see *New York Times*, Oct. 6, 1946, p. 1E; on demands of New York City Council, see *New York Times*, Oct. 7, 1946, p. 1.

On October 9, with public pressure mounting, Clark Clifford (an aide of the President), Anderson, Porter, Hannegan, and other officials met to discuss possible solutions to the meat shortage. Among the alternatives available to the Administration were importation of Argentine beef, seizure of meat in packing houses, farm set-asides on livestock, and special price incentive for quick marketings. The only other answer to the shortage was abandonment of controls. On the 10th, the largest press conference since V–J Day gathered to question Truman on the meat issue, but he had little to say. Then on October 14, some two weeks after he assured the country that it would not happen, the President ended price ceilings on meat. Truman later claimed that he retreated because he had come to believe that the farmers would lose money rather than accept controls. The combination of Hannegan and the farmers had proved too much. OPA was finished. The price of steers doubled in two days, and the great postwar inflation rolled on without impediment.[42]

But Truman's decision came too late to help the Democrats, if indeed anything could have prevented their defeat in 1946. In one and one-half years Truman had suceeded in alienating laborers, businessmen, and farmers of all shades of opinion, along with liberal intellectuals. Administration errors in judgment and bad luck had provided the Republicans with a wealth of good issues. Thus the public hostility to labor took the form of opposition to the Democrats. Shortages always seemed to be the fault of the bureaucrats in Washington. The Wallace–Truman feud had split the Democratic party, and concern over communism became a

[42] For a report of the meeting and alternatives open to it, see *New York Times*, Oct. 10, 1946, pp. 1 and 35; on Truman's press conference, see *Public Papers of the Presidents: Harry S. Truman, 1946* pp. 446–448; for Truman's announcement ending controls, see same volume, pp. 451–455; Truman's later statement on reasons for his retreat were given in an interview with the author, July 27, 1961; on the price of steers, see *New York Times*, Sept. 17, 1946, p. 1.

dangerous weapon in skillful Republican hands. But the best issue for the Republicans was meat. Meat gave special meaning to that shrug of despair that was their campaign slogan. "Had enough?", they asked. Truman's prestige had sunk so low that throughout the campaign the party leaders imposed a silence on him that spoke eloquently of his political weakness. The only real question was how bad would the thrashing be.[43]

The results surprised even the most optimistic Republicans. Both farmers and city dwellers had turned decisively against the Democrats: the party lost eleven seats in the Senate and fifty-three in the House. Surveying the wreckage, Senator William J. Fulbright, Democrat of Arkansas, suggested that Truman appoint a Republican as Secretary of State and then resign from the presidency. As for the Republicans, they looked forward gleefully to their first chance in sixteen years to control the Congress. There would be no more OPA to disturb their labors on behalf of a free market. But, alas, there would be a very regrettable inflation.[44]

[43] For a summary of campaign issues, see *New York Times*, Nov. 3, 1946, p. 1E; for an account of the campaign, see "Politics: Bad Breaks for the Democrats," *Newsweek*, 28:33–34 (Oct. 14, 1946); see also "Upon the Winter Air," *Time Magazine*, 48:23–24 (Nov. 4, 1946).

[44] For results of the election, see *Time Magazine*, 48:22–23 (Nov. 18, 1946); for Fulbright's suggestion, see *New York Times*, Nov. 7, 1946, p. 3.

4 THE POLITICS OF DEFEAT

By election day, 1946, the delicate fabric that was F.D.R.'s New Deal coalition lay in tatters. Defections had been occurring since 1937, but the peculiar prosperity of the war and its aftermath caused the most serious damage to Roosevelt's handiwork. Overnight, prosperity and the inflation that accompanied it transformed the political and economic landscape of America. The chief executive suddenly found that he was no longer the broker among the special interests; price and wage control made him instead their common opponent. Farmers and workers now joined businessmen in protesting against the restraining hand of government. As long as there was war, Roosevelt was able successfully to champion the public interest, but peace inaugurated a rancorous and destructive struggle among the competing groups for consolidation of their uncertain wartime gains. Even had Truman possessed Roosevelt's political virtuosity, which he did not, the cleavages in the old alliance had gone too deep to permit quick repair. The farmers, for instance, had repudiated the New Deal coalition in a fury that could not soon be assuaged. Allied now with business in opposition to OPA and to the demands of union labor, they turned away from the Democratic party. Thus in the election of 1946, from Michigan to the Dakotas, from Ohio to Kansas, not a single Democrat in predominantly rural congressional districts survived the crushing Republican sweep.[1]

The cross currents of interest group politics revealed themselves in the struggle of the farm bloc in Congress to revise the parity formula. It was not enough that net farm income had tripled since 1940 or that farm prices had risen 78 percent in the last six years while industrial prices went up only 29 percent. Prosperity had merely whetted the appetite of the farmers for greater returns. The quickest way to raise farm income, reasoned farm congressmen, was to tamper with parity, for the government had committed itself to support most important farm products at 90 percent of parity, however defined, for the two years following the end of the war. Moreover, OPA was prevented by law from setting ceiling prices on food below 100 percent of parity. Representative Stephen Pace of Georgia introduced a bill to include the cost of all farm labor (including the estimated value of the proprietor's and his family) in the computation of the index of what farmers buy. The cost of farm labor had risen so greatly since the 1910–1914 base period that the effect of its inclusion in this index would have been to raise parity prices one third. During the war, the proposal had twice passed the House, only to be thwarted in the Senate by Administration concern over inflation. When Pace resurrected the proposal in the 79th Congress, OPA again denounced it, joined for once by Clinton Anderson, who feared that a too violent jump in farm prices would encourage unnecessary production.[2]

[1] On fate of Democrats in predominantly rural congressional districts in 1946, see Charles M. Hardin, *The Politics of Agriculture* (Glencoe, Ill.: The Free Press, 1952), p. 151.

[2] For a good discussion of the Pace bill and reasons for Anderson's opposition, see "30% Rise for Farmers?", *Business Week* (Nov. 10, 1945), pp. 19–20; see also Keith Hutchinson, "Stretching for Inflation," *Nation*, 162:427 (April 13, 1946).

But the House Committee on Agriculture reported the bill unanimously in November, 1945. It justified the proposed windfall by reference to labor's supposed gains and made some hostile remarks on the rash of strikes that had lately brought victory to the unions. Pleading for equal treatment for the farmer, the Committee's report ended by quoting generous portions of Markham's "Man With the Hoe" (in which the farmer is called among other things "brother of the ox" and "this dark terror"). The strategy of the House managers was to let the matter rest until the Senate took action on a similar bill of its own.[3]

It was not until March, 1946, that the issue re-emerged, this time by way of a strange and revealing parliamentary maneuver. Senator Richard B. Russell of Georgia moved that a version of the Pace bill be attached as an amendment to the Administration's minimum wage bill, which until that moment had been moving easily through the Senate. Russell acted in full knowledge that President Truman would veto a wage bill so amended. Farm senators, especially of the Southern variety, joyously embraced this opportunity to demonstrate their love of the farmer and at the same time defeat the favorite measure of labor by subterfuge. The Farm Bureau and the Grange had already expressed opposition to the minimum wage bill. Curiously the farm organizations also opposed the Pace bill, on the grounds that in depressions labor costs decline so drastically that parity prices would actually fall below levels attainable under the existing formula. But the combined opposition of OPA, Clinton Anderson, all the farm organizations, and organized labor was unable to overcome the determination of the farm sena-

[3] "Inclusion of Farm Wages in Determining Price of Agricultural Commodities," House Report No. 1185, *House Miscellaneous Reports*, V, 1945, 79th Cong., 1st sess.

tors. On March 29, 1946, the Senate passed the Russell Amendment 43 to 31.[4]

The managers of the minimum wage bill then attempted a compromise. They would reduce the minimum wage provision in the bill from seventy-five to sixty cents, and in return the farm bloc was to supply votes to kill the Russell amendment. Accordingly the Senate overwhelmingly agreed to the fifteen-cent reduction, but on the subsequent motion to kill the Russell amendment, the needed votes were not delivered. On April 5, the minimum wage bill, heavily burdened by the unwanted rider, went to the House and to certain doom. As Senator Robert M. La Follette commented, the bill was now a "legislative dead duck," for the assurance of a presidential veto precluded serious consideration. To such a sorry pass had come the farmer-labor alliance of the thirties.[5]

Rebirth of antilabor sentiment, opposition to price control, and disappearance of economic privation were some of the reasons for the flight of the farmer from the Administration to the Republicans. But American agriculture has never been monolithic, and among its diverse components there existed some elements possessing a natural affinity to a Democratic Administration. Discounting the ambiguous contribution of the Southern farmer, whose representatives would probably oppose Truman's domestic policies, the Administration at its inception could look forward to the almost certain support of two farm organizations: the National Farmers Union and the Midwestern farmer committees of the Agricultural Adjustment Agency (AAA). One measure of the early difficulties of the Administration was that it alienated these groups, though they had no place to go but the Democratic party.

In spite of their considerable influence, no farm organizations have ever wielded decisive political power in any por-

[4] *Congressional Record*, 79th Cong., 2nd sess., vol. 92, pt. 2, 2661; pt. 3, 2786, 2815, 2818.

[5] *Congressional Record*, 79th Cong., 2nd sess., vol. 92, pt. 2, 3093–3096, 3108–3113, 3205.

tion of rural America. The Farmers Union, great rival of the conservative Farm Bureau and heir to agriculture's radical past, has found most of its membership in the predominantly Republican wheat states of the Middle West, where it has been disappointed in its few overt efforts to elect liberals. State farm bureaus similarly have failed to demonstrate much political potency in attempts to unseat liberals in the Corn Belt, where the bureaus have their greatest strength. Both of these organizations, like the politically passive Grange, gain members because of their social functions, their insurance programs, and their marketing and other cooperative enterprises, rather than by the appeal of their political programs. Indeed, in the realm of politics and farm policy, the leadership often has used the influence of these groups in ways that fail to reflect the opinions of the membership.

Nominally part of the bureaucracy of the Department of Agriculture, the AAA administered the action programs of the Department through state committees appointed in Washington and county committees elected by farmers themselves. In the Middle West, the deep commitment of these committees to the programs of the New Deal led them into politics where they exerted pressures on Congress on behalf of their agency and attempted on occasion to influence elections. In certain parts of the Middle West, they regarded themselves as an arm of the Democratic party, to which they owed existence and gratitude for services rendered in the Depression. But like the other farm groups, the AAA committees were powerless whenever the tide was rolling away from their favored candidates. As one close student of farm politics has written, "it is most difficult to discern any effect (of AAA efforts) upon election returns." [6]

Though not too effective as reapers of votes, the farm

---

[6] Hardin, *Politics of Agriculture*, 149–155; for background on Farm Bureau, Grange, and Farmers Union, see Wesley McCune, *Who's Behind Our Farm Policy* (New York: Frederick A. Praeger, 1956), pp. 15–52.

organizations have always been of considerable political importance. Above all, they are lobbyists without peer. In the 1940's, the Farm Bureau was exercising power over farm legislation rivaling that of the Department of Agriculture, while the Farmers Union and the AAA had great influence with certain congressmen in the Middle West. In addition, the farm organizations do much to create that unmeasurable but significant factor: the political atmosphere. For these reasons, Truman could have used whatever help he could get in farm circles, but partly because of the policies of Clinton Anderson, the Administration by November, 1946, could claim no ally in the whole of organized American agriculture.

After 1940, when he became its president, James Patton was chief architect of the liberal policies of the Farmers Union. A man of wide interests and unbounded idealism, he worked not only for liberal agricultural programs, but also for the foreign policy of Henry Wallace, for farmer cooperation with organized labor, and for the extension of the New Deal into all facets of American life. In accord with other liberals in agriculture, his chief goal for the postwar period was that government abandon the restrictionist economics of the Depression and replace the policy of reduced production with one of broadened consumption.

As long as Anderson advocated abundant production, as he did during the last months of the war, Patton was his friend. But soon after the war's sudden end, Anderson became obsessed with the fear that continued high production would soon bring on precipitous price declines. One day in October, Anderson informed a Farm Bureau delegation that the Government's production goals for the next year might call for decreased output. In contradiction to Patton's policy hopes, Anderson argued that production goals set by the Department should ask farmers to produce only what the public could buy. Patton quickly issued a statement saying that he hoped Anderson "will not permit the impression to continue to be spread that he favors a return to restrictionism of the kind advocated by the Farm Bureau Federation." The world food shortages quickly rendered all fear of surpluses obsolete, but the incident revealed significant differences between Patton and Anderson.[7]

In December, 1945, Anderson made some changes in his Department that further antagonized Patton. No agency in the Department commanded higher esteem among liberals in and out of agriculture than the Farm Security Administration (FSA). Assisting subsistence farmers, tenants, and migrant workers with sometimes bold and controversial policies, the FSA had been under severe attack from the Farm Bureau and congressional conservatives since 1941. Its chief defender was James Patton, who consequently regarded the FSA as his special province. Late in 1945 the job of Administrator of the FSA fell vacant. Anderson ignored Patton's nominee and chose instead a man whose appointment Patton called a "bitter betrayal of millions of small farmers." Patton was soon to learn, however, that FSA had more dangerous foes than Anderson. In 1946, Congress, abetted by Anderson's indifference, would kill FSA, replace it with the innocuous Farmers Home Administration, and thereby postpone indefinitely further assaults on rural poverty.[8]

Another agency favored by Patton and the liberals was the Bureau of Agricultural Economics (BAE). Under the leadership of Howard Tolley, the BAE had revealed concern for agriculture's disinherited and dissatisfaction with the restrictionist policies of the thirties. Like the FSA, it had en-

[7] FU press release, Oct. 11, 1945, Press Release file, FUL.

[8] For background on FSA and conservative opposition to it, see Grant McConnell, *The Decline of Agrarian Democracy* (Berkeley and Los Angeles: University of California Press, 1953), pp. 84–111; for Patton on the appointment of a new FSA chief, see FU press release, Nov. 15, 1945, Press Release file, FUL; FU press release, Dec. 11, 1945, same file.

dured the rage of congressional conservatives. In December, 1945, Anderson announced the transfer of all planning activities from the Bureau, where Henry Wallace had put them in 1938, to the Secretary's office. BAE would lose its independent influence on policy. Soon Congress would make drastic cuts in its appropriations, Tolley would resign, and the Bureau would fall under conservative influence. Patton would blame the decline of BAE on Anderson's December order and on his failure to come to the Bureau's defense before the Congress.[9]

By February, 1946, Anderson's growing hostility to OPA earned him another fusillade of Patton's angry rhetoric. Patton attacked Anderson's position on subsidies and on the dairy problem, and accused him of conducting a "conspiracy against price control." Charging that Anderson was giving aid to all of the opponents of OPA, Patton urged the President "to read the riot act to all those of his subordinates who are opposing his own attempts . . . to stay runaway inflation." Later in the month, the Farmers Union designated Chester Bowles as the man who had done most for agriculture in 1945.[10]

When Anderson failed to appear before the House Ways and Means Committee to testify in favor of social security for farmers and farm workers, he widened still further the nearly impassable gulf between himself and Patton. While the hearings were still in progress, Patton obtained an appointment with the President and protested Anderson's si-

[9] For history of BAE's troubles, see Charles M. Hardin, "The Bureau of Agricultural Economics Under Fire," *Journal of Farm Economics,* 28:635–668 (Aug., 1946); for Anderson's order on BAE's new functions, USDA press release, Dec. 12, 1946, Reorganization of the Bureau files, Records of BAE, N.A.; for Patton criticisms of Anderson's role in weakening BAE, Patton to the President, May 2, 1946, OF I–Misc. file, TP, TL.; and FU press release, May 14, 1946, Press Release file, FUL.

[10] FU press release, Feb. 4, 1946, Press Release file, FUL; FU press release, Feb. 14, 1946, same file.

lence. Truman was apparently moved by Patton's plea for support of the social security measure, for shortly thereafter he wrote Anderson an unusual letter in which he said, "I think it is essential . . . that you request an opportunity to testify before the Committee and that you submit material supporting these proposals." The implied rebuke and explicit instructions were contrary to Truman's usual way of dealing with subordinates. There is, however, no evidence in the Committee's published hearings that Anderson ever did testify. No doubt his inaction pleased agriculture's conservatives (the Farm Bureau did not testify either), but they were already lost to the Administration.[11]

By April, Patton and the Farmers Union were joining the growing chorus of criticism against the Administration's relief policies. Condemning dependence on voluntary methods of conserving food, Patton called for a bonus plan for grain, similar to the one soon to be adopted, and suggested an increase in the export goal. In May, Patton said that Anderson's "fumbling, fluctuating policies" were "directly responsible for the United States' present difficulties in meeting its obligations to feed the distressed abroad." [12]

On May 1, 1946, the rupture was complete. On that day, Anderson made his ambiguous comment before the Senate Banking and Currency Committee regarding controls on meat. The next day Patton wrote the President, saying that Anderson had "issued an open invitation to the packers to continue their tremendous campaign to smash price control." He went on to compose a long indictment of Anderson's

[11] On Patton's conversation with Truman, interview of James G. Patton by author, Aug. 1, 1961; Truman to Anderson, March 27, 1946, in U.S. Dept. of Agriculture Documents, TL; for hearings at which Anderson did not appear, see "Amendments to Social Security Act," Hearings before Committee on Ways and Means, U.S. House of Representatives, 79th Cong., 2nd sess.

[12] FU press release, April 5, 1946, Press Release file, FUL; Patton to the President, May 2, 1946.

tenure, complete with a detailed account of the many episodes in which the Secretary betrayed the hopes of the liberals. Inevitably Patton concluded by asking Truman to fire Anderson. On May 4 Truman replied to Patton. "I think you are entirely misinformed in [the Secretary's] attitude," he wrote. "I think he is as able a Secretary of Agriculture as the Country has ever had and I intend to keep him." [13]

Two months later Patton announced that the Farmers Union was "pulling out of Washington." Only one man of the previous fifteen-member staff would remain behind. "The Union," he said, "has lost confidence in the Truman Administration's doing anything about legislation we consider important." The object of his wrath was no longer merely the Secretary of Agriculture. President Truman, he said, had failed to push liberal measures and had helped bring inflation. Soon, Patton prophesied, the people would call for another New Deal. Thus before the campaign of 1946, the Farmers Union entered the growing ranks of Truman's opponents. It is a revealing commentary on Truman's early presidency that the Farm Bureau and the Farmers Union could denounce him with equal vehemence.[14]

The alienation of the AAA farmer committees grew out of Anderson's attempts to impose order on the administrative anarchy of his department. Appalled by the bureaucratic monster over which he had nominal control, Anderson quickly appointed an advisory committee on reorganization chaired by Milton Eisenhower of Kansas State University, and composed of men in and out of the Department long associated with agriculture. From their hasty labors emerged an ill-conceived agency, the Production and Marketing Administration (PMA), which Anderson created by fiat in August of

[13] Patton to the President, May 2, 1946; Truman to Patton, May 4, 1946, OF I–Misc. file, TP, TL.
[14] New York Times, July 12, 1946, p. 10.

1945. By the terms of Anderson's order, twelve previously independent agencies and staff offices of the Department were broken up and recomposed into branches of the PMA. Some of the branches handled commodity problems (for example, the Cotton Branch) and others served functional purposes (Marketing Facilities Branch, Food Distribution Branch). In addition a field service branch carried "to the field, through state and county agricultural committees, programs dealing directly with farmers." This branch was the old Washington office of the Agricultural Adjustment Agency, created by the New Deal to combat farm depression. Staffed by the same people as before, it would retain the old committee system, with state committees still composed of farmers appointed in Washington, and local committees still elected in the counties. But now the farmer committees would administer policies conceived in the PMA branches rather than by an independent AAA, though the field service branch would still have its own conservation program. The committees were even forced to abandon the initials AAA, symbolic of the heroic struggles of the depression, and to accept instead the strange letters, PMA.[15]

From the beginning there was grumbling about the reorganization. Critics said that in a marriage of marketing and production, marketing officials hoping for lucrative jobs in the processing industries might predominate over farmer-minded production men. The transformed AAA might lose its role as aggressive farmer spokesmen and fade into a mere executor of the policies of others. As an administrative reform, PMA seemed to create more problems than it solved, for it was so huge and powerful that its administrator might some day rival the Secretary himself. But in August, 1945, the

[15] For announcement and description of the new order, USDA press release, Aug. 18, 1945, PMA file, Senator Anderson's office, Washington.

PMA was only words in a press release and its flaws too vague or distant to arouse concerted opposition.

On September 27, 1946, over a year after he created the PMA, Anderson announced a reorganization of the reorganization. The Field Service Branch (the old Washington office of the AAA), was to be abolished and replaced by an Assistant Administrator for Field Operations. From now on, all action programs would originate in the remaining PMA branches and be passed directly to the state and local committees for execution. To its enemies this order meant the destruction of the last vestiges of the AAA and farmer influence in Washington. They claimed that Anderson either had acted to destroy an AAA which he suspected of disloyalty or that he was the guileless dupe of that agency's many opponents in the Department. To Anderson, however, the reorganization was merely a logical step in achieving efficiency in his Department. He simply did not understand all the implications of his own reorganization. What he did not seem to realize was that in the bureaucratic jungle of the USDA, separation of administration from policy is impossible. Had Anderson foreseen the storm of criticism that was to engulf him, he never would have made his announcement when he did.[16]

Outside the Department, Anderson's reorganization provoked a nearly unanimous protest. Even the Farm Bureau was opposed, though at first glance the abolition of the Field Service Branch seemed to play into its hands. Having as its goal the control of all farm policy, the Farm Bureau should have welcomed the destruction of a rival as formidable as the AAA, but it apparently decided that marketing control of the Department was more to be feared than farmer control. The case of all the farm organizations

[16] For announcement of reorganization order, USDA press release, 9–30–46, PMA file, Senator Anderson's office, Washington.

including the farmer committees was summarized in a telegram from Patton to the President. Farmer influence, Patton said, would now wither both in Washington and at the grass roots. "Processor-dominated officials will control instructions issued to the field by 17 separate branches." The result, Patton predicted, would be administrative chaos and alienation of the farmers.[17]

Anderson found himself vulnerable to attack not because of the cogency of these arguments but because of his own bad timing. Unfortunately for him, the election of 1946 was only a month away. Patton bluntly warned the President that the reorganization "will cause a widespread revolt among farmers with serious results . . . for the Democratic party." This was not empty prophecy. Already state AAA committees had expressed their resentment of Anderson's order to the state Democratic chiefs, who in turn protested to Democratic headquarters in Washington. Less than two weeks after Anderson issued the order, Truman announced its suspension.[18]

But suspension was not enough to satisfy the opponents of the reorganization. They wanted its abandonment. Ironically, it was Anderson himself who unwittingly provided them the opportunity to mount a counterattack. In the quiet time before his order, Anderson invited the forty-eight directors of the state committees and one committeeman from each state to meet in Washington for an agricultural outlook meeting. Thus on October 7 at the height of the controversy over the reorganization, Anderson's most vigorous opponents gathered to defend the agency to which they were so de-

[17] Edward O'Neal, President of American Farm Bureau Federation, to Anderson, Oct. 10, 1946, Organization 1 file, Records of Office of Sec. of Ag., Gen'l Cor., N.A.; telegram from Patton to the President, Oct. 9, 1946, OF 1–Y, TP, TL.

[18] Patton's telegram, Oct. 9, 1946; for a copy of Truman's reply to Patton informing him of the suspension of the order, FU press release, Oct. 9, 1946, Press Release file, FUL.

voted. During the four days of the outlook meeting, the directors spent most of their time lobbying against Anderson's proposal and framing a petition of protest, which thirty-six of them signed. Dated October 11, 1946, the petition asked that Anderson rescind his order and remove certain designated officials in the Washington office of PMA who were presumably under the influence of the food processing industry.[19]

Anderson's luck continued bad, for confusion in the Department mails delayed delivery of the petition to his office until late in the day of October 15. A few hours earlier, he had left Washington for a three-week vacation in New Mexico. The state directors, who had been waiting for four days for some response from the Secretary, interpreted his departure as arrogant disregard of their just complaint, and they returned home nursing grievances against the tyrant in the Department of Agriculture. Anderson later chided the directors for not personally delivering their petition or approaching him at the outlook conference to air their opinions.[20]

The antagonism engendered by this episode profited only the enemies of the Administration. As the election drew near, false rumors circulated that Anderson intended to fire large numbers of the state directors. The Secretary darkly hinted that the source of the rumors was the Farm Bureau, which was trying to use the furor over the reorganization to hurt the Democrats in the Middle West. How many votes the whole controversy lost for the Democrats is impossible to say. That it threw the farmer committees into an uproar and helped pollute the political atmosphere is beyond question. Anderson himself believed that the opposition made

[19] For the petition, see state PMA Directors to Clinton Anderson, Oct. 11, 1946, PMA file, Senator Anderson's office, Washington.
[20] Anderson, "Statement to the Signers of the Oct. 11 petition," Nov. 12, 1946, PMA file, Senator Anderson's office, Washington.

76

good use of the issue in Iowa, Illinois, Indiana, and Missouri. At an inopportune time, Anderson's well-intentioned decree had alienated the last farmer ally of the Administration.[21]

The debate raged on after the election. Anderson never abandoned his intention of someday implementing his order, and he took great pains to explain its purpose. The reorganization, he claimed, would actually strengthen farmer committees. No longer would any intermediary stand between the committees and the makers of policy. In addition the end of the Field Service Branch would eliminate useless personnel from the Government payroll.[22] Anderson's defense failed to answer the widespread fear that the end of AAA in Washington left the career people, who had an eye on better jobs in industry, in control of policy.

The farmer committees, therefore, were not swayed by Anderson's arguments. The Secretary and the state directors carried on a prolonged correspondence and exchanged veiled charges, but the only result was that Anderson slowly lost his temper and finally lashed at his tormentors in a series of revealing and angry letters.

> I am a tax payer. I pay the Government every year several times as much in income taxes as it pays me in salary as a cabinet officer. When I see people in the Department loafing because they have no work to do and realize that I am prevented from removing them . . . from the payroll by abolishing branches of our Production and Marketing Administration, then I feel a little upset because I know that some of my money is being used to keep those people on the payroll.

As he wrote, his anger mounted:

> You need have no worry as to whether I am perfectly sincere in promoting the reorganization. . . The people who are not

[21] Anderson to J. Frank Hobbs, Chairman of Tennessee State Democratic Committee, Nov. 20, 1946, OF I–Misc., TP, TL.
[22] Anderson to Albert J. Gross, Oct. 30, 1946, PMA file, Senator Anderson's office, Washington.

sincere are the people who circulated rumors that I was going to discharge great numbers of State Directors; rumors that I was going to be kicked out by the President right after election; rumors that my health was so bad that I could never come back to Washington from New Mexico; rumors that I have refused to see state Directors after their petition was presented to me . . .[23]

In the end Anderson had the last word. On July 1, 1947, the disputed order went into effect and the Field Service Branch—the AAA—was no more.

Had a man with a shrewder grasp of the politics of agriculture held the office of Secretary, Harry Truman might not have found himself so isolated from the American farmer in 1946. Anderson had made the political position of the Administration worse than it had to be. Truman's task now was to win back the various disaffected interest groups before the election of 1948. But as long as Clinton Anderson served in his Cabinet, there was little hope for alliance with even the liberals of American agriculture.

[23] Anderson to Lee M. Gentry, Illinois PMA Committee, Dec. 2, 1946, Organization 1–2 file, Records of Office of Sec. of Ag., Gen'l Cor., N.A.

5 THE DILEMMA OF TRADE

❧ While politicians fought the battles of relief and price control and maneuvered in the daily struggle for office and influence, the civil servants wrestled with the long-range problems that were left by the war. Indeed, even before the Allied war machine had begun to fashion victories in the field, small armies of technicians in the State and Agriculture Departments were drafting plans for the postwar world. Inevitably, from their separate labors, clashing visions of the future emerged.

To the State Department, Utopia corresponded strikingly to the Age of Queen Victoria, to the world as it was before 1914, an era when free trade and world peace seemed each the necessary condition to the other. No memory of the interwar period more disturbed the architects at the State Department than the trade rivalries that darkened the years of the Depression. There must be an end, they said, to the complicated machinery that distorted the natural flow of trade. There must be an end to high tariffs, import quotas, export subsidies, preferential customs arrangements, currency depreciations, bartering, and private cartels. They preached, as Secretary Cordell Hull had been doing for years, that if only the blood of trade could flow freely and in ample volume, the new world order would have life and health and be bound into a harmonious whole.[1]

[1] For the State Department's trade program, see Clair Wilcox,

FARM POLICIES AND POLITICS

The struggle to commit Great Britain to freer trade policies began in August, 1941, when Roosevelt got Churchill to approve Article IV of the Atlantic Charter, which committed both their peoples to strive for equal access for all nations "to the trade and raw materials of the world." In the Mutual Aid Agreement of February, 1942, Britain agreed to undertake conversations to implement this goal. In the talks that followed, the State Department hoped above all to shake the British loose from the imperial preference system, but on this crucial point, Britain would not budge. Imperial preferences had been negotiated at Ottawa in 1932 and marked the termination of a century of British free trade policies. Under their terms, English manufactured goods paid less duty in the Dominions than products from other nations; and food and raw materials from within the empire entered England less burdened than materials from elsewhere. It was just this sort of discrimination that the State Department wanted to abolish, but Britain correctly argued that the expected exhaustion of her dollar resources by the end of the war would long delay any loosening of trade restrictions. Only when Britain found herself desperate for an American loan in the bleak winter of 1945 did she seem to surrender to the State Department. Among the terms of the loan was British agreement to abandon, in principle, the imperial preference system.[2]

With Britain now reluctantly following the American lead, a technical staff within the United States Government completed work on a pamphlet entitled *Proposals for Expansion of World Trade and Employment*. Issued by the State Department in November, 1945, the *Proposals* briefly suggested a series of desirable rules for the liberation of trade and

"Organization to Liberate World Trade," *Annals of the American Academy of Political and Social Science*, 246:95–100 (July 1946).

[2] William Adams Brown, Jr., *The United States and the Restoration of World Trade* (Washington, D.C.: The Brookings Institute, 1950), pp. 47–49, 54–56.

elimination of restrictive practices. If the nations of the world favorably received the *Proposals,* an international conference on trade and employment would convene to discuss details and incorporate the American proposals into a charter for an International Trade Organization (ITO).[3] World approval of ITO became a major objective of American foreign policy. The British, on the other hand, regarded ITO and State's free trade policies as a serious threat to their security. As a legacy of depression and war, they found themselves committed to devices, such as inconvertibility of pounds to dollars, that had become essential for economic survival. In face of evidence soon to mount that its policies were irrelevant for a world devastated by war, the State Department would maintain its laissez-faire convictions with undiminished fervor.

The Department of Agriculture viewed recent history from a much different perspective than State. To it, the tragedy of the Depression was not trade rivalry, but poverty on the farms of America. Its hero was not Cordell Hull, apostle of free trade, but Henry A. Wallace, champion of farm relief. Indeed, the struggle between the two Departments over foreign trade had its roots in the 1930's. The New Deal farm program was a notorious example of economic nationalism and stood in obvious conflict with Hull's reciprocal trade agreements program. Under the Agricultural Adjustment Acts, the Department supported the price of certain domestic farm products above the level of the world market. In 1935, to protect supported domestic commodities from lower priced imports, Congress empowered the President to impose import quotas whenever domestic price support operations were endangered. Congress also authorized the Government to spend 30 percent of the gross customs receipts to encourage, among other things, the export of farm products. In other words, the

[3] *Proposals for Expansion of World Trade and Employment,* developed by the United States Government (Washington: U.S. Department of State, Publication 2411, Nov. 1945).

Government could subsidize exports so that they sold for lower prices in the foreign than in the domestic market. Officially, in the early 1940's, the Department was toying with the notion of abandoning the price support system after the war. But in its daily operations, it regarded free trade as the harbinger of farm depression, while import quotas and export subsidies were cherished weapons in the war against rural poverty.

In April, 1945, the Department of Agriculture published its own blueprint for the future, entitled *A Postwar Foreign Trade Program for United States Agriculture*. This pamphlet was a manifesto on behalf of massive interference in the operations of world commodity markets. Relaxation of trade barriers, said the Department, "could not remedy a serious world surplus situation, nor could it prevent widespread agricultural depression." The Department's solution to surpluses was the international commodity agreement. During the Depression, agreements for tea, rubber, sugar, and coffee had been negotiated in order to divide up the world market among the exporters and commit them to production restrictions. Restrictionism now was discredited, however. Any future agreements would be designed not only to stabilize prices but to encourage increased consumption. The Department proposed that the nations of the world agree on maximum and minimum prices for primary commodities. If free market prices should fall to the minimum, the managers of national or international buffer stocks would begin buying to protect the sellers; conversely, if the world price reached the agreed maximum, they would start selling to protect the buyer. Bargain sales to underdeveloped areas could provide relief from excessive stock accumulations. Thus rational intervention would replace the vicious workings of the free markets.[4]

[4] USDA, *A Postwar Foreign Trade Program for United States Agriculture*, developed by the Interbureau Committee on Post-War Programs (Washington: USDA, April 1945).

At the same time that the State Department was debating with Britain on the nature of trade rules, it was negotiating a separate agreement with Agriculture in an effort to win that Department's approval of the ITO. As a result of long discussions, State's *Proposals* had to allow an exception to the provision against import quotas, permitting them whenever they might be needed to protect national programs limiting production of surplus products. In the article proscribing export subsidies, State's *Proposals* made limited exceptions for any commodity in burdensome world surplus. The question of commodity agreements proved especially difficult. The State Department favored a provision expressing general disapproval of them but recognizing their use as a transitional aid in shifting resources away from surplus production. The Department of Agriculture sought to remove commodity agreements entirely from the province of ITO and place them instead under the more sympathetic eye of the Food and Agriculture Organization of the United Nations (FAO). Though State successfully prevented this transfer, the other concessions that it made to Agriculture seriously weakened the American effort to pry other nations away from their own special restrictive devices. If American agriculture were protected, why not infant industries in underdeveloped countries or British exports?[5]

The FAO had its origin in a conference held in Hot Springs, Virginia, in 1943. Committed to raising the nutritional levels of the world's people, the first annual conference convened in Quebec in November, 1945, to define the tasks more fully and to build necessary machinery. The autumn

---

[5] On import quotas, export subsidies, and commodity agreements, *Proposals for Expansion of World Trade* . . . (Nov. 1945), pp. 13, 15–16, 20–23; on interagency conflict on commodity agreements, Leslie A. Wheeler to the Secretary of Agriculture, July 3, 1945, Foreign Relations File, Records of Office of Sec. of Ag., Gen'l Cor., N.A.; and Executive Committee on Economic Foreign Policy to the President, attached to Wheeler's letter to the Secretary.

of 1945 was that brief season when the Allies could enjoy undisturbed their victory over fascism and peer hopefully into a future not yet darkened by Communist intractability. As State's *Proposals* phrased it, "The main prize in the victory of the United Nations is a limited and temporary power to establish the kind of world we want to live in." Supported by a seemingly worldwide consensus, the delegates were ready to transform the rhetoric of internationalism into a concrete program for elimination of hunger. But a prophetic shadow soon fell over the conference. While the work of creating administrative machinery progressed smoothly, differences developed concerning the purposes to which the machinery should be put. Was FAO to serve as dispenser of technology and patron of research, or should it become an action agency devoted to solving the problems of distribution as well as production? Countries like South Africa and Australia, burdened by surpluses since World War I, alluded to the need for programs of distribution. Backward agricultural nations like China spoke only of technical improvements. By electing Sir John Boyd Orr, Scottish farmer-scientist and expert on nutrition, as the director-general of FAO, the delegates gave at least temporary victory to the activists rather than the educators. Orr was determined to resolve that worst of the paradoxes of a free market: hunger amid surplus. He was an advocate of an international buffer stock scheme, similar to the one proposed by the Department of Agriculture. Though the conference dispersed without defining FAO's future, the prevailing mood remained optimistic. Said Sir John, "FAO is the answer to the atom bomb." To many others, the creation of FAO's machinery was the prelude to a great and humane venture in international relations. Like hunger itself, disagreements among members must prove conquerable.[6]

[6] For quotation from State's *Proposals*, p. 1; FAO, *Proceedings of*

In the year that followed, FAO conducted surveys and provided useful assistance in the fight against famine. To Orr, however, FAO must become more than a clearing house for information, and, on instructions from an emergency session in May, 1946, he published his *Proposals for a World Food Board* for submission to the annual conference. So great was the sense of urgency surrounding the appearance of this document that the annual conference convened two months earlier than scheduled.[7]

Like Agriculture's own proposals, Orr's World Food Board would set maximum and minimum world prices for storable agricultural commodities and maintain these prices through management of buffer stocks. By buying cheap and selling dear, the Board could pay for the considerable costs of storage. Unmarketable surpluses would be diverted to that half of the world's population too poor to afford an adequate diet. Orr's scheme boldly resolved some of the ambiguities in the Department of Agriculture's *Trade Program* by insisting that operations for all commodities be conducted by a single agency functioning as an independent, international entity. Deceptively simple, the World Food Board idea, as even Orr admitted, presented many practical difficulties. How, for instance, would subsidized distribution of chronic surpluses be financed and how managed so that regular markets would not be disrupted? Skeptics could justifiably ask for cost estimates and for suggestions on how prices could be set to satisfy both consumers and producers. Unencumbered as it was by essential detail, the concept was nevertheless the most imaginative ever advanced to solve the great dilemma

---

the First Session of the Conference (Washington, FAO: Jan. 1946), pp. 32–36, 40–44, 113–117, 119-126, 37–38; the quotation from Sir John is in the *New York Times*, Oct. 30, 1945, p. 8.

[7] On background of Sir John's proposals, "Report of the United States Delegation to the Third Session of the Conference, FAO," Nov. 11, 1947, Reports file, Records of Office of Sec. of Ag., Gen'l Cor., N.A.

of world agriculture, and it was so regarded in the Department of Agriculture. At the State Department, the defenders of free trade prepared for battle.[8]

Leading the opposition to the Orr plan for State was William L. Clayton, Assistant Secretary for Economic Affairs since 1944 and one of the world's great cotton merchants. Once described by a subordinate as an unreconstructed Manchester liberal, Clayton had left the Democratic party in the early 1930's and joined the Liberty League in protest against New Deal farm policies, but he returned to support Roosevelt in 1936 when Alf Landon attacked the reciprocal trade agreements program. It was Clayton who chaired the interagency committee that wrote the *Proposals for Expansion of World Trade and Employment*. Naturally he rejected the interventionist premises of the World Food Board. Thus State and Agriculture found themselves in a conflict of ideologies that had significant effects on postwar internationalism.[9]

On August 13, 1946, two weeks before the second annual conference of FAO convened in Copenhagen, Secretary of Commerce Henry Wallace told the press that the Cabinet had voted approval in principle of Orr's plan, which Wallace called an international ever-normal granary. The United States delegation, Wallace said, would recommend study of this and alternative proposals. But the secret instructions prepared by the State Department and approved by President Truman for the American delegation contained no endorsement, even in principle, of the World Food Board. As summarized by Under Secretary of State Dean Acheson,

[8] *Proposals for a World Food Board,* prepared by director general of FAO for the second session of the conference (Washington: FAO, July 5, 1945).

[9] On Clayton, see "Freer Trade vs. Control," *Fortune,* 35:2–4 (Feb. 1947); see also *Current Biography,* ed. Anna Roth (New York: H. W. Wilson Company, 1944), pp. 95–99.

these instructions stated "(1) that the problems of stabilizing agricultural prices and improving nutrition are important, (2) that international action is needed, (3) that the Conference should do no more on these problems than establish a committee to study alternative solutions." These instructions were obviously intended to convey polite indifference, and the conference would understand that the proposed committee was to serve as a graveyard for the embarrassing proposals.[10]

The delegates gathered on September 2, 1946, in the great upper chamber of the Parliament building in Copenhagen to hear King Christian X welcome the conference. Two days later, Orr delivered a sober and restrained address explaining his proposals and pleading for a solution to the world food problem that would vindicate the concept of internationalism. Norris E. Dodd, chief of the American delegation, spoke next.[11]

Dodd was an Oregon rancher and wheat farmer who had gone to work for the Agricultural Adjustment Agency during the Depression. By the time Clinton Anderson became Secretary, Dodd was chief of the AAA. In an apparent effort to weaken the power of the Agency in the Department, Anderson promoted Dodd to Under Secretary and confined his assignments to foreign agricultural affairs. Dodd's plain manner and quiet competence had won him wide respect in farm circles and provided striking contrast to the polished style of the professional diplomats with whom his new position brought him into frequent contact. Since the conference had no knowledge of the American position, Dodd began his speech amid noticeable suspense. After some remarks on the anomaly of overproduction in an underfed world, he shocked the State Department by declaring, "We in the

[10] *New York Times,* Aug. 14, 1946, p. 10; Dean Acheson to the President, Aug. 29, 1946, OF 85–n, TP, TL.

[11] FAO, *Proceedings of the Second Session of the Conference* (Washington, FAO: May 1947), pp. 3–4, 38–48.

United States . . . strongly favor the general objectives laid down by Sir John Boyd Orr." Dodd supported creation of an FAO commission to put the Orr proposals into final form. Seizing hopefully on the indecision in the Administration and interpreting his instructions with a liberality approaching disobedience, Dodd had placed the United States on record in favor of the World Food Board. When Dodd concluded, according to one observer at Copenhagen, "a sigh of profound relief swept the great upper council Chamber." It remained to be seen whether his revolt would be sustained at home.[12]

John Strachey, the British delegate, followed Dodd and maintained the forward momentum of the conference. Since Britain was a major importer and a broker of much of the world's trade in primary commodities, she was expected to oppose creation of an independent board with powers to control world farm prices, but Strachey informed the conference that Orr's plan had "in principle the full support of His Majesty's Government." The British, however, differed from Dodd and Orr on the question of who was to work out the details. Strachey talked of the dangers of a World Food Board twisted from its original intention into an instrument of restrictionism; he talked too of the need to include nations, like Russia, which were members of the United Nations but not the FAO. To prevent isolation of FAO and assure its compatibility with the principles of other world organizations, he proposed submitting the Orr plan to the Economic and Social Council of the United Nations. Since the World Food Board now received support from even the nations which a year earlier had stressed only technical progress, the real debate centered on the appropriate agency to formulate the details.[13]

[12] For Dodd's biography, see *Current Biography*, 1949, pp. 156–158; for Dodd's speech, *Proceedings of the Second Session*, pp. 43–46; for a knowledgeable account of this incident, see Russel Smith, "FAO: Copenhagen Story," *New Republic*, 115:471 (Oct. 14, 1946).

[13] FAO, *Proceedings of the Second Session*, pp. 46–52.

At stake was more than a procedural question. The FAO under its dedicated director general stood committed to the buffer stock concept. Who knew what delays or unforeseen opposition might await the proposals in perhaps less friendly councils? The State Department was especially quick to see the implication of removing the issue from FAO. Informed beforehand of the British position, State maneuvered to have the United States support the British, but the effort did not quite succeed. The Copenhagen conference, therefore, set up a preparatory commission under its own jurisdiction to meet no later than November 1, 1946, in Washington to consider the Orr proposals and any others addressing themselves to the great problem of world agriculture.[14]

Perhaps because Clinton Anderson only weakly supported the position of his Department, the State Department in the weeks after adjournment of the conference was able to bring the Administration firmly on its side of the argument. Dodd's gamble had failed. At the Washington meeting of the preparatory commission, he suffered the humiliation of having to inform the delegates that the Americans were reversing their position. The ITO, according to the new American view, provided a blueprint for solving world food problems. Without quantitative controls on supply, the United States doubted that the World Food Board would succeed. "Well," said Orr, "the State Department has won. But it's better to get it out in the open."[15]

[14] On State's efforts to obtain new instructions, Acheson's memo to the President, Aug. 29, 1946; on failure of State to change the instructions, see Smith, "FAO: Copenhagen Story," New Republic.

[15] Anderson's views of WFB were given in an interview with the author, July 24, 1962; for the American position at the meeting of the preparatory commission, "Position to Be Taken by the U.S. Representatives on the FAO Preparatory Commission," Oct. 25, 1946, FAO Preparatory Commission file, Records of BAE, International Organizations, Committees, and Conferences, N.A.; for Orr's quotation, see New York Times, Oct. 29, 1946, p. 4; on embarrassment caused by reversal of American position, see "The Lonely Furrow," Time, 48:31 (Nov. 11, 1946).

Nevertheless, the delegates worked in Washington for two months to salvage something from their ruined expectations. Frightened by a temporary threat of wheat surpluses, the United States retreated somewhat from its negativism late in December, 1946, and endorsed the principle of bargain sales to the undernourished. In January, 1947, the preparatory commission issued a report recommending "accumulation of limited reserves, sometimes known as buffer stocks, for commodities subject to seasonal and cyclical fluctuations but not likely to be in world surplus. Having regard to the financial obligations involved, we feel that . . . such stocks should be held nationally but administrated under internationally agreed rules." The commission endorsed the principle of bargain sales to poorer countries. The real meaning of the report was that FAO was abandoning all pretense of becoming a major force in world food matters. It surrendered even the small responsibility for overseeing future commodity negotiations to other international agencies. The real control over trade in food would remain in the hands of the separate governments whose policies had created the destructive rivalries of the recent past, and a unique opportunity for achieving a solution to the surplus problem was lost. "The State Department's objections to the world food board," said the *Nation*, "seem to be wholly doctrinaire, with no recognition of the significant difference between restrictive nationalistic controls and international controls which have as their aim stimulation of production and trade."[16]

Rescue of the ITO from the imaginary dangers of the

[16] On effects of possible wheat surplus on the American position, see *New York Times*, Dec. 21, 1946, p. 2; on revised American position, "Proposals for Consideration by Committee I," presented by U.S. Delegates, Nov. 12, 1946, FAO Preparatory Commission file, Records of BAE, Organizations, Committees, and Conferences, N.A.; *Report of FAO Preparatory Commission on World Food Proposals*, 1947, FAO Preparatory Commission File, Records of BAE; "Food and Trade," *Nation*, 163:516–517 (Nov. 9, 1946).

World Food Board did not end the struggle between State and Agriculture. Faced again with the prospect of managing surplus production nationally, Agriculture continued to regard free trade with fear. On the other hand, Agriculture was always eager to expand farm exports and realized that selective tariff reduction could have that result. Consequently, Agriculture never mounted any consistent attack on State's policies; its opposition most often took the form of guerrilla warfare on specific issues rather than conflict over general principles. In spite of the hesitancy of its challenge, the Department of Agriculture proved a serious annoyance to William L. Clayton and the Department of State.

State had been making steady progress toward establishment of ITO during 1946. In February, the United Nations Social and Economic Council summoned a committee to prepare for an International Conference on Trade and Employment. Meeting in London in the fall of that year, the preparatory committee debated the American proposals for an ITO and made large strides toward settling most of the issues separating the interested governments. The committee, however, had to make certain strategic retreats from the original American proposals, including dilution of the provisions regarding preferential tariff systems. The committee recommended that a second preparatory meeting be held in Geneva in April, 1947, both to continue discussion of the proposed charter and to undertake multilateral negotiations for reduction of tariffs.[17]

Since the London draft of the ITO charter (issued December, 1946) retained the exceptions needed by the Department of Agriculture to protect itself, the only peril to Agriculture's tranquillity as 1947 began came from the proposed multilateral tariff negotiations, known later as the General Agree-

[17] See *Charter for an International Trade Organization,* articles drafted at London (Dec. 1946).

ments on Tariff and Trade (GATT). A historic pronouncement by the Southern Commissioners of Agriculture illustrated the anxiety of American agriculture as the State Department began to drag it reluctantly from behind its trade barricades.

> The thirty-seven millions of citizens of the great Southland and their duly elected state officials, the Southern Commissioners of Agriculture, are each one sprung from the loins of those who for more than one hundred years carried the standards of the Democratic party in never-ending struggle and even on the field of battle . . . to support the economic theory and doctrine of "free trade" versus the "protective tariff." These stalwarts and Democratic Southern peoples, after long trials and due to the kaleidoscopic changes attending the national economy of the United States in a more modern world, are with reluctance compelled to burn all bridges behind them and to make prayer to their Chief Executive that he now retain on behalf of their agricultural products the vestiges of tariff protection which still remain in the Act of 1930.

With cotton supported above the world price, the Southern farmer was deserting the faith of his fathers.[18]

"Insofar as we have been able to ascertain," wrote the Acting Administrator of the Production and Marketing Administration to the Secretary on January 10, 1947, "there has been no well-defined or even general policy in the Department of Agriculture" on the coming tariff negotiations. Late that same month, however, the Department's Committee on Foreign Relations began the painful task of hammering out Agriculture's position on the various farm products to be discussed at Geneva. Inevitably the Department of Agriculture found its recommendations considerably less generous than those desired by State. Two weeks before the opening of the Geneva conference, Anderson wrote Will Clayton to

[18] The statement by the Southern Commissioners is reproduced in "Freer Trade vs. Control," *Fortune*, 35:2–4 (Feb. 1947).

appeal for more sympathetic consideration of Agriculture's problems. Price support programs must be protected from tariff reductions, he said. In cases where reductions are possible, these should be applicable only on a specified quantity of imports. The Department opposed duty reductions on livestock (though it would allow the quota to be doubled), most dairy products, poultry, eggs, grains, most vegetables, and wool. It agreed to a 50 percent reduction on certain cheeses, cabbage, Brazil nuts, and certain fats and oils.[19]

While State squabbled with Agriculture, Congress and the National Wool Growers Association were raising obstacles of their own to the Geneva conference. For months the Government had realized that one of the crucial issues of the conference would be wool. Undoubtedly the British Commonwealth would refuse to alter the empire preference system unless the United States made concessions on wool imports from Australia, New Zealand, and South Africa. But no group in America had more to lose from free trade than the sheep men.

During World War II the American sheep industry was crippled by rising costs and labor shortages. Even with heavy duties on wool imports, American sheep growers in the war years were unable to compete with the more efficient producers of the British Commonwealth. In 1943, to keep the industry alive, the Government decided that wool was a strategic material and began to purchase domestic supplies for storage at prices substantially above the world market. Once embarked on this program, the Department of Agriculture was reluctant to thrust the sheep men back into the

[19] Acting Administrator, PMA, to the Secretary, Jan. 10, 1947, Foreign Relations 2 file, Records of Office of Sec. of Ag., Gen'l Cor., N.A.; for a summary of Departmental preparations for forthcoming conference, L. A. Wheeler to the Secretary of Agriculture, Jan. 23, 1947; Foreign Relations 3 file, Records of Office of Sec. of Ag., Gen'l Cor., N.A.: Anderson to Clayton, March 25, 1947, Foreign Relations 2 file, Records of Office of Sec. of Ag., Gen'l Cor., N.A.

competitive market, and the Government continued to purchase and store American wool after the end of the war. With stocks mounting ever higher, Secretary Anderson finally announced that the program would be terminated on April 15, 1947, unless Congress decided otherwise. By March of that year, the Department was the sad owner of 460 million pounds of wool, considerably more than a year's domestic production.[20]

In time, the wool lobby, the wool Senators, and the Administration reached agreement on a new wool program. The Commodity Credit Corporation (CCC) would continue for two more years to buy domestic wool at prices above the world market, but henceforth it could resell its stocks in the domestic market at prices competitive with foreign imports. The Government, of course, would absorb a heavy financial loss. Though this tampering with the world trade in wool disturbed the State Department, the Department realistically acquiesced, and the bill seemed headed for easy passage. Then late in March, 1947, Norris Dodd, recently outmaneuvered at Copenhagen by State, evened the score with Will Clayton. Dodd warned a congressional committee that government losses might be substantial under the proposed wool program and predicted that whenever the Commodity Credit Corporation announced a price on its wool low enough to meet foreign competition, the foreign suppliers would undoubtedly drop their prices still lower to retain their American markets. To protect the CCC and facilitate disposal of its stocks, Dodd proposed that Congress authorize extra import fees or quotas to be employed whenever foreign wool posed serious obstacles to the new program. The House Committee on Agriculture obliged Dodd by reporting a wool bill on

[20] For background on the wool problem, see "Providing Support for Wool," Hearings before Committee on Agriculture, U.S. House of Representatives, 80th Cong., 1st sess., pp. 12–18; and *Congressional Record*, same sess., vol. 93, pt. 5, 5679.

April 15, 1947, complete with a provision authorizing the Secretary of Agriculture to impose import fees up to 50 percent ad valorem whenever the wool program needed protection.[21]

At Geneva, meanwhile, the conference began to bargain in an atmosphere heavy with pessimism. Plagued by trade deficits and sterling debts, Great Britain was reluctant to compromise the preference system which had given her partial defense against American imports. Few were surprised when Britain replied to early American offers with almost no concessions of her own. "The British attitude," one delegate wrote home in early May, "continues to be somewhat less than cooperative." But it was wool that posed the gravest obstacle to success at Geneva. Wool accounted for ninety percent of Australian exports to the United States, and Australia was the pivotal nation at the conference. Unless the Americans made concessions on the wool tariff, Australia would refuse to lower any of its tariff preferences currently favoring British imports and would in turn refuse to consent to any British modification of empire preferences affecting Australian exports to Britain—assuming Britain could be persuaded to make such concessions in the first place. When the United States offered only to freeze the wool tariff where it was, the Australian delegation threatened to go home. The rest of the Commonwealth used Australian dissatisfaction as an excuse for making poor offers of their own, and soon negotiations with New Zealand and South Africa were at a

[21] For proposed new program, see a copy of Senate Bill 814 in "Price Support Program for Wool," Hearings before Committee on Agriculture and Forestry, U.S. Senate, 80th Cong., 1st sess., pp. 3–4; for views of the State Department, see "Providing Support for Wool," Hearings before Committee on Agriculture, U.S. House of Representatives, same sess., pp. 157–160; for Dodd's testimony on quotas and fees, "Price Support for Wool," Senate hearings, pp. 45, 120–125; "Providing Support for Wool," April 15, 1947, House Report No. 257, *House Miscellaneous Reports,* vol. V, same sess.

standstill. If Congress should attach new import restrictions to the pending wool bill, the American negotiators might even have to withdraw their offer to freeze the wool duty. Passage of the bill, reported the *New York Times* correspondent at Geneva, would most likely force the nations of the British Empire to reconsider the whole concept of an International Trade Organization. The eighteen nations at Geneva could do little until the American and Commonwealth delegations came to terms. By mid-May, the conference seemed to be staggering to a regrettable climax.[22]

Attention shifted back to the House of Representatives where the wool bill was to come up for debate on May 22, 1947. Rallying to the support of the import fee were not only wool Democrats and their cotton friends, but also all those Republicans who had never really felt comfortable with the bipartisan foreign policy. Regarding the Hawley–Smoot Tariff as a national blessing and the State Department as a haven for "do-gooders," these Republicans used the wool bill to fight a rearguard action on behalf of protectionism and the past. So insistent was their rancor that they carried with them the leadership of the party. Members of the House Republican Steering Committee met secretly to redraft the controversial tariff provision to make it less distasteful to the moderates. A few days before the House debated the bill, Congressman Clifford Hope, Republican from Kansas, presented the revised version to a meeting of the House Committee on Agriculture. Unaware that the Hope amendment was really part of Republican strategy, the Democrats on the Committee accepted it as a reasonable compromise. The new version gave authority to impose import fees to the President instead of to the Secretary of Agriculture

[22] For a discussion of British attitude at Geneva and obstacles posed by American wool, Robert B. Schwenger to L. A. Wheeler, May 13, 1947, Meetings file, Records of OFAR, Gen'l Cor., N.A.; *New York Times*, June 12, 1947, pp. 1 and 18.

and provided for preliminary hearings by the Tariff Commission. If the President finds the wool program endangered by imports, said the amendment, "he shall by proclamation . . . impose fees."[23]

Faced with deadlock at Geneva and sabotage in the House, Will Clayton, who was serving as chairman of the Geneva conference, decided to fly home to oppose the Hope amendment in person. He quickly wrote a letter to Democratic Representative Harold D. Cooley of North Carolina, ranking Democrat on the Committee on Agriculture, and stated his case. "If at this time," Clayton said, "when we are actually negotiating with the other countries at Geneva for the lowering of trade barriers, we raise new barriers as this bill proposes, we stand convicted of insincerity." Wool, he said, accounts for only one half of one percent of American agricultural income. Unless America offers a reasonable proposal on wool, we shall lose the cooperation of the British Empire and consequently an opportunity to make a better world. Said Republican Representative Robert F. Rich of Pennsylvania, "I am for the tariff . . . If you want to help American labor . . . let us have a tariff . . . let us bring Clayton back . . . let the foreign countries take care of themselves." Cooley, for one, was persuaded that his previous support of the Hope amendment was wrong, and he did his best to win over the other Democrats. It did neither Clayton nor Cooley much good that their opponents could claim the Department of Agriculture as an early supporter of import restrictions on wool. When Cooley proposed an amendment to give reciprocal trade agreements precedence over the tariff provision in the bill, he was defeated 102 to a scant 27. The House passed the wool bill with the Hope amendment. In Canberra, Australia, Prime Minister Joseph B. Chifley

[23] On role of Republican Steering Committee, see *Congressional Record*, 80th Congress, 1st sess., vol. 93, pt. 5, 5695; for text of Hope amendment, *ibid.*, pp. 5750–5751.

told his parliament that he was "confounded and astonished" by the action of the American House of Representatives.[24]

In the resulting Senate–House conference committee, the senators fought for two weeks to eliminate the Hope amendment, but the House conferees would not yield and the provision remained. When the House began debating the conference committee's report, Cooley rose to tell his colleagues that the wool bill "is nothing more or less than an insidious effort to undermine the reciprocal trade treaty program." No one disputed his charge. In spite of a determined effort by Administration forces and pleas from Secretary of State Marshall and former Secretaries Stimson and Hull, the bill passed 191 to 166. Three days later, on June 19, 1947, the Senate too accepted the conference bill (48–38). Australia let it be known that if the bill became law, she would move the adjournment of the conference. Though the Farm Bureau and other defenders of wool appealed to him to accept the bill, President Truman had to support the State Department. In his veto message, Truman said that if he had signed the bill, it "would be interpreted around the world as a first step on the same road to economic isolationism down which we and other countries travelled after the First World War with such disastrous consequences." Shortly thereafter, a new bill, free of provisions for fees or quotas, passed the Congress and was signed by the President. Though it had taken a presidential veto to rescue his policies from a resurgent isolationism, Clayton could return to Geneva secure in the knowledge that American sincerity had been vindicated.[25]

[24] For Clayton's letter to Cooley, see the copy in *Congressional Record*, 80th Cong., 1st sess., vol. 93, pt. 5, 5692; for Rep. Rich's statement, *ibid.*, p. 5678; on Cooley's amendment, *ibid.*, pp. 5751, 5760; for the reaction of Australian Prime Minister, see "Some Wool over the Ayes," *Newsweek*, 29:34 (June 9, 1947).

[25] For Cooley's statement, see *Congressional Record*, 80th Cong., 1st

Though negotiators at Geneva could now proceed undisturbed by the rumbling of Congress, the wool duty still remained the principal problem. Unless Australia received a cut in the duty, imperial preferences would stand. Moreover, without a wool concession, Australia felt unable to lower her own tariff duties on goods from other nations, who in turn could not settle with each other or the United States until they reached agreement with Australia. "And so," the New York Times reported, "by a kind of chain reaction, nearly every negotiation going on here runs into the block caused by the American wool policy." Finally in early August, 1947, the American delegates offered to cut the wool duty 25 percent, and under pressure from South Africa, Australia reluctantly accepted.[26]

But new problems had already arisen at the conference to dwarf the old ones. The irony of Geneva was that while the delegates were striving to reduce trade barriers and define trade rules, the very foundations of world trade were crumbling. The summer of 1947 saw the nations of western Europe poised at the brink of bankruptcy, their industrial plant still unredeemed from the ravages of war, their dollar resources perilously close to exhaustion, their peoples once more menaced by famine. These nations, and especially Great Britain, dependent for her life on trade, regarded with fear the reforms taking shape under the aegis of the State Department. Let them talk of free trade at Geneva. In London, the Government was struggling to prevent economic catastrophe and would employ whatever measures were

---

sess., vol. 93, pt. 6, 7105; for appeals of Marshall, Stimson, and Hull, *Congressional Record*, same sess., p. 7103; for House vote, *ibid.*, p. 7112; for Senate vote, *ibid.*, pp. 7284–7285; on Australian threat, see *New York Times*, June 24, 1947, p. 17; "Wool Act 1947–Veto Message," Senate Doc. 68, *Senate Miscellaneous Documents*, 80th Cong., 1st sess.

[26] On these developments, see *New York Times*, July 25, 1947, p. 7; Aug. 10, 1947, p. 27; Aug. 12, 1947, p. 37.

necessary for self-defense. As the clouds gathered over Europe, Clement Atlee told the United States, in August, 1947, that his country could sign no multilateral trade agreement unless permitted temporarily to retain her discriminatory import controls. The United States had no choice but to accede to the request. Soon afterward, the British announced that they were curbing American agricultural imports by 600 million dollars a year in an effort to conserve dollars. A week later Britain suspended free convertibility of sterling to dollars, an obligation undertaken less than a month before at the insistence of the United States Government.[27]

All this had its effects on the Geneva conference. The British negotiators, of course, clung more jealously than ever to the imperial preference system. Of the total trade represented at the conference, 70 percent passed between England and the United States. Without agreement between the two giants, there could be no meaningful conclusion to the negotiations. Through August, Britain held firm, and hopes kept fading. Then in September, she made enough concessions to keep the conference going. By October, 1947, the United States could take satisfaction from several important reductions in British preferences, which, while not sweeping or deep, were still enough to make the conference a success. After six months of arduous negotiation, the delegates had as their reward 123 separate agreements involving one half of the world's trade.[28] Though the American farmer made con-

[27] On Britain's dollar crisis, Telegram from No. 4291 to Secretary of State, London, Aug. 8, 1947, Records of OFAR, Gen'l Cor., N.A.; on British insistence on temporary discriminatory import controls, see *New York Times*, Aug. 2, 1947, p. 1; on curtailment of American agricultural imports, N. E. Dodd to Robert A. Lovett, Aug. 14, 1947, Foreign Relations 2 file, Records of Office of Sec. of Ag., Gen'l Cor., N.A.; on suspension of convertibility, see *New York Times*, Aug. 21, 1947, p. 1.

[28] *New York Times*, Sept. 9, 1947, p. 4; Oct. 10, 1947, pp. 1 and 3; Oct. 30, 1947, p. 1.

cessions on wool, butter, beef, sugar, wheat, and a host of less important products, many of these either lowered duties only on the small quantities permitted by quotas or merely reduced inflated tariffs. The wheat duty, for instance, fell from 42 cents to 21 cents, but since the wheat quota was only 800,000 bushels per year, the concession was meaningless. Agriculture had defended its interests with great skill. The State Department, of course, had realized that if it aroused the anger of farm congressmen, the whole reciprocal trade agreement program would be in jeopardy. As for his exports, the American farmer received such benefits as removal of the 20 percent Canadian duty on most fresh fruit, inclusion of apples on the British free list, a flat 10 percent duty without quota on all dried fruits sent to France and a 66 percent reduction of the French wheat duty. The work done at Geneva to reduce tariffs worked no hardships on the American farmer. But from agriculture's view, the simultaneous negotiations on the ITO charter had not gone so well.[29]

Midway through the Geneva conference, a subcommittee unexpectedly rewrote the articles on export subsidies, making them unacceptable to the Americans. The United States was paying export subsidies only on cotton in 1947, but the Government realized that if surpluses returned, it might have to make more extensive use of this device. The new provisions stipulated that beginning two years after the formation of ITO, nations could pay export subsidies only with ITO's permission. In addition, the Geneva articles applied only to the American method of subsidizing exports and excepted the kind of subsidies used by other countries. Because the Americans supported farm prices above the world market,

[29] On important agricultural provisions of GATT, see Minutes of Staff Meeting, Nov. 20, 1947, Meetings 6 file, Records of Office of Sec. of Ag., Gen'l Cor., N.A.; for a discussion of American concessions, see Allan Rau, *Agricultural Policy and Trade Liberalization in the United States* (Geneva: Librairie E. Drouz, 1957), pp. 113–115.

their subsidies were open and direct.[30] Other nations supported income rather than price, thereby financing exports in a hidden but nonetheless effective manner. The United States asserted its right to make its own decision on the use of subsidies and protested against the unfair application of the provisions. With the adjournment of GATT in the fall of 1947, the work of the preparatory commission was over, and the discussions on the ITO charter moved to Havana, site of the United Nations Conference on Trade and Employment.

In Washington, Clinton Anderson made it quite clear to the State Department that there could be no compromise on the subsidy issue. He wrote State in November, 1947, that the subsidy provision as it stood would "make it practically impossible for the Department to discharge its responsibilities under existing agricultural price support legislation." Consequently, the United States delegation in Havana introduced a new subsidy proposal in which the only real limitation on the right to pay subsidies was that they should not be used to capture more than a fair share of the world market. The original State Department position of 1945 had imposed stricter limitations on subsidies, but in view of growing skepticism in American farm circles toward the charter, it now seemed politic to reduce the areas of possible domestic contention as much as possible.[31]

The controversy over subsidies soon laid bare the real hostility of Agriculture to the whole ITO idea. For years, State had been trying to undermine the basis of the Agriculture

[30] *Report of Second Session of the Preparatory Committee of the United Nations Conference on Trade and Employment* (U.N. Publication E/PC/T/186), 1947, pp. 26–28.
[31] Clinton Anderson to Willard Thorp, Nov. 13, 1947, Meetings—ITO–Havana file, Records of OFAR, Gen'l Cor., N.A.; "Proposed U.S. Position . . . Regarding the Provisions of the Draft Charter Relating to Subsidies," Nov. 13, 1947, same file.

Department's programs, rarely showing any sympathy for the problems of the farmers, and making necessary compromises with ill-concealed regret. Agriculture's criticism of the Geneva subsidy provision soon burst into an over-all attack on the charter. "I have been gravely concerned," Anderson wrote Secretary Marshall in December, 1947, "as to the effect that the proposed charter might have, if it were adopted, on the welfare of the farmers of this country." Anderson pointed first, of course, to the provision on export subsidies. Next, and for the first time, he warned of the dread results that might occur should import quotas be permitted only in times of surplus. And finally, "article 21, granting escape from many of the restrictions for countries experiencing balance of payments difficulties, seems to me to grant a blanket escape to almost all the countries of the world except the United States and one or two others." After this assault, which accomplished nothing, the Department lapsed again into semiacquiescence.[32]

In Havana, Canada and Brazil led the opposition to the United States on the question of subsidies. Canada, with wheat markets to protect, and Brazil, hopeful of increasing foreign cotton sales, had much to gain from a successful attack on American export subsidies. With less apparent reasons, Britain too lined up with the opposition, as she had done in Geneva. After two months of negotiating, Canada and the United States reached a compromise: Though ITO had power to determine what was a fair share of the world market, each nation would decide on what commodities it would pay subsidies. Moreover, income payments (indirect subsidies) would be considered a form of export subsidy. Hopeful that she would receive sympathetic treatment from ITO, Brazil also accepted the compromise. But Britain, who

---

[32] Clinton Anderson to George C. Marshall, Dec. 15, 1947, Foreign Relations 2 file, Records of Office of Sec. of Ag., Gen'l Cor., N.A.

had earlier explained her support of the Geneva draft in terms of loyalty to a Commonwealth partner, suddenly stood forth alone and with belligerence against the compromise. Subsidies, Britain now said, were wrong in principle. Previous to this display of highmindedness, the American delegation interpreted Britain's stand on subsidies as a ruse for extorting more favorable consideration for discriminatory import practices. Actually the British had been hoping all along that the subsidy issue would deadlock the conference and that there never would be a charter or an ITO. But Britain could not hold out indefinitely by herself, and finally she, too, accepted the new provision. The delegates successfully resolved all other differences, put the finishing touches on the charter, and adjourned in March, 1948.[33]

The subsidies dispute revealed much about the ITO episode, including Agriculture's basic antagonism to the concept, the reluctance of Britain to abandon her restrictive practices, and the gradual erosion of the original principles to accommodate necessity. In the words of Agriculture's delegate to Havana, the "Charter is no longer a Charter for the reduction of trade barriers as much as an undertaking of the signatory countries to work together and consult on matters of economic interest." The *Proposals* drafted in 1945 had been twisted beyond recognition by the addition of escape clauses and exceptions. At the same time that these alterations made the charter palatable to a great many conflicting international interests, they alienated necessary sources of support at home.

[33] On opposition of Brazil, Canada, and Britain, Robert B. Schwenger's "Report on Subsidies in the ITO Charter, as of Dec. 13, 1947," Meetings file, Records of OFAR, Gen'l Cor., N.A.; and Robert B. Schwenger to Clair Wilcox, Feb. 3, 1948, Meetings–ITO–Havana file, Records of OFAR, Gen'l Cor., N.A.; on subsidy compromise and continuing British opposition, "Report on Status of Havana Subsidies Negotiations as of Feb. 8, 1948," same file; on American suspicions that Britain did not want a charter, Schwenger to L. A. Wheeler, Feb. 18, 1948, same file.

The Chamber of Commerce and the National Association of Manufacturers regarded the document as a betrayal of free enterprise. *Fortune,* long a supporter of Clayton's policies, denounced the work done at Havana, and said that further pursuit of an ITO would be futile. That the Farm Bureau and Farmers Union eventually supported ITO was striking evidence of how far the charter had strayed from its original purpose. Indeed the Havana compromises that had changed the character of ITO were in large part made necessary by the State Department's original concessions to Agriculture. No congressional committee ever reported the charter, and in December, 1950, President Truman announced that he would not again submit it to Congress. Two months later, the British also declared that as far as they were concerned, ITO was dead. Like American agriculture, the nations of the world had been unable to make the economic realities fit the theories of the State Department.[34]

It had been Agriculture's contention all along that the only solution to global surpluses was not free trade, but massive intervention. Commodity agreements that set prices or allocated markets or created buffer stocks would impose order on the chaos of national competition. Thus while ITO moved slowly on its way to oblivion, Agriculture was trying out its own answer to the dilemma of trade. In July, 1945, the International Cotton Study Group drafted proposals to allot shares of the world market among the exporting nations. But be-

[34] For comment of American delegate, see R. B. Schwenger to Eric Englund, April 18, 1948, Meetings–ITO–Havana file, Records of OFAR, Gen'l Cor., N.A.; for views on the charter of the Chamber of Commerce, N.A.M., and the farm organizations, see "Membership and Participation by the United States in the International Trade Organization," Hearings before Committee on Foreign Affairs, House of Representatives, 81st Cong., 2nd sess., pp. 407–440, 561–570, 335–349, 764–765; for views of *Fortune,* see "ITO Charter," *Fortune,* 40:61–62 (July 1949); on fate of ITO, see "International Trade Organization," *International Organization,* vol. V (May 1951), 384.

cause the Liverpool Cotton Exchange opposed restrictions on its control over cotton prices, the British Government was somewhat less than excited by the prospect of an agreement, and the long meetings of 1946 and 1947 came to nothing. Efforts dragged on for some years more, got nowhere, and were finally abandoned. The story for wheat was somewhat different.[35]

Since 1933 interested governments had been trying to negotiate a workable wheat agreement. Finally in March, 1948, their persistence seemed ready for its reward. Thirty-three importing countries agreed to buy 500,000,000 bushels of wheat (about half the amount entering world trade), from three of the four major exporters (Canada, Australia, and the United States) at prices that were within a predetermined range. During the five years of the agreement, maximum prices were to be $2.00; minimum prices would begin at $1.50 and would fall ten cents each year to $1.10. This agreement differed markedly from most earlier efforts, for it imposed no limits on the quantity of wheat passing into international trade. If scarcity drove wheat prices upward, importers were assured of at least some supplies at the $2.00 price. If surpluses sent the world price beneath the minimum, exporters knew that a portion of their production would bring from $1.50 to $1.10. The result, it was hoped, would be a measure of price stability in world wheat markets. If wheat prices in the United States exceeded the $2.00 maximum, the Government would pay producers an export subsidy on the 185 million bushels that it had committed under the agreement.[36]

[35] International Cotton Study Group, "Tentative Agreements," July 20, 1945, Foreign Relations file, Records of Office of Sec. of Ag., Gen'l Cor., N.A.; on reasons for failure to reach agreement, interview with Leslie A. Wheeler, Aug. 2, 1962.

[36] On past efforts to negotiate an agreement, see H. Tyszynski, "Economics of the Wheat Agreement," *Economica*, 16:27–39 (Feb.

Innocuous though the agreement seemed, it nevertheless provoked great fears among the grain traders. In their testimony before a subcommittee of the Senate Foreign Relations Committee, they offered many ingenious criticisms of the agreement, warning especially of infringements of national sovereignty and potentially high subsidy costs. But John L. Locke of the Millers National Federation spoke their real objection: "Government control of prices in one segment of a trade always leads to demands that controls be extended to all segments of that trade . . . Thus if the agreement is ratified, it may result in government control of all domestic as well as international transactions in wheat." (These fears eventually proved entirely groundless.) The grain traders spent considerable time early in the summer of 1948 button-holing members of the subcommittee to counter the testimony of the Farm Bureau and the Department of Agriculture, with the result that consideration of the agreement was postponed until the next session. Charles F. Brannan, recently appointed Secretary of Agriculture, informed the subcommittee that failure to ratify by August, 1948, would be tantamount to rejection. The importing countries were anticipating benefits from the agreement in the next crop year and would demand new negotiations if America delayed acceptance until 1949. His appeal failed to move the subcommittee, and the Department of Agriculture watched still another opportunity slip away. The Democrats did not neglect to point out to the farmers in the election of 1948 that a Republican Senate preferred grain traders to wheat farmers.[37]

1949); for provisions of the 1948 agreement, see "International Wheat Agreement," Hearings before Committee on Foreign Relations, U.S. Senate, 80th Cong., 2nd sess., pp. 6–30.

[37] "International Wheat Agreement," Hearings before Committee on Foreign Relations, U.S. Senate, 80th Cong., 2nd sess., pp. 68–84; on lobbying by grain traders, N. E. Dodd to Russel Smith, May 20, 1948, Foreign Relations 3 file, Records of Office of Sec. of Ag., Gen'l

The negotiations of 1949 took place in a radically different atmosphere. The sudden end of the world wheat shortage had sent prices sliding downward. After lengthy haggling, the exporters had to accept a maximum price of only $1.80. Less attractive for United States farmers than the agreement of 1948, this one passed the Senate under the determined prodding of the farm organizations, and the first and only commodity agreement of the postwar period went into effect.[38]

On its very face, the international wheat agreement was much too puny an instrument to deal with the problem of chronic surpluses, and in spite of the early hopes of its sponsors, it achieved only paltry results. During the life of the first agreement, unforeseen developments such as bad weather and the Korean War, kept world prices so high that the exporting countries had to pay heavy subsidies to farmers on wheat shipped under the agreement. In 1953, when the agreement was renegotiated, it raised the maximum from $1.80 to $2.05 and the minimum from $1.20 to $1.55. But as Britain correctly prophesied when she refused to adhere, prices set in the new agreement were now too high. Only Canadian manipulation of export prices in contradiction to the terms of the agreement kept prices from falling to the minimum. Indeed the agreement had no perceptible effects at all in determining world prices. Surpluses began mounting during the 1953 agreement, and they continued to mount under future agreements. The real problem was overproduction rather than price instability, and the feeble provisions of the wheat agreements offered no cure.[39]

Cor., N.A.; Charles F. Brannan to Henry Cabot Lodge, June 16, 1948, same file.

[38] Helen C. Farnsworth, "International Wheat Agreement and Problems, 1949–1956," *Quarterly Journal of Economics*, 70:221–223 (May 1956).

[39] Farnsworth, "International Wheat Agreements," *QJE*, pp. 228–232,

The fault lay not with Agriculture's basic concept, but with the practical difficulties of bringing together a profusion of conflicting international interests. Governments overwhelmed by short-run problems could not command the vision needed to negotiate agreements providing for buffer stocks, or orderly surplus disposal to the undernourished, or production curbs. In the end, then, the efforts of both State and Agriculture were in vain. Each had helped to undermine the design of the other, but both were doomed to defeat by the sheer complexity of economic life in the postwar world.

246–247; for statistics on world production and trade of wheat, see "Problems of Wheat," *The Economist*, 195:895 (May 28, 1960).

6   THE PROBLEM OF ABUNDANCE

✌ During Truman's first term, agricultural policy makers devised new ways to deal with the problems of abundance that had plagued farmers between the world wars. In the postwar era, the planners argued, right policy would convert abundance into a blessing. From their creative labors issued ideas that were new and bold, but, unfortunately, obsolete from the moment of their conception. For America was in the midst of an agricultural revolution that had begun with the advent of World War II and would continue for at least two decades after the return of peace, but whose true magnitude proved beyond the imagination of the planners in the 1940's to grasp. Unable to perceive the dimension of the technological changes already transforming agriculture, their efforts were condemned to failure.

The term *revolution* is by no means an exaggeration to describe what happened to farming after 1940. Only the Civil War period saw changes of comparable significance. Then farmers took giant steps toward shifting from manpower to animal power, as mechanical reapers, corn planters, threshers, and other machinery drawn by the horse, came into common use. Spurred by wartime demand and record prices, farmers in the Civil War hastened to use the backlog of invention that had been accumulating since 1830. By 1880 the shift to animal power was complete, and from then until

1940 productivity gains occurred at a slower rate. The second agricultural revolution, initiated by World War II, was also possible only because of the technological advances made in the previous twenty years, advances that drought and depression had discouraged farmers from using. After 1940, given wartime incentive and severe labor shortages, farmers hastened to employ every bit of available technology to increase production, and, of course, profits. The interwar accumulation of unused potential production had gone largely unnoticed, and so the dramatic impact of its employment after 1940 proved startling. By 1946, with less labor than before the war, American agriculture was producing 33 percent more food and fiber than the 1935–1939 average. But what observers did not see was that this was only the beginning, and it was this understandable failure of vision that would betray the policy-makers. After 1945, as industry converted to a peacetime basis, resources became available to produce more of the fertilizer, chemicals, and steel machinery that helped to make the revolution possible. Even in the 1950's, when agriculture again plunged into depression, farmers continued to seize on technological advances in an effort to cut costs and so avoid extinction.[1] By 1957–1959, farmers were producing 60 percent more food and fiber than the prewar average; by 1963, 75 percent more. In 1940 one farm worker supplied all the farm products needed by eleven people. In 1945 that same worker could supply the needs of fourteen people; by 1956, sixteen people; in 1963, thirty people.[2]

If the first agricultural revolution brought the change from manpower to animal power, then the second hastened the

[1] Wayne D. Rasmussen, "The Impact of Technological Change in American Agriculture, 1862–1962," *Journal of Economic History*, 22: 578–591 (Dec. 1962).

[2] USDA, *Changes in Farm Production and Efficiency*, Statistical Bulletin No. 233, revised (July 1964), pp. 7, 44.

transformation from animal power to mechanical power made possible principally by the gasoline tractor. In 1940, over one and one-half million tractors were already on American farms. By the end of the war, farmers were using 2.3 million tractors, and by 1963, 4.6 million.[3] In the South, where mechanization had lagged far behind other regions, the exigencies of war brought tractors into common use for the first time. By doing some of the work of farm labor, tractors served after the war to encourage Southern landowners to use the new cotton picking machines that could complete the mechanization process. In 1947, 2 percent of the cotton crop was harvested mechanically; by 1955, 23 percent.[4] Tractors not only did the plowing on American farms; they also supplied the power for such machines as the corn picker and the grain combine, whose wider use was also facilitated by World War II. The number of grain combines on farms, for instance, doubled during the war years and continued to rise rapidly thereafter.[5] The mechanization process steadily eliminated the need for horses and mules, and in 1962 the Department of Agriculture discontinued reporting their numbers.[6] Between 1920 and 1950, fifty-five million acres that had sustained farm animals used for power were freed for production of marketable commodities. Mechanization not only contributed to productivity; it also vastly improved the quality of American farm life by reducing the drudgery of farm labor.[7]

The rapid application of technology to agriculture after 1940 brought better balanced feeding of livestock, widespread use

[3] USDA, *Changes in Farm Production and Efficiency*, pp. 29, 30.

[4] James H. Street, *The New Revolution in the Cotton Economy* (Chapel Hill: North Carolina University Press, 1957), p. 158.

[5] Sherman E. Johnson, *Changes in American Farming*, USDA Misc. Pub. No. 707 (Dec. 1949), p. 13.

[6] Rasmussen, "The Impact of Technological Change in American Agriculture," p. 578.

[7] Johnson, *Changes in American Farming*, p. 15.

of chemicals for such purposes as weed killers and defoliants, and more effective methods to control insects and disease. Improved conservation practices, most notably the use of cover crops, gained greatly in popularity. But most of all came the miracles achieved by genetics and fertilizer.[8]

By the time of World War I experimenters knew that self-fertilization in corn plants tended both to purify and weaken strains, but that crossbreeding the inbred strains could restore vigor. Careful breeding, therefore, might produce corn strains far superior to anything known before. Though ready for commercial use by the early 1920's, modern hybrid seed corn had found its way to only one percent of the nation's corn acreage by 1933 and to 15 percent of the corn acreage by 1938. But by the end of the war, the percentage had risen to 69, and in 1960, all but 4 percent of the nation's corn acreage was in hybrid seed. Merely by itself, hybrid corn raised yield expectancy by 20 percent. In combination and other improvements, it did even more. The average yield per acre of corn rose from 23 bushels in 1933 to 62 bushels in 1964.

After the success of hybrid corn, new breeding techniques spread to other crops. By 1958 half the acreage planted in sorghum feed grain was sown with hybrid seed. Yields increased from 19 bushels per acre in 1951 to 41 bushels in 1964. Scientific breeding produced improved strains of wheat and various vegetables. Advances in livestock breeding were slower but no less real. Crosses of American hogs with the Danish Landrace hog and subsequent intermating of the progeny produced several new, mildly inbred lines that gave more lean meat, less fat, and larger litters. In the sheep industry, crossbreeding followed by intermating and selection

[8] Wayne D. Rasmussen, "Scientific Agriculture," (in manuscript form for a forthcoming publication, *History of Technology*, ed. Melvin Kranzberg).

achieved major changes. In the American beef cattle industry, productivity gains resulted mainly from improved nutritional practices, but crossbreeding did produce lines well suited to the peculiar agricultural conditions of the South. Genetic advances in the dairy cattle industry, however, were great. Discovery that certain sires regularly produced milk cows of superior productivity led after 1940 to widespread adoption of artificial insemination. In 1939 only 646 herds with 7,539 cows were using artificial breeding methods. By 1962, 7.7 million cows in 862,000 herds were bred artificially. In 1961, the average amount of milk produced yearly by a daughter of a proved sire was 11,172 pounds, compared to the average productivity of all dairy cows of 7,223 pounds.[9]

The greatest gains made in agricultural production came from increased use of lime and fertilizers. Lime is not a fertilizer, but by reducing soil acidity it enables commercial fertilizers, especially phosphates, to perform more effectively By the end of the war, farmers were using three times as much lime as they had before the war. With the chemical industry producing better products, the appetite of the American land for mixed chemical fertilizers seemed insatiable. During the war years alone, farmers took advantage of such chemical fertilizers as concentrated superphosphate (developed by the Tennessee Valley Authority) and the latest synthetic nitrogenous preparations to double the amount of all plant nutrients that they were adding to the soil. After the war, the increase was even more rapid. In 1939, for instance, farmers were spreading 398,000 tons of nitrogen over the land. By the war's end, the quantity had mounted to 635,000, and by 1963 was 3,770,000 tons. The results for production were astounding. The Department of Agriculture has estimated that increased use of fertilizers accounted for 55 percent of

[9] Rasmussen, "Scientific Agriculture"; also on genetics, see Johnson, *Changes in American Farming*, pp. 4, 32–46.

the productivity gains per crop acre that occurred from 1940 to 1955. These triumphs of fertilizer and of other technological improvements had an ironic result. They created huge price-depressing surpluses, which by the 1950's, in combinatinn with insufficient migration from the farm, impoverished large portions of rural America. Only the famine in Europe and the Korean War saved the farmer from depression in the Truman years.[10]

In 1945, though aware that important changes had already occurred on American farms, agricultural economists could not yet see how many more changes were to come. Consequently what most impressed them about the wartime experience was not increased production but rather the inability of farmers to satiate the nation's appetite during the prosperous war years. Overnight, full employment and war had transformed the surpluses of the 1930's into the shortages of the 1940's. As many suspected all along, underconsumption, not overproduction, had been the real problem of the Depression. Let factories in the city continue to hum, the economists said, and the average American would yearly consume 160 pounds of meat instead of the 130 that he ate before the war. He would buy 30 pounds of poultry instead of 20; 75 pounds of citrus fruit instead of 49; 350 eggs instead of 300. His table would groan under ever larger quantities of fruits, milk, and vegetables. If only he had enough money in his pocket, the American citizen would eat most of the so-called surpluses. By 1945, in the Bureau of Agricultural Economics and on campuses throughout the country, the word *abundance* came to summarize a hopeful view of the farm problem, a view holding that not crop controls but full industrial employment in the coming peace was the best

[10] Rasmussen, "Scientific Agriculture"; the statistical data for this discussion is in Johnson, *Changes in American Farming*, pp. 24–25; and USDA, *Changes in Farm Production and Efficiency*, pp. 21–22.

farm program. By rejecting restrictionist economics, the advocates of abundance broke sharply with the New Deal and created in effect a new liberalism.[11]

According to its advocates, abundance was not merely inescapable; it was a positive blessing. Assuming full employment, the Bureau of Agricultural Economics estimated that Americans would want to buy 18 percent more food and fiber in 1950 than before the war. At current levels of technology, the task of meeting this volume of domestic demand and maintaining exports would require 369 million acres of land or 19 million acres more than were actually under cultivation in 1945. But what if technological advances should continue, asked BAE. On the basis of estimates that seriously underestimated the future pace of change, BAE calculated that continuing productivity gains might reduce the number of needed acres in 1950 to 327 million acres or 23 million fewer than were currently cultivated. To solve the problem of the possible surplus acres, the new liberals proposed to widen the scope of farm policy and make it an instrument in the fight against poverty.[12]

Since, the liberals argued, a large portion of the American people would lack adequate nutrition even in times of full employment, the extra acres should be used to feed the undernourished through subsidized consumption programs. The New Dealers had attacked the problem of low farm income by restricting production; the liberal of 1945 would prevent the problem by expanding consumption. To some the needs

[11] For the major statement of the new liberalism, see USDA, *What Peace Can Mean to American Farmers: Agricultural Policy*, Misc. Pub. No. 589 (Dec. 1945); for estimates on per capita consumption of various products in times of full employment and a good statement of the new liberalism, see Clinton P. Anderson, "Is the Farmer Heading for Trouble Again?", *Saturday Evening Post*, 213:18–19, 94–96 (Dec. 22, 1945).

[12] USDA, *What Peace Can Mean to American Farmers: Post-War Agriculture and Employment*, Misc. Pub. No. 562 (May 1945).

of the undernourished seemed so great that the farmer could grow more food indefinitely. But the Department of Agriculture was considerably less optimistic. If the government undertook to provide all families earning less than $1,500 a year "a low income adequate diet," only five million more acres would be used. A high quality diet for these families would, of course, put many more acres to work, but the Department left the number unspecified. To avoid overproduction and underemployment in agriculture, said BAE, farm labor should fall from nine and one-half to eight million.[13]

And what of the farmer in all this? The BAE estimated that in 1950, under full employment and without price supports, the general level of his farm prices would be at about 100 percent of parity compared with 119 percent in 1943. Reasonable prosperity would be a gift of the free market, and the elaborate machinery of the Depression could be thrown away. Among the refuse would be the notion of parity, that is, that there is an ideal price for a commodity not related to its market situation. The first commandment of agrarian fundamentalism had been that the price a farmer received for his product should have purchasing power equal to what it possessed in some favorable period in the past, usually 1910–1914. The peculiar marriage of parity and price supports stood as the foremost obstacle in bringing production into line with the desires of the consuming public. By freezing prices in some faraway relationship, the concept of parity ignored changes in consumer taste and cost of production, thereby overpricing certain products and encouraging farmers to grow too much of them during periods of price support. Relatively, it cost much more to produce livestock and much less to grow wheat in 1945 than in 1914; yet the parity

[13] USDA, *What Peace Can Mean* . . . , Nos. 562 and 589; for an overoptimistic statement of the new liberalism, see Arthur Moore, "Feeding the Forty Million," *Atlantic Monthly*, 175:101–103 (May 1945).

formula allowed no adequate alteration in their 1910–1914 relationship. By abandoning price supports and parity, the Government would restore sanity to farm prices and keep American agriculture competitive in international trade.[14]

The doctrines of the liberals were a far cry, however, from those of the doctrinaire advocates of free enterprise. The liberals did not intend to abandon the farmer during the painful transition from the protected and booming market of the war years to the free market of peacetime. The BAE, for instance, felt special anxiety for the cotton farmers who, in 1945, were laboring under the heavy burden of tremendous stocks, bleak export prospects, and the threat of competition from synthetic fibers. Cotton prices, said the liberals, must fall to the world level, a process which could drive many farmers into poverty. But technical assistance and cash payments to aid in conversion to other forms of production would ease the adjustment. In areas like the Southern Appalachians, the program would require retraining for nonfarm employment.[15]

In times of unemployment and depression, the Government would resume its role of protector of the farmer by undertaking to assure him a fair share of the national income. This share would not be determined by some percentage fixed by the distant past; rather, it would be equivalent to total farm income under most recent, peacetime, full employment conditions. Farmers would receive the difference between actual

[14] USDA, *What Peace Can Mean* . . . , Nos. 562 and 589; a critique of the notion of parity can also be found in Arthur C. Bunce, "Our Agricultural Policies," in *Agricultural Adjustment and Income,* Postwar Economic Studies, no. 2 (Board of Governors of the Federal Reserve System: Washington, Oct. 1945), pp. 13–14.

[15] USDA, *What Peace Can Mean* . . . , Nos. 562 and 589; for a detailed statement of transitional cotton policy, *Production Programs for Transition and Post-War Years* (prepared by Post-War Program Committee), file date 4–30–45, Economics 6–1 file, Records of Office of Sec. of Ag., Gen'l Cor., N.A.

and guaranteed income from direct payments rather than price supports. Liberals could point out that income rather than price was the real measure of rural health and that direct payments caused less interference in world trade than price supports.[16]

The liberal vision, therefore, was of an America free of malnutrition and a farm population producing for use at a profit. Abundance rather than restriction, subsidized consumption rather than surpluses, free market prices instead of the parity price, and in depression, income payments rather than price supports—this was their basic program. There were, of course, variations.

John D. Black of Harvard, an influential agricultural economist who had helped to shape New Deal farm policies, joined the crusade against restrictionism. Black told a congressional committee, "We were spending $725,000,000 a year in 1937, 1938, and 1939, on a production-adjustment program. Let's consider spending something like that on a consumption-adjustment program instead, and see if it will not accomplish more." Like the BAE, Black knew that expanded consumption would not be enough to prevent the reappearance of surpluses. But rather than suggest a migration of workers from the farms, he proposed a program that would encourage farmers to shift from cotton, wheat, rye, rice, beets, and potatoes for human consumption, to pasture, grass, and feed grains for livestock. Forty million acres converted to livestock production were equivalent to taking 36,000,000 acres of tillage out of use, "and that," said Black, "will go a very long way toward getting rid of our agricultural surplus." The higher cost of a meat diet made consumer subsidies essential to the success of his plan.[17]

[16] USDA, *What Peace Can Mean* . . . , No. 589.

[17] For Black's views, see his testimony in "Post-War Economic Policy and Planning," Hearings before the Subcommittee on Agriculture and Mining, Special Committee on Post-War Economic Planning, U.S. House

Though Black had tried to learn from the failure of the Depression, other survivors of those bleak days proved less flexible. Above all, agriculture's conservatives decisively rejected the doctrines of abundance—not because they peered into the future and saw the effects of the technological revolution, but because they fixed their gaze everlastingly on the Depression and clung to the policies that had helped then to rescue them. Edward A. O'Neal, an aging Alabama aristocrat, spoke the dogmas of conservatism with unchallenged authority. Owner of a huge plantation and president of the American Farm Bureau Federation, he was regarded with a mixture of awe and fear by Congress. During the Depression, Henry Wallace and Ed O'Neal had worked together closely in building New Deal programs for agriculture, but toward the end of the 1930's, they began to go separate ways. Though always a staunch foe of liberal programs to help farm tenants and laborers, O'Neal never abandoned his loyalty to the basic farm program of the New Deal. By 1945, defense of the old programs had become a new conservatism.[18]

O'Neal disputed the very first principle of the new liberals. To imply that agricultural prosperity was a function of industrial full employment was to distort the true relationship. Since the number of workers in factories was only slightly higher than on farms, there could be no prosperity anywhere unless farmers were receiving a fair price for their crops.

---

of Representatives, 78th Cong., 2nd sess. and 79th Cong., 1st sess., pp. 1486–1491; for an example of Black's former adherence to production control and a hint of his later position, see Nourse, Davis, and Black, *Three Years of the Agricultural Adjustment Administration* (Washington, D.C.: The Brookings Institution, 1937), pp. 480–508.

[18] For biographical material on O'Neal, see *Current Biography*, ed. Anna Roth (New York, H. W. Wilson Company, 1946), pp. 436–438; for O'Neal's collaboration with the New Deal, see Orville M. Kile, *Farm Bureau Through Three Decades* (Baltimore: Waverly Press, 1948), pp. 170–253; for an account of later differences between O'Neal and the New Deal, see C. M. Campbell, *The Farm Bureau and the New Deal* (Urbana: University of Illinois Press, 1962), pp. 156–178.

O'Neal refuted only by silence the arguments of the economists that since agricultural production is relatively stable it is the great fluctuations in industrial production that create economic instability and therefore farm depression. Pay the farmer parity prices as defined with wisdom and justice in current legislation, said O'Neal, and the industrial worker will have markets for the products of his labor.

His prognosis of the state of the postwar market shared none of the optimism of the liberals. O'Neal foresaw a threat of giant, price-depressing surpluses generated by the extraordinary but transient needs of the war. The menace of surpluses, however, could be conquered merely "through retention and strengthening . . . of these basic laws," the laws passed during the crisis of the 1930's. When surpluses threatened, farmers would gladly submit to production controls, which would beget parity prices and stable markets.

So great was O'Neal's faith in the efficacy of the parity price that to him agriculture needed little else. As long as prices were fair, there was no need, for instance, to decrease the farm population. He regarded the joys of sharecropping on twenty-eight acres as being real and abundant. In fact, he told a House committee, his tenants were making more money than members of Congress. As long as the legislation of the 1930's remained the basis of farm policy, life on the farm, any farm, would be good indeed.[19]

The man who provided the theoretical rationale for the conservative's fear of the postwar market was Theodore W. Schultz of the University of Chicago who, with John D. Black, was the most influential academic agricultural economist of the day. Though based partly on a prophecy of an industrial depression that never occurred, Schultz's views came closer than anyone else's to grasping the conditions that would pre-

[19] For O'Neal's views, see his testimony in "Post-War Economic Policy and Planning," Hearings before House Subcommittee, pp. 1509–1540.

vail in the farmer's future market. In spite of occasional inconsistencies, he evolved a searching critique of the notion that the farmer could grow all he wanted and enjoy high income at the same time. Demand, said Schultz, would soon fall behind supply, because population growth in the future would be slower than growth in agricultural production. Schultz granted that per capita income had gone up at least 40 percent since the war began, but even if this gain should be maintained, which he doubted, demand would still not be sufficient to absorb increased production. The conclusion rested on Schultz's empirical studies which led him to the belief that Americans spend far less of their income gains on food than had been generally assumed. In short, the income elasticity of food is low. Surpluses, he said, would soon re-emerge, and "the per capita income of farm people . . . is likely to drop at least one-third, and it may go as much as two-fifths below current levels." At times Schultz talked of subsidizing consumption in the same way the orthodox liberals did, but in his work, these subsidies never played an important role and never moderated his basic pessimism.[20]

Schultz, however, was no conservative. He denied the worth of crop control as a means of restoring prosperity to the farmer. Restrictionism was, first, destructive of real wealth and, second, impossible. His own policy proposals found a wide hearing. Prices, he said, should not be supported but should be set by the Government in ways that would en-

[20] For his views of future growth of population and agricultural production, see Theodore W. Schultz, "Food and Agriculture in a Developing Economy," in *Food for the World*, ed. T. W. Schultz (Chicago: University of Chicago Press, 1945), pp. 306–320; on income elasticity of food, see testimony in "Post-War Economic Policy and Planning," Hearings before House subcommittee, p. 1631; for prediction of drastic drop in per capita farm income, see Theodore Schultz, "Which Way Will Farmers Turn?", *Foreign Affairs*, 23:632 (July 1945); on subsidizing consumption see Theodore Schultz, *Agriculture in an Unstable Economy* (New York and London: McGraw-Hill Book Company, Inc., 1945), pp. 241-242.

courage production of needed products and discourage un-economic use of resources. Calling this proposal forward pric-ing, Schultz considered it of the first importance but failed to clothe it in needed detail. Moreover, since forward pricing pre-sumably would not diminish total supply, it could not solve the basic problem of overproduction. Though the conservatives found little to praise in his constructive proposals and especially objected to his advocacy of income payments instead of price supports in depression, Schultz had nevertheless given academic respectability to their grim view of the future.[21]

Many others besides O'Neal and Schultz harbored fears of new surpluses. Powerful farm congressmen like Republican Clifford Hope of Kansas told the farmers, "Call it what you will—over-production or under-consumption—there will be times in the future when the supply of agriculture products will exceed demand." Fortunately, added Hope, Congress had wisely provided machinery for acreage restriction to handle the problem. The grim pronouncements of Theodore Schultz found a ready audience in silent corners of the De-partment of Agriculture, in portions of the AAA, for instance, where the calculations of BAE could never convert the old-timers. And on the farms of America, the depressing predic-tions of some of the experts merely reinforced a by now deep fear of the future.[22]

The debate over postwar policy was both creative and quixotic: creative because it developed the concept of abun-dance; quixotic because farm policy for the transition period had been fixed by law in 1942. The Steagall amendment to

[21] Schultz, *Agriculture in an Unstable Economy*, pp. 166–175, 262–264, 221–235.

[22] For Clifford Hope's remarks, see *Congressional Record*, 79th Cong., 2nd sess., vol. 92, pt. 9, A636–638; for evidence that many in the Department of Agriculture shared Schultz's views, G. B. L. Arner to J. M. Letiche, July 25, 1945, Foreign Affairs Trade files, Records of OFAR, Gen'l Cor., N.A.; for description of views of AAA, interview with Nathan Koenig, Sept. 11, 1961.

the Emergency Price Control Act stipulated that all commodities for which the Secretary of Agriculture requested production increases must be supported at 90 percent of parity for two years after the official termination of the war. The justification for this sweeping measure was that if farmers responded to the war emergency by raising larger crops, they should be protected from a recurrence of the price collapse that had followed World War One. Defenders compared the amendment to various cancellation payments in industrial contracts. But the Steagall amendment threatened to prevent the readjustment to peacetime which was one of the aims of the amendment. Encouraged by high levels of support, farmers might maintain expanded production of certain commodities, some of them perishable, that were no longer in high demand.

By 1945 the laws of Congress required price supports at 90 percent of parity for the basic commodities corn, wheat, rice, and tobacco and 92 percent for cotton. In addition the Government had to extend 90 percent supports to the thirteen commodities that came under the terms of the Steagall amendment: hogs, eggs, chickens, turkeys, milk and butterfat, dry peas, dry beans, soybeans, flaxseed, peanuts for oil, American-Egyptian cotton, sweet potatoes, and potatoes.[23] Since President Truman did not officially end war hostilities until December 31, 1946, the Steagall amendment had to be the foundation of farm policy through 1948, regardless of the visions of the liberals. Only the prolonged and unexpected European relief crisis rescued the Department from an impossible task. For the whole of the Steagall period, farmers continued to find markets at record prices for almost any-

[23] On Steagall amendment, see Walter W. Wilcox, *Farmers in the Second World War* (Ames, Iowa: The Iowa State College Press, 1947), pp. 243–248; for the list of Steagall commodities, see "Potato Surpluses and Prevention of Wastage," Hearings before Committee on Agriculture, U.S. House of Representatives, 80th Cong., 1st sess., pp. 86–87.

thing they could produce, with two exceptions—superabundant eggs, which became an annoyance, and potatoes, which became a disaster. As if to demonstrate both the havoc that the Steagall amendment could have caused under different circumstances and the futility of the Government's basic farm policies, the lowly potato grew as it never grew before. Only Henry Wallace's little pigs provoked greater public outrage. No other incident so well reveals the complexity and inadequacy of the farm program. To those who were willing to see, the potato problem also showed how the program of abundance could be destroyed by a rampant technology.

The potato had been a small problem even in the Depression, when the Department of Agriculture had purchased from 3.3 million bushels in 1934 to 21.1 million bushels in 1940 in an effort to support potato prices. The Government was encouraged, however, by the steady decline in acreage from 3.8 million in 1934 to 2.8 million in 1942. But the nation was at war in 1942, and the armies and the allies began to place large orders for potatoes. Spurred by memories of the World War I potato shortage and of angry demonstrations made then by potato-starved housewives, the Department of Agriculture asked farmers to increase production for 1943. This request, of course, made potatoes a Steagall commodity and guaranteed a support price equal to 90 percent of parity from then until two years after the end of the war. It also began one of the most unhappy chapters in the history of the Department.[24]

Even in 1943 the farmer grew more potatoes than the Government had asked for and surpluses materialized. But it was not until 1946 that the problem grew serious. In that

[24] For figures on potato support operations in 1940 and before, see "Potato Surpluses and Prevention of Wastage," House hearings, p. 61; on wartime background, see "Potato Situation," Minutes from the Secretary's Staff Meeting, March 9, 1950, Potatoes file, Records of Office of Sec. of Ag., Gen'l Cor., N.A.; also see Wilcox, *Farmers in the Second World War*, pp. 209–213.

year potato growers broke all production records and sent 484 million bushels to market. To keep prices at 90 percent of parity the Commodity Credit Corporation bought 108 million bushels, which it then attempted to distribute in any way it could outside commercial channels. Such distribution resulted in a loss to the Government amounting to 91 million dollars. Notwithstanding mighty efforts by the CCC to find an outlet for every bushel, some potatoes went to waste.[25]

The European famine of 1946 made the plethora of potatoes doubly embarrassing. Newspapers carried stories of starvation on one page and pictures of rotting potatoes on another. Moralists and conservatives alike joined to denounce waste and demand that potatoes be shipped abroad. A leading moralist (but certainly no conservative) was Fiorello La Guardia, Director General of UNRRA and bitter critic of potato wastage. In anticipation of the surpluses, La Guardia met with potato congressmen and helped draft an amendment to an appropriation bill that eventually was enacted. The amendment authorized the CCC to dehydrate its potatoes and sell them at a loss for relief purposes. (Fresh potatoes are generally too perishable and bulky for export.) UNRRA subsequently placed an order for 50,000 tons of dehydrated potatoes and offered to pay one cent per pound. The Department replied that the cost of buying and dehydrating potatoes was twenty-five cents per pound and that, regardless of statutory authority, the loss would be unreasonably large. La Guardia wrote President Truman to explain that UNRRA could not afford to pay Department prices and asked Truman to intervene on UNRRA's behalf. In answer to a presidential inquiry, Agriculture replied that it would lose 20 million dollars more by selling to UNRRA than by handling potatoes

[25] "Potato Situation," Minutes from Staff Meeting, March 9, 1950; Tables on Potato Price Supports, Potatoes file, Records of Office of Sec. of Ag., Gen'l Cor., N.A.

in its usual way, and that consequently the sale was "contrary to the public interest." Truman did not intervene, and La Guardia did not get his potatoes.[26]

In the meantime, the Department made vigorous efforts to dispose of the ever growing mountain of surplus potatoes in any other way it could. The school lunch program and charitable organizations eventually took three million bushels. Hungry European nations like Belgium, able to pay transport costs and willing to take a chance on fresh potatoes, purchased 10½ million more. Livestock growers in need of feed bought 11 million bushels, and starch mills, 10½ million. But the greatest market for surplus potatoes was the distilling industry. Noting that 30 million bushels had been converted to alcohol, Anderson moaned, "We will be criticized at the next W.C.T.U. convention." Sprayed blue to prevent unlawful resale, 22 million bushels lay rotting in the fields.[27]

The Department spent a great deal of time analyzing how it had come to this sorry impasse. Had not farmers planted the number of acres requested by the Government? It turned out that they had. But good weather and increased use of fertilizers and insecticides raised the yield per acre from 155 bushels in 1945 to 185 in 1948. Yields had long been increasing, but never before had technology achieved such dramatic results in a single year. The Department uneasily acknowledged that while the CCC was fighting surpluses, the research bureaus of the Department were developing ever more effective ways of increasing yields. Consumers, for their part, had slowly been turning away from the potato to fruits and

[26] F. H. La Guardia to President Truman, Sept. 12, 1946, OF 786, TP, TL; Clinton P. Anderson to the President, Oct. 10, 1946, same title.
[27] Efforts to dispose of the surplus are described in USDA press release, Oct. 1946, OF 786, TP, TL; and Clinton Anderson to Elmer Thomas, Nov. 26, 1946, File of Kenneth Heckler, TL; the quotation from Anderson is taken from "Spuds, Spuds, Spuds," *Time*, 28:77–78 (Sept. 2, 1946).

other vegetables. In 1910 the average American ate 190 pounds of potatoes a year; in 1940, 133 pounds of potatoes a year; in 1946, only 128. Meanwhile the inflexible provisions of the Steagall amendment greatly overpriced potatoes and assured continued overproduction for at least two more years.[28]

Secretary Anderson asked Congress to consider the problem of how best to prepare for the deluge of 1947, received no advice, and then decided to act on his own. Production control being his only recourse, he broke down national acreage goals for 1947 into goals for states, counties, and individual farms. Only those farmers who kept within assigned acreage could receive price supports. As anticipated, however, this program did not prevent small local surpluses in 1947 of highly perishable early potatoes, and by mid-May, the Government had been forced to buy nearly 100,000 bushels in Alabama, most of which it quickly distributed. Local agents of the Department then poured kerosene on some of the 30,000 bushels still remaining and thereby caused a political conflagration that lit up the Washington skies. Across the country on May 18, a shocked public looked at pictures of the mutilation in its newspapers, and in the next week an outraged Congress authorized an investigation of the whole potato program. Except for a recommendation that potatoes never again be intentionally destroyed, no constructive suggestion resulted from congressional concern. The real problem, of course, was the Steagall amendment, but no one in a responsible position dared to challenge the farm bloc by proposing an alteration of the basic program. Actually, though the Department lacked authority to penalize farmers who ex-

[28] Statistics are derived from "Potato Surpluses and Prevention of Wastage," House hearings, pp. 50–57; Minutes of Secretary's Staff Meeting, March 9, 1950; Tables of Potato Price Support.

ceeded their goals, acreage in 1947 fell, as the Government had asked, from 2.6 million acres to 2.1 million acres, while yield per acre remained constant. Even so, surpluses accumulated, but since these were only half the 1946 quantity and were generally distributed without spoilage, the Government regarded the year as a kind of triumph.[29]

The year 1948 was the last chance for potato farmers to enjoy the high prices guaranteed by the Steagall amendment. Casting aside restraint, most of them ignored their government goals, and those who acquiesced planted closer and used more fertilizer and DDT. As in 1946, yields per acre made a huge jump, this time from 185 bushels to 215. The long-run decline in consumption accelerated with alarming speed, falling from 118 pounds per capita in 1947 to 104 pounds in 1948. Potatoes began to pile up in the generous arms of the Government. The farmers who ignored their goals often made more money than cooperators, because Government purchases from cooperators had the effect of bolstering the market for all potatoes. Before the nightmare was over, the Government bought 139 million bushels of potatoes (total production was 455 million), which it distributed at a loss to itself of 223 million dollars. Incredibly the Department managed to avoid dumping a single bushel. To persuade industrial users to take its potatoes, the Department spent fifty-five million dollars to pay transport and

[29] On Anderson's request for congressional consideration of the problem, Anderson to Elmer Thomas, Nov. 26, 1946, File of Kenneth Heckler, TL; on Anderson's decision to declare acreage allotments, Clinton Anderson to August Andresen, May 28, 1947, Files of Kenneth Heckler, TL; on the incident in Alabama, see "Potato Surplus and Prevention of Wastage," House hearings, pp. 135–148; for congressional reaction to the kerosene incident, see *Congressional Record*, 80th Cong., 1st sess., vol. 93, pt. 5, 5733–5734; 5735–5736; 6101–6105; 5645–5647; for summary of Department's experience with potatoes in 1947, Clinton Anderson to Arthur Capper, Feb. 26, 1948, Heckler files, Agriculture folder, TL.

other marketing costs. The 370,000 farmers who grew one or more acres of white potatoes brought the Steagall period to an inglorious conclusion.[30]

There was more to the story, however. The Agricultural Act of 1948 required the Secretary of Agriculture to support 1949 potatoes at anywhere from 60 to 90 percent of parity. The new Secretary of Agriculture, Charles F. Brannan, lowered the support rate to 60 percent, causing acreage to fall from 2.1 million acres to 1.9 million. But intensive planting wiped out much of the advantage, and production reached 411 million bushels instead of the 350 million target. Even at 60 percent of parity, the supported price was attractive enough to encourage overproduction. Eventually the Government had to enter the market to buy 75 million bushels. Acreage allotments without marketing controls, Brannan concluded, were worthless. The Department once again faced the problem of distributing a surplus. When Brannan announced that henceforth all recipients of bargain rate potatoes would have to pay transport costs, alcohol plants and livestock growers immediately cut their orders. Consequently, most of the surplus stayed on the farms where it was grown, was dyed blue to keep it there, and then sold back to the farmer for one cent per hundred pounds for use as fertilizer. In short, the Government dumped its potatoes. In 1950, with support still at 60 percent of parity, the CCC had to buy 94.2 million bushels at a net loss of 64 million dollars. Since 1943, the Government had spent nearly one-half billion dollars in its potato operation. In 1950, finally exasperated, Congress

[30] For an account of potato price support operations in 1948, Minutes of the Secretary's Staff Meeting, March 9, 1950; also, USDA press release, April 21, 1949, Heckler files, Ag. Folder, TL; for statistical data, Tables on Potato Price Supports; for a summary of reasons for 1948 surplus, see "Five Minus Two Equals Eight," *Newsweek*, 33:17–18 (Feb. 21, 1949).

effectively terminated support beginning the next year. So in 1951, without any support at all, farmers finally responded as the Government wished, dropped their acreage to a mere 1.3 million, and produced only 325 million bushels. In the meantime, the Korean War had broken out, demand for potatoes suddenly spurted upward, a sizable shortage developed, and prices rose so fast that the Government had to put potatoes under price control.[31]

Much could be learned from the saga of the white potato. The incident served, for instance, to dramatize again the dilemma of American trade policies. The ability of Canadian farmers to undersell American producers even with a tariff of seventy-five cents per hundred pounds on imports meant that in 1949, while the American Government was purchasing seventy-five million bushels to keep the prices high, Canada complicated the task by exporting nine million bushels at lower prices. For the liberals, the potato scandal provided additional evidence of the absurdity of a parity formula that failed to recognize radical changes in the market situation and encouraged uneconomic production. The ingenuity of the farmers in defeating efforts to curb production strengthened further the liberal case. On the other hand, the dismaying rate of technological progress should have given pause to the liberals, for the ability of the producer to grow potatoes had quickly surpassed the Government's efforts to expand consumption. The potato illustrated anew the failure of the old policies and raised serious doubts about the wisdom of the new. As for the Department of Agriculture, it could only rejoice that the Steagall amendment would expire December

[31] On 1949 potato operations, "The Present Potato Situation" (a statement by Secretary Brannan), Jan. 31, 1950, Heckler files, Ag. Folder, TL; for an announcement of potato price control, OPS press release, April 30, 1950, file IV B2, Korean War, ERS, ESA, Ag. Hist. Br., USDA.

31, 1948, and continue to lay plans for the years that were to follow.[32]

By 1945 the BAE had formulated its bold pronouncements in behalf of abundance, and the critics had established the grounds for their dissent. As for Secretary Anderson, his views on agricultural problems were mildly liberal, but he believed that Department programs should reflect the views of the permanent bureaucracy rather than transient secretaries. "I hate to start talking about agricultural policy and economics," he once admitted, "because I am not schooled in it at all." On January 2, 1946, Anderson asked D. A. FitzGerald to assume responsibility for long-range planning recently removed from BAE. Anderson suggested that Fitz-Gerald assemble estimates of crop needs for 1949 and devise methods "to taper off and adjust our agriculture to meet that 1949 pattern." By 1949, Anderson thought, agriculture would be ready to prosper without price supports in a free economy. Anderson expected FitzGerald's job to take two weeks. It took two years. FitzGerald got involved in the famine crisis of 1946 and left the Department in the spring to head a temporary international famine committee. Since the Department still had to endure two more Steagall years, no good reason existed to rush matters. Not until December 30, 1946, when Anderson appointed Charles F. Brannan as chairman of a Program and Policy Committee, did work on long-range planning resume. President Truman had recently offered Brannan a place on the Indian Claims Commission, but Anderson induced Brannan to remain in the Department by giving him this new responsibility.[33]

[32] On reports of Canadian potatoes, K. T. Hutchinson to Milton R. Young, March 3, 1950, Potatoes file, Records of Office of Sec. of Ag., Gen'l Cor., N.A.; see also "The Potato Invasion," *Newsweek*, 35:65–66 (Feb. 20, 1950).

[33] The quotation from Anderson on agricultural economics is in "Agricultural Price Support Policy," Hearings before House Committee

The main task of the new committee was to take the vision of abundance so well enunciated by the BAE and accommodate it to reality. Painful experience had already taught Clinton Anderson the penalties of advocating policies merely because they were rational. In November, 1945, the Secretary had gone into the South and delivered speeches on the cotton problem prepared for him by the BAE. The Secretary told his audiences to mechanize production, lower costs, and make cotton competitive again by bringing prices back to the world level. "It seems like plain common sense," he said, "to set prices that can be reached in normal times with full employment." If market returns proved inadequate, then the government should make payments to the farmers sufficient to assure decent income. Above all, three million workers, many of whom would be displaced by machines, must be moved off the land. To cotton congressmen, wedded loyally to the New Deal cotton program, such heresies were intolerable. Stung by bitter Southern criticism, Anderson disavowed his speeches and left Howard Tolley of BAE alone to absorb congressional venom. However original in conception, the Department's postwar programs would have to recognize the existence of Congress, or the new liberalism would pass into oblivion.[34]

---

on Agriculture, 80th Cong., 1st sess., p. 27; for Anderson's views on role of bureaucracy in policy-making, interview with Nathan Koenig (Anderson's executive assistant in the Department), Sept. 11, 1961; for Anderson's instructions to FitzGerald on long-range planning, Anderson to FitzGerald, Jan. 2, 1946, Public Relations 11 file, Records of Office of Sec. of Ag., Gen'l Cor., N.A.; on Brannan's decision to stay in the Department, interview with Charles F. Brannan, July 31, 1961.

[34] For Anderson's speeches in the South on the cotton problem, USDA press release, Nov. 12, 1945, World War II Records, ERS, ESA, Ag. Hist. Br., USDA; and *Congressional Record*, 79th Cong., 1st sess., vol. 91, pt. 13, A4989–4991; for an example of congressional rage, see Senator John H. Bankhead's savage cross-examination of Howard Tolley in "Agricultural Department Appropriations Bill, 1947," Hearings before Committee on Appropriations, U.S. Senate, 79th Cong., 2nd sess., pp. 93-104.

Throughout 1947 Brannan's group met to shape a farm program. Opening the House hearings on long-range policy in April, Anderson presented the general outline of the Department's ideas. In October Department witnesses returned to the Hill to offer the most searching and extensive review of farm life and the farm problem ever made in America. Though the witnesses covered everything from telephone service to sanitation, the core of the testimony concerned production and price policies and was a masterful reconciliation of the doctrines of abundance with political reality.

In accord with the canons of the new liberalism, the Department began its analysis by estimating what consumers really wanted rather than what they could afford to buy. There was, said the Department, a vast and unsatisfied desire among Americans for more meat and dairy products. If farmers increased livestock numbers to satisfy this appetite, grain growers could stop worrying about surpluses, unneeded tillage would become grass and pasture, and tired soils would be fertilized. "Livestock farming," said Anderson, "is in itself a good farm program." Assuming that farmers made the adjustment, the Department estimated total cropland in 1950 at 415 million acres, compared with 403 million in 1946. "This is just about as much farm land as we have available," Brannan noted. To assure markets for the farmer and good diets to the consumer, the Government would subsidize consumption through school lunch and industrial feeding programs and especially a food allotment plan for low income families. There could be no turning back to the policies of the restrictionists, the Department said. There was no real alternative to "organized, sustained and realistic abundance."[35]

[35] The general outline of the Department's program was presented by Secretary Anderson in "Long-Range Agricultural Policy," Hearings before Committee on Agriculture, U.S. House of Representatives, 80th Cong., 1st sess., pp. 2–28. For Anderson's livestock remark, see p. 6 and for his remark on abundance, see p. 2. For Brannan's amplification

At this point, the Department made its departures from the earlier liberal program, departures that were both economically reasonable and politically necessary. Price supports, production control, and the concept of parity would all survive in altered form. First of all, since the farm bloc would never surrender parity, the Department decided to seek only its modernization. The Department proposed a formula that recognized recent market changes while retaining the 1910–1914 relationship of all farm prices to nonfarm prices. Price supports would be mandatory only for storable commodities and would be fixed "considerably below the general level of prices sought to be achieved over a period of years." Thus a relatively free market would once again influence allocation of resources and shifts of production. A reasonable support level, say 75 percent of parity, would prevent disastrous price declines and might even serve to maintain an ever normal granary for America. Price supports for perishable commodities should be entirely discretionary with the Department. Production controls could combat chronic surpluses of individual crops and would be used to bring shifts from one crop to another rather than to curb over-all production. The Department's departures from the liberal program were not serious, and its vision of abundance remained undimmed.[36]

The year 1947 saw not only a return to realism in the Department; it saw also a radical alteration of the political landscape of American agriculture. In that year, the American

---

of the Department's program, see "Long Range Agricultural Policy," Hearings before a subcommittee of the Committee on Agriculture and Forestry, U.S. Senate, and the Committee on Agriculture, U.S. House of Representatives, pp. 4–49. For Brannan's remark on acreage, see p. 24.

[36] The Department's position in regard to these subjects was given by C. C. Farrington, Assistant Administrator of PMA, in "Long-Range Agricultural Policy," Hearings before a subcommittee of the Committee on Agriculture and Forestry, U.S. Senate, and the Committee on Agriculture, U.S. House of Representatives, pp. 149–174.

Farm Bureau Federation, the giant among the farm organizations, suffered internal divisions that almost split it into two. The end result of a hard struggle was a shift in power from the farm bureaus of the Southern states to those of the Middle West, with immense consequences for the future of farm policy. During the New Deal, the Federation had achieved within its ranks a "marriage of corn and cotton," that is, cooperation between the midwestern corn belt and the cotton South, and on this cooperation rested Farm Bureau influence. But beginning in 1940, the question of low versus high supports began to strain the unity of the Federation.

Corn farmers, who formed a majority of Farm Bureau membership, marketed most of their crop in the form of hogs. Since demand for meat is elastic (that is, sales rise more than proportionally as prices fall), many hog farmers saw no advantage in limiting supply to keep prices high. Also those farmers who sold their corn to deficit feed areas outside the Middle West feared that high prices would encourage farmers in other sections to begin producing corn or other feed grains in competition with the corn belt. The corn belt farmers also opposed high supports for cotton and wheat, for they foresaw that the accompanying production controls would free lands in the South and the Plain states for production of feed grains. Relatively prosperous in the 1940's, many corn farmers (but by no means all) preferred the risks of a relatively free market to government control of their production. The cotton South, on the other hand, sent its crop directly to market and saw only gain in high, fixed price supports. Never too far from poverty, cotton farmers welcomed protection from disastrous surpluses afforded them by rigid crop control. As one Farm Bureau spokesman explained after the war, "farmers in the South, where agricultural income is lower, are more anxious to use marketing quotas as a means of adjusting production to market demands than are producers of other regions. This affords them an opportunity to adjust supplies to demand before their industry is in trouble." In 1940 both sections agreed to accept price supports at 85 percent of parity, a level too high in the view of the midwestern farm bureaus and too low to suit the South.[37]

As committees of Congress held hearings on long-range policy in 1947, evidence began to accumulate that the sectional split, reflected in Farm Bureau internal tensions, was deepening. Throughout the South, farmers expressed their strong preference for high supports. The president of the Alabama Farm Bureau succinctly summarized the views of his section: "The Farm Bureau in this state," he said, "has been on record for many years for loans on basic commodities at 100 percent of parity." Production controls, he continued, would be the principal means of preventing overproduction and maintaining high prices. As for modernizing parity (which would lower the parity price for cotton), "I think that would be like modernizing the Ten Commandments." But the president of the Iowa Farm Bureau, a rising farm politician named Allan B. Kline, challenged all these dogmas and advocated a policy of abundance very close in substance to what the Brannan committee had recommended. Kline called for full farm production and subsidized consumption, and at the same time disparaged crop controls. The only function of price supports, in Kline's opinion, was to put a floor under prices to prevent disastrous declines rather than to keep prices artificially high. Faced by this regional split, Ed O'Neal, president of the Federation, discreetly avoided

[37] On early friction between corn and cotton and the 1940 compromise, see C. M. Campbell, *The Farm Bureau and the New Deal*, pp. 134–139; on reasons for midwestern opposition to high supports, letters from Allan B. Kline to the author, July 20, 1964, and Aug. 4, 1964; the quotation on reason for the Southern position on production control is in "Agricultural Act of 1948," Hearings before the Committee on Agriculture and Forestry, 80th Congress, 2nd session, p. 71.

mention of support levels in his own 1947 testimony before Congress. O'Neal, however, did not disguise his contempt for the doctrines of abundance. Calling the Department's program impractical, he saved his harshest criticism for consumer subsidies. Production control, O'Neal said, was still the best solution to the surplus problem. By implication, therefore, O'Neal was remaining loyal to his native South and the doctrines of conservatism.[38]

On the eve of the great 1948 debate on farm legislation, the Farm Bureau squarely faced the policy split. The Federation's annual convention, meeting in Chicago late in December, 1947, became a battleground between the South and the Middle West. After fifteen years in office, Ed O'Neal was resigning from the presidency. The South could not change his mind, nor persuade Earl Smith of Illinois, long associated with O'Neal's policies, to run for the office. Allan Kline, the candidate of the Middle West, consequently won without opposition. Victory on the policy question also went to the Middle West, for the convention endorsed "mandatory variable price supports—with or without quotas,"—that is, flexible price supports. Southerners left Chicago sullen and unconvinced, perhaps sensing that the Farm Bureau had just undergone a revolution that would permanently alter its character. Like the Department of Agriculture, the Farm Bureau was turning its back on the farm program of the New Deal.[39]

[38] For views of the president of the Alabama Farm Bureau, see "Long-Range Agricultural Policy," Hearings before the House Committee, pp. 1016–1017; for views of Allan Kline, see "Long-Range Agricultural Policy and Program," Hearings before subcommittee of Committee on Agriculture and Forestry, U.S. Senate, 80th Cong., 1st sess., pp. 760–774; for O'Neal's testimony, same hearing, pp. 2–49.

[39] For accounts of the convention, see *New York Times,* Dec. 18, 1947, p. 34; and Dec. 19, 1947, p. 29; on maneuvering for Federation's presidency, see *Wallace's Farmer and Iowa Homestead,* Jan. 3, 1948, p. 7; for convention's resolution on price supports, see *American Farm Bureau Official Newsletter,* Dec. 24, 1947, p. 1.

Though less powerful than the Farm Bureau, the Farmers Union also had a measure of influence to bring to bear on agricultural policy. But in 1947 it too proved unable to bend conflicting aspirations into coherent policy. In his testimony before Congress James G. Patton championed price supports at a rigid 90 percent of parity. Patton persisted in viewing farmers as a disadvantaged group for whom simple justice required maximum governmental protection. Moreover, the wheat belt where most Union membership is concentrated had sound economic reasons for favoring high, fixed supports. Demand for wheat is relatively inelastic, so that lower prices would not increase sales proportionately and would result in diminished income. Patton, however, had always taken the liberal side of every argument, and he now found himself unable entirely to oppose the new doctrines. So in his testimony he also advocated abundant production and rejected production controls. By opposing controls while advocating support levels that could generate surpluses, Patton faced a dilemma he could not solve. His contradictory testimony on long-range policy deserved the general indifference with which it was greeted.[40]

The decisive voice had yet to speak. Congress had sent committees throughout America in 1947 to gather testimony on long-range policy from economists, bureaucrats, lobbyists, and farmers. With the Steagall Amendment due to expire on December 31, 1948, Congress could no longer avoid the task of passing new legislation. The Senate Committee on Agriculture and Forestry opened the farm debate of 1948 by drafting a bill that generally followed the proposals of the Department of Agriculture and the midwestern farm bureaus. Parity was modernized. The basic commodities, defined now as cotton, corn, wheat, rice, tobacco, peanuts, and wool (wool was later given different though still special treatment)

[40] "Long-Range Agricultural Policy," House hearings, pp. 131–174.

would receive mandatory price supports according to the following scale:

If the estimated supply is	the level of support shall be the following percentage of parity
not more than 70% of normal	90%
more than 70 but not more that 82%	85%
more than 82 but not more than 94%	80%
more than 94 but not more than 106%	75%
more than 106 but not more than 118%	70%
more than 118 but not more than 130%	65%
more than 130% of normal	60%

The Committee had such faith in this sliding scale (or flexible supports as it was also called) that it made no provision for production controls. Since the sliding scale would encourage needed production shifts by lowering supports in periods of oversupply, there would most likely be no surpluses at all. At the same time, the producer of the basic commodities had assurance that prices would never fall below 60 percent of parity. Significantly, the Committee's bill made no provision for consumer subsidies, the favorite measure of the liberals. The terms of controversy were narrowing. What had begun in 1945 as a promising episode in the history of farm policy would end as a fruitless debate over rigid 90 percent supports versus the sliding scale.[41]

Secretary Anderson told the Senate Committee that while his Department was in sympathy with the spirit of the proposed bill, it regretted the absence of provisions to expand consumption, to control production in times of emergency, and to support nonbasic commodities. Anderson was wary of

[41] For a copy of the bill, see "Agricultural Act of 1948," Hearings before the Committee on Agriculture and Forestry, 80th Cong., 2nd sess., pp. 1–14.

the inexorable movements of the sliding scale and asked that the Secretary be given discretionary authority to set supports anywhere between 60 and 90 percent on basics and zero and 90 percent for all other commodities. Allan Kline, now president of the Farm Bureau Federation, told the Committee that he was in basic agreement with the bill, but he, too, felt that authority to control production should be added. To propitiate the South, Kline suggested "an amendment which would permit the producers of cotton to vote on marketing quotas whenever the supply is normal or above, and the price is 90 percent or less of parity." Even James Patton was seduced by the sliding scale and temporarily abandoned his campaign for high, rigid supports. Thus, in 1948, for one brief moment, the Farm Bureau, the Farmers Union, and the Department of Agriculture stood together on a question of price policy. To accommodate the consensus, the Senate Committee rewrote its bill to permit production controls in times of serious oversupply, adjusted the sliding scale to between 72 percent and 90 percent for crops under production control, and gave the Secretary discretionary authority to support nonbasic commodities. The bill went to the Senate floor with the unanimous approval of the Senate Committee on Agriculture and Forestry.[42]

The real strength of the farm bloc lay in the House of Representatives. The House Committee on Agriculture had little tolerance for the sliding scale and other retreats from guaranteed farm prosperity. Clifford Hope, Republican Chairman of the Committee, sponsored a measure to extend price supports at 90 percent for basic commodities until June 30, 1950. Moreover, rather than abandon Steagall commodities

[42] For Anderson's reactions to the Committee's bill, see "Agricultural Act of 1948," Senate hearings, pp. 15–59; for Kline's views, see same hearings, pp. 61–87; for Patton's views, see same hearing, pp. 111–133; for the revised bill, see S2318, "A Bill to Provide a Coordinated Agricultural Program," May 17, 1948, 80th Cong., 2nd sess.

to a free market or to the unpredictable impulses of the Secretary of Agriculture, Hope proposed to give these commodities mandatory supports ranging between 60 and 90 percent during the same period. How, asked advocates of the Hope bill, could farmers adjust to normal conditions while the extraordinary European demand persisted? Another Steagall period was, in their view, clearly in order. The political situation on the floor of the House as debate on the Hope bill began was more than unusually confused. The Administration was against the Hope bill, but most Democrats, especially those from the South and West, favored it. Most Republicans agreed with the Truman Administration that the sliding scale was the policy of wisdom, but a strong minority from deep within farm country stayed loyal to 90 percent. After perfunctory debate, the advocates of 90 percent in the House triumphed, and the Hope bill passed by a voice vote.[43]

A few days later, the Senate debated its long-range bill, sponsored by Vermont's liberal Republican, George Aiken. At first it seemed as if high supports would win even in the Senate. By a vote of 41 to 40, Democrats from all sections and a handful of Republicans voted to give tobacco unvarying 90 percent price supports. But when Georgia's Senator Russell attempted to substitute the Hope bill for the Aiken bill, he discovered that only 24 Democrats, almost all from the South, would follow him, while the other 16 Democrats voted with the Administration and for flexible supports. With all but three Republicans opposed to 90 percent, Russell went down to defeat by 27–55. The Senate then voted overwhelmingly for the Aiken bill. By the time the House and

---

[43] For the report on the Hope bill by the House Committee, see House Report No. 1776, *House Miscellaneous Reports,* III, 80th Cong., 2nd sess.; for House debate on Hope bill, see *Congressional Record,* same sess., vol. 94, pt. 6, 7983–8014.

Senate appointed members to a conference committee to reconcile the conflicting bills, it had become clear that most Democrats in Congress favored 90 percent and most Republicans, the sliding scale. Neither party had shown much interest in using abundant production to conquer malnutrition.[44]

Suffusing the conference room in Washington was a strong odor of partisan politics blowing in from Philadelphia, where Republican delegates were assembling to choose a presidential candidate. Amid the confusion of approaching adjournment, the conferees found themselves deadlocked. For two days, the House conferees, Democrats and Republicans alike, insisted on the Hope bill, while the Senate, with equal adamancy, stood by the Aiken bill and the sliding scale. But the Republican leadership, with an eye on the coming election, decided to add long-range farm legislation to the list of the achievements of the Eightieth Congress. It persuaded Republican Congressman Reid F. Murray of Wisconsin to resign his conference seat and appointed in his stead someone who could accept the sliding scale. Late on Saturday, June 19, 1948, the Republicans from the House deserted their Democratic colleagues and accepted a compromise that would make the Hope bill, with its provision for 90 percent, operative only until January 1, 1950, after which the Aiken bill and flexible supports would become the permanent farm law. The Democratic conferees from the House cried that their chamber had been "raped" by this partial desertion of the House Republicans to the sliding scale, and they refused to sign the report, which nevertheless won easy approval in both houses of Congress. President Truman regretted that the sliding scale would not become law until 1950 but signed the Hope–Aiken bill into law. Thus the culmination of three years' planning was a hurried compromise that pleased no one. In

[44] *Congressional Record*, 80th sess., vol. 94, pt. 7, 8537–8544, 8556–8557, 8567–8568, 8598, 8612.

spite of the partisan recriminations that attended the birth of the farm act of 1948, price supports did not become an issue in the coming campaign. After all, the Truman Administration had shared responsibility with Congressional Republicans for the new direction of farm policy enacted in the Aiken bill.[45]

But as many suspected, the passage of the Hope bill for one year was merely the prelude to destruction of the Aiken bill in the next congressional session. Congress had lost a unique opportunity to enact a long-range program. Perhaps never again would all the farm organizations and the Department of Agriculture unite on an important question of policy. Though the Aiken bill had been in many ways a disappointment to the advocates of abundance, it came as close to liberal desires as was politically possible. But in truth, history cannot lament the failure of the Aiken bill to become law. In the 1950's the sliding scale would be found sadly inadequate in preventing surpluses, for no such device could cope with an annual rise in agricultural production of 2.5 percent per year, while population was advancing only 1.8 percent a year.[46] As Theodore Schultz had correctly foreseen, production would increase faster than population, while the income inelasticity of food would decline. Thus even if every American were a full consumer, which was the dream of the liberals in the mid-40's, immense stocks would still have cluttered the countryside. Not too many years after Senator Aiken hoped that production controls would never have to be used again, the revolution in agricultural production forced a return to the restrictionist policies of the 1930's.

[45] The story of political maneuvers centering around the conference committee is found in *Congressional Record*, 80th sess., vol. 94, pt. 7, 9345–9346.

[46] Willard W. Cochrane, "Farm Technology, Foreign Disposal and Domestic Supply Control," *Journal of Farm Economics*, 41:885–889 (Dec. 1959).

7 CRISIS IN EUROPE

In the years between 1945 and 1948, at the same time that the Government was devising trade and agricultural policies for the future, it had to face the recurrent problem of European crisis. Progressive deterioration of European society after the end of the war posed a threat to the democracies almost as menacing as Hitler himself had been. Her energies sapped by prolonged and chronic hunger, Europe left undone the tasks of reconstruction and watched the rise of Communist parties readying themselves to rule by default. Only America, her wealth and power augmented by the very war that left Europe in ruins, could prevent the catastrophe that seemed imminent. America's vast resources, and above all, the abundance of her agriculture, could alone stave off collapse.

For a long time, Europe underestimated the seriousness of her condition. On the basis of the rapid recovery following World War I, she expected that, after one difficult year, steady progress would soon return her to prosperity. This optimism was especially prevalent in the summer and autumn of 1946. Indeed, during these months, factories and transport systems actually did make hasty improvement so that by the end of the year, industrial production in many countries was approaching prewar levels, and agriculture too had made sizable gains. America, of course, was anxious to believe that the crisis was over. During the summer of 1946, the

American Government, supported by Canada and Great Britain, announced that it would soon cut off funds for the international "gravy train," as Will Clayton called UNRRA. This decision resulted not only from the apparent easing of the food shortage, but also from the State Department's reluctance to continue financing those UNRRA countries now under Communist domination. Clinton Anderson was second to none in the fullness of his optimism. The American corn and wheat crops were going to be so bountiful, he said, that America could "meet all essential foreign demand for wheat and other grains." Caution, however, led him to avoid making export "commitments," which had created so much trouble for him in the previous year. In the crop year July 1, 1946–June 30, 1947, he established only "goals," and for a beginning he set a mere 6.7 million tons for wheat exports (compared with 10.3 in the last crop year) and 4 million tons of corn. The goal for all grains was therefore only 10.7. "As for bread rationing," he wrote one Government official, "I believe that the possible need for it can be disregarded for all practical purposes."[1]

By the middle of August, 1946, Anderson actually began to fear that grain was too abundant. The American harvest was going to exceed the most generous of predictions, and only a few requests for grain were trickling into the Department from abroad. Anderson remembered, of course, that it had not been until late December of the year before that he received requests for larger exports, but since oversupply seemed more probable than renewed famine, he began to

[1] On premature optimism in Europe, see "Meeting of the Committee on European Economic Cooperation: Statement by Rapporteur General and the Summary of the General Report," U.S. Department of State Bulletin, 17:681–687 (Oct. 5, 1947); Clayton's phrase is quoted in T. J. Hamilton, "After UNRRA, What?", Nation, 164:123–125 (Feb. 1, 1947); on wheat crop and rationing, Clinton Anderson to Paul Porter, Aug. 18, 1946, War 6 file, Records of Office of Sec. of Ag., Gen'l Cor., N.A.

consider abandonment of some of the limitations on wheat consumption that had been decreed by the President months before.[2] First up for review was the order that raised the wheat extraction rate from 70 to 80 percent. This measure had cut down wheat wastage, but it gave white bread a grayish color and greatly annoyed the baking industry.

One of the dissenters from the current optimism was D. A. FitzGerald, now Director General of the International Emergency Food Council (IEFC) whose job it was to allocate available supplies among claimant nations. In mid-August, 1946, he wrote his old chief to appeal for continuance of all American limitations on grain consumption. According to his estimates, the world would require perhaps 26.7 million tons (one billion bushels) of exported grain in the 1946–47 crop year, but only 20 million tons would actually be available. In contrast to Anderson's figures, FitzGerald said that requests for American wheat already far exceeded the American goal. Several countries, he continued, would again face critical shortages. "How will these countries react to the removal of all restrictions on the use of wheat in the United States, particularly since we in IEFC have been insisting that they do not increase their very low rations?" FitzGerald asked. The same day that FitzGerald made this plea, Anderson himself verified its implications by writing to the Secretary of War to inform him that, in view of new threats of mass starvation in India, the Army would receive a small grain allocation in September.[3]

Nevertheless, Anderson rescinded the order raising the extraction rate. The British Food Minister reported that he

[2] Secretary Anderson to J. B. Hasselman, Aug. 15, 1946, Publications 1 file, Records of Office of Sec. of Ag., Gen'l Cor., N.A.

[3] D. A. FitzGerald to Secretary of Agriculture, Aug. 16, 1946, Grain 3 file, Records of Office of Sec. of Ag., Gen'l Cor., N.A.; Secretary of Agriculture to the Secretary of War, Aug. 16, 1946, Grain file, Records of Office of Sec. of Ag., Gen'l Cor., N.A.

was "perturbed" and asked Anderson to explain "what reasons moved the United States Government to cancel the restrictions previously imposed." Impolitic though it was, Anderson's decision affected the wheat supply only in a small way. It signified, however, a general lack of concern with world food problems in the summer of 1946 and could only be interpreted by the public as evidence that the time of shortages was over. "Most Americans apparently believe," reported the *Nation*, "that the need for belt-tightening on our part has passed." The liberal Catholic journal *Commonweal*, still worrying about the possibility of renewed famine abroad, said, "the symbol of [Anderson's] failure will perhaps be recorded in the history books as the return of white bread." Meanwhile in a little-publicized report of September 2, 1946, the Food and Agriculture Organization issued a solemn warning: "Evidence of serious malnutrition is accumulating. In the worst areas, many adults have suffered 15–25 percent loss in weight. The hospital cases of hunger are numerous and increasing. There have been some deaths from starvation. If the food scarcity continues to be so acute for another twelve months, the permanent damage to health is unpredictable. It is vitally necessary that rations . . . be raised at least to the minimum subsistence level." Two months later, on November 26, 1946, assuring the President that the need for sacrifice was over, Anderson recommended an end to all remaining important limitations on the use of grain by brewers, bakers, and distillers. As far as he was concerned, the only obstacle to adequate American exports was the critical shortage of boxcars to transport grains to portside.[4]

[4] On reaction of British Food Minister, Henry Hardman to Clinton Anderson, Aug. 29, 1946, Grain file, Records of Office of Sec. of Ag., Gen'l Cor., N.A.; "The Shape of Things," *Nation*, 163:543 (Nov. 16, 1946); "Eating Your Cake and Having It," *Commonweal*, 44:492–493 (Sept. 6, 1946); FAO, *World Food Appraisal for 1946–1947* (Copenhagen, Sept. 2, 1946), p. 2; Anderson to the President, Aug. 23, 1946, White House file, Senator Anderson's Office, Washington.

Though lax on relief, Anderson maintained the Department's campaign for full farm production. Conditions in Europe testified to the wisdom of this policy, but many, including Anderson himself, regarded it as potential folly. In case of full recovery abroad, surpluses could well depress domestic markets. "I can just hear the lambasting I will get about a year from now because of my stupidity in calling for a large production in 1947," Anderson said. Criticism of the high production goals that he issued in October, 1946, was widespread in farm circles and even provoked protests from the usually timid Grange.[5]

Anderson's call for full production was soon vindicated. The severity of the winter of 1946–47 in Europe and a lag in American grain exports due to transport difficulties ended the period of recovery and restored a sense of crisis. As a committee of experts later stated, "the European economy, still at the convalescent stage, suffered a most serious setback as a result of the continued shortage of coal, the increased cost of primary products, and the prolonged world shortage of food and other essential commodities." The period of optimism was over.[6]

On January 17, 1947, the British Food Mission to America told Anderson that it was very disappointed by the February allocations for Great Britain, that at any moment, some British flour mills might have to close down, that "we are hovering on the brink all the time," and that delay in shipment could lead to a breakdown in the British ration. The other area near the brink was central Europe, which for the

[5] On call for full production, USDA press release, Nov. 8, 1946, Releases 5–2 file, Records of Office of Information, USDA, N.A.; the quotation from Anderson is taken from Anderson to Editor of the *New York Times*, Nov. 12, 1946, Publications 1 file, Records of Office of Sec. of Ag., Gen'l Cor., N.A.; on criticism for high production goals, see *Wallace's Farmer and Iowa Homestead*, Jan. 4, 1947, p. 20.

[6] Report of the Paris Conference on the Marshall Plan (text reprinted in *New York Times*, Sept. 24, 1947).

past two years had been supplied by UNRRA. But UNRRA's funds were running out. In Hungary, Italy, Poland, Austria, Greece, and Yugoslavia, mortality rates for infants and young children were accelerating, foreign exchange to finance new imports was vanishing, and food stocks were nearly exhausted. In November, 1946, La Guardia, Director General of UNRRA, had proposed that members of the United Nations provide 400 million dollars for continued assistance to UNRRA countries, the money to be distributed by the UN according to need. La Guardia condemned the United States for destroying international relief work merely because it disapproved of some of the recipients. Dean Acheson replied for the United States that regular commercial transactions were adequate for food distribution and that, if necessary, the United States would supply loans and grants to needy nations to finance food purchases. By February, 1947, the time had clearly come for making loans and grants. President Truman asked Congress for 350 million dollars for those liberated areas once fed by UNRRA and still in need of help. Sensitive to charges that it was playing politics with relief, the State Department had included the Communist countries of Poland and Hungary. Displaying a lack of prescience, Will Clayton said, "if sufficient assistance is provided promptly, there is every reason for anticipating that, with the possible exception of Austria, these countries will not need further relief after 1947." Though not sure it approved of giving money to Poland and Hungary, Congress finally passed the aid bill in May, 1947. A few months later, the Government decided that Russia was able to supply her satellites, and all American aid to them was halted.[7]

[7] On imminent breakdown of British ration, Henry Hardman to Clinton Anderson, Jan. 17, 1947, Foreign Relations 2–1 file, Records of Office of Sec. of Ag., Gen'l Cor., N.A.; for La Guardia's proposal for continued funds for UNRRA, see *New York Times*, Nov. 12, 1946, p. 6; Dean Acheson, "U.S. Position Regarding UNRRA," *U.S. Department*

The decision in February, 1947, to aid the UNRRA countries did not solve the problems of Europe. The worst winter in the memory of man continued to erase the progress of the last year. In March cold and floods brought Great Britain to the verge of catastrophe, while April in France saw drastic reduction in food rations. In May, the Italian Ambassador informed the American Government that breakdown in the bread ration in Italy was approaching and asked for 60,000 tons of wheat. In Germany, during the spring of 1947, daily rations in certain important industrial centers fell to 1,000 calories a day. By mid-May the experts were forecasting that no nation on the continent would be spared a reduction of rations during the next two months. "More and more," reported Anne O'Hare McCormick from Europe, "it is borne in on policy-makers that everything comes back to food."[8]

During that hungry winter, the only good news for Europe came from America. After the solution of the transport problem, grain began flowing across the Atlantic in record quantities, and by May 1, 1947, the 10.7-million-ton export goal had been exceeded. Fearing that continued heavy purchases would aggravate the already serious inflation in food prices, Anderson then ceased procurement. Soon afterward, however, apparently on instructions from the White House, buying for export resumed, and by June 30, the Government had shipped

---

of State Bulletin, 15:1107–1108 (Dec. 15, 1946); for Truman's February request, see Public Papers of the Presidents: Harry S. Truman, 1947 (Washington: U.S. Government Printing Office, 1963), pp. 149–150; Clayton's quotation is taken from "Relief Assistance to Countries Devastated by War," Hearings before the Committee on Foreign Affairs, U.S. House of Representatives, 80th Cong., 1st sess., p. 3; for debate, see Congressional Record, 80th Cong., 1st sess., vol. 93, pt. 5, 5619–5626.

[8] Summary of plea of Italian Ambassador is contained in John Steelman to the President, May 1, 1947, OF 174, TP, TL; on predictions of experts on ration reductions, see New York Times, May 11, 1947, p. 5E; for the estimate of German rations and also her quotation, see Anne O'Hare McCormick, New York Times, May 10, 1947, p. 12.

15 million tons of wheat and corn which, while a record, was far short of need.[9]

By the spring of 1947, policy-makers on both sides of the Atlantic realized that Europe's problem was more than merely bad weather. A crisis dwarfing all others of the postwar period lay just ahead, a crisis that could not be relieved by another emergency loan. The billions poured into Europe since the end of the war had purchased survival but not recovery, and the economies of the still devastated nations were slowly falling apart. The widespread destruction of industrial plants and transport systems, of banking facilities and sound currencies had proved too thorough for Europe to repair alone. No small cause of faltering industrial production was the chronic hunger that weakened the workers of the cities. Unsatisfied demand for even the necessities of life sparked an uncontrollable inflation that discouraged commerce. Indeed, the farmer could find little to buy with the proceeds of his labor, and lacking incentive to trade with the city, he began to curtail his production for market. While Europe's population had increased 8 percent since the beginning of the war, food production had fallen 20 percent, and inequitable distribution left the cities near desperation. Workers grew ever more hungry and industrial production fell further behind. Only America had the grain and other commodities that could break the debilitating cycle. But by the spring of 1947, Europe was importing one billion dollars more a month from America than she exported to America. The foreign exchange that had been financing this deficit was almost gone, and the American Congress had made no provision for new credits.

Against this background of industrial and agricultural col-

[9] On gratifying rate of export in early months of 1947, see *Public Papers of the Presidents: Harry S. Truman, 1947*, pp. 159–161; also Stanley Andrews to the Secretary, March 18, 1947, Grain file, Records of Office of Sec. of Ag., Gen'l Cor., N.A.; for summary of American exports in 1946–47, see *New York Times*, July 6, 1947, p. 29.

lapse, Secretary of State George C. Marshall delivered his extraordinary address to the Harvard Commencement on June 5, 1947. Focusing on the breakdown of market agriculture in Europe as the source of the problem, Marshall proposed that America finance the vast requirements of food and other products needed in the next three or four years, and in return, the European nations would have to work together to draft long-range plans for their own rehabilitation. The long period of drift, improvisation, and premature optimism was over.[10]

Europe responded quickly to Marshall's offer. By mid-July, sixteen non-Communist nations were getting ready to join the British and French in Paris to begin a survey of their resources and requirements. Preliminary to this meeting, an International Cereals Conference examined the most important problem of all. According to its estimates, the world would need exports of 50 million tons of grain in the year 1947–48, but only 32 million tons would be available. Clinton Anderson, then traveling in Europe to examine conditions firsthand, thought estimated grain requirements much too high. Yet in a few weeks, continuing bad weather forced the experts to lower estimates of world exports from 32 to 29 million tons, while requirements, according to D. A. FitzGerald of IEFC, would probably exceed 50 million.[11]

Anderson had good cause to be uneasy about the grain situation, for it threatened to become the most distressing aspect not only of foreign but of domestic policy. The full

[10] Remarks by the Secretary of State, "European Initiative Essential to Economic Recovery," U.S. Department of State Bulletin, 16:1159–1160 (June 15, 1947); the best book on the subject is Harry Bayard Price, The Marshall Plan and Its Meaning (Ithaca, N.Y.: Cornell University Press, 1955).

[11] On response to Marshall Plan, see Price, The Marshall Plan, pp. 26–29; for Anderson's comments on grain requirements, see New York Times, July 13, 1947, p. 7; address by D. A. FitzGerald to FAO, Aug. 30, 1947, FAO Conferences file, Records of BAE, International Organizations, Committees and Conferences, N.A.

American wheat crop for 1947 was forecast at 37.3 million tons, an all-time record that would exceed the last harvest by 6.4 million tons. But in the Corn Belt, the news was all bad. On June 1, 1947, between 20 and 25 percent of corn acreage was still unseeded. "You can't harvest corn that isn't planted," said the *New York Times*, "and you can't plant corn when it's raining three days out of four, as it did throughout April and May over much of the country's corn territory." By August, the Department of Agriculture estimated that probable corn yields in October would be 17.5 million tons below the previous year; by September, the estimate was 24.7 million tons below. Suddenly it seemed like the spring of 1946 all over again. Without adequate corn supplies for their livestock, farmers might use wheat for feed just when wheat had become indispensable for European survival.[12]

Renewal of galloping inflation was one inevitable result of the corn shortage. By mid-August of 1947, corn was selling higher than wheat for the first time in years, and hog and cattle prices surged rapidly upward. During September, when the autumn harvest should have been depressing prices, some food items jumped 10 to 30 percent in a single day. Throughout the summer, Anderson had been aggressively buying grain to meet the 1947–48 export goal, which was set at 10.7 million tons of wheat and 1.9 million tons of corn. Because of the poor corn crop, Anderson set a grain goal (12.6 million tons) that was 2.5 million tons below 1946–47 exports. By the end of August, Anderson had purchased 5.3 million tons and intended to procure grain thereafter on a

[12] On record wheat crop, see *New York Times*, June 11, 1947, p. 41; on bad news from Corn Belt, Summaries of Reports by State Directors of Extension in Mid-Western States Relative to Current Planting and Crop Conditions, June 16, 1947, Reports file, Records of Office of Sec. of Ag., Gen'l Cor., N.A.; for quotation from the *Times*, see *New York Times*, Aug. 14, 1947, p. 22; for corn crop forecast, USDA press release, Sept. 10, 1947, Releases 5–2 file, Records of Office of Sec. of Ag., Gen'l Cor., N.A.

monthly basis to meet the rest of the goal. But the incredible September inflation caused him to change plans, and he announced a temporary suspension of all procurement.[13]

September, 1947, found the Administration groping painfully for a policy to meet the accumulating problems of foreign need and domestic inflation. On the tenth day of the month, Secretary Marshall informed the press that the program for economic reconstruction of Europe would begin too late to rescue that continent from the perhaps fatal hardships of the coming winter. The emergence of unanticipated problems, he said, required the United States to provide interim aid sometime before the end of 1947. The depletion of European dollar and gold reserves, which had been greatly accelerated by the American price inflation, had already forced some nations to curtail food and fuel purchases. Admitting that Congress alone could authorize emergency relief, Marshall, by implication, was calling for a special session of Congress. From somewhere in the Atlantic, where he was enjoying an extended cruise, President Truman issued a curt "no comment" to inquiries about a special session. Less reticent, Clinton Anderson told the press that such a session would be futile; moreover, as for the price controls lately espoused by labor, he was against them, too.[14]

When Truman returned to Washington early in the third week of September, his desk was piled high with reports and recommendations concerning the developing crisis. Chief among them was a statement on policy from the Cabinet

[13] On inflation in August and September, see *New York Times*, Aug. 18, 1947, p. 1; Sept. 13, 1947, p. 1; Sept. 18, 1947, p. 10; on Department's procurement of wheat, press release, Report of President's Committee on Foreign Aid, "Grain Export Program," Sept. 26, 1947, OF 307, TP, TL.

[14] Statement by the Secretary of State, *U.S. Department of State Bulletin*, 17:590 (Sept. 21, 1947); for Truman's refusal to comment, see *New York Times*, Sept. 13, 1947, p. 1; on Anderson's remarks, see *New York Times*, Sept. 20, 1947, p. 11.

155

Food Committee, whose members were Anderson (the chairman), General Marshall, and Secretary of Commerce W. Averell Harriman. The report merely summarized the current program of the Department of Agriculture and reflected the views of neither Marshall nor Harriman, though both signed the report. Justifying the low export goal of 12.6 million tons as a consequence of the poor corn crop, the report acknowledged the worsening plight of Europe and recommended a voluntary conservation program as one possible way to save grain and increase exports. On the question of resuming procurement, the report was silent.[15]

A few days later, the Committee on Foreign Aid dissented from Anderson's policies. Chaired by Secretary Harriman, this Committee of distinguished private citizens had been formed to advise the President on the problems of the Marshall Plan. In the Committee's opinion, the Administration faced a painful dilemma. Either it had to resume procurement of grains and force up prices, or it could delay procurement and risk discovering in a few months that no wheat for export remained. "A policy decision needs to be made as to which horn of the dilemma to seize," the Committee said. For its part, the Committee recommended not only that procurement be resumed but that, in view of the worsening European crisis, the grain export goal be raised. Were the Government to reduce the carry-over to a precarious 2.7 million tons and rescue 4 million tons of wheat from livestock feeders who were currently expected to utilize a huge 10.7 million tons, the Administration could raise the goal from 12.6 million tons to 15.2 million, a total equal to grain exports of the previous crop year. To implement these policies, the Committee could

[15] USDA press release, "Report on Food Situation by Cabinet Food Committee," Sept. 22, 1947, Releases 5–2 file, Records of Office of Information, USDA, N.A.

suggest nothing more bold than a voluntary food conservation campaign.[16]

On October 1, 1947, at a conservation meeting in the White House, Anderson defended his policies. To enter the market on the scale recommended by Harriman's Committee would aggravate the inflation. "I am advised," Anderson said, "that an increase of fifty cents a bushel in wheat prices, with smaller increases for other grains, could in the present situation increase the annual cost of food alone to the American consumer by two and one-half billion dollars." As for reducing the carry-over, dry weather was threatening to delay and perhaps discourage planting of winter wheat. A reasonable carry-over was the only insurance against the menace of wheat famine next year. Throughout most of October, Anderson worried about drought in the Great Plains, but by the end of the month, pressure from the State Department and possibly from within the White House forced him to accept a compromise goal of 13.9 million tons and resume aggressive procurement.[17]

The one policy recommended by both Anderson's Cabinet Food Committee and Harriman's Committee on Foreign Aid was voluntary food conservation. As recently as June, 1947, John R. Steelman, assistant to the President, had said that the Administration regarded voluntary conservation as useless. But in September, ignoring the failure of the Emergency Famine Committee of 1946 and reluctant to advocate stronger measures, the Administration embraced a conservation cam-

[16] Press release, Report of President's Committee on Foreign Aid, "Grain Exports Program," Sept. 26, 1947, OF 307, TP, TL.

[17] Statement by the Secretary of Agriculture, Oct. 1, 1947, Public Relations 11–5 file, Records of Office of Sec. of Ag., Gen'l Cor., N.A.; on Anderson's anxiety about drought in the Great Plains, Anderson to the President, Oct. 27, 1947, OF 426, TP, TL; for evidence of preference in the White House for 15.2-million-ton goal, Jim to John R. Steelman, Oct. 29, 1947, OF 307, TP, TL.

157

paign as the best alternative to no policy at all. On September 25, Truman called a press conference and announced formation of a Citizens Food Committee to lead America on a campaign to save food for Europe. At the same press conference, Truman announced that he was inviting congressional leaders to Washington for a briefing on the crisis. Would he call a special session? Perhaps that would prove necessary, but the President did not know yet. Did he favor return of price controls and rationing? "I will wait and see," he said. The one topic on which the President had definitely made up his mind was the importance of the voluntary conservation campaign.[18]

The object of the voluntary conservation drive was to push exports to the full 15.2 million tons recommended by the Harriman Committee. On the theory that selling conservation was like selling soap, President Truman appointed Charles Luckman, thirty-eight-year-old president of Lever Brothers, to be chairman of the Citizens Food Committee. Serving with Luckman were such notables as George Gallup, Henry Luce, Chester Davis, Herbert Lehman, Philip Murray, and Spyros Skouras. Five days after its creation, the Committee convened in Washington, heard Luckman explain his plan for voluntary rationing, and, according to press reports, voted it down on the grounds that it had been discredited by unhappy experience. A few days later, Luckman staged a radio show starring President Truman, with Harriman, Anderson, Marshall, and himself in supporting roles. The climax was Truman's announcement of the program so inhospitably received by Luckman's Committee only a few days before. "The program," said the President, "is simple and straightforward. Learn it, memorize it . . . (1) use no meat on

[18] On Steelman's view of voluntary conservation, Steelman to Anna G. Rosenberg, June 7, 1947, OF 426, TP, TL; for Truman's press conference, see *Public Papers of the Presidents: Harry S. Truman, 1947*, pp. 437–443.

Tuesdays; (2) use no poultry or eggs on Thursday; (3) save a slice of bread every day . . ."[19]

The program might seem simple to the President, but, according to the press, it baffled the public. Many Americans just "couldn't understand," said *Newsweek*, "how Europe would be fed if they merely ate poultry instead of meat on Tuesdays, and meat instead of poultry on Thursdays. Besides, wouldn't eating less poultry create an embarrassing chicken surplus and didn't a chicken go on eating grain even if it wasn't itself eaten?" Indeed, some even doubted that the President himself really understood. At one press conference, a reporter asked, "If you ate more poultry, wouldn't you have fewer chickens to eat the grain?" Answered the President, "Now that's like which came first, the chicken or the egg. Can't answer a question like that. Can't answer that question."[20]

But the real work of the Citizens Food Committee was negotiating with food processing industries to limit their use of wheat and corn. Hoping ultimately to conserve 2.7 million tons of grain, Luckman began his campaign with the distilling industry. The distillers agreed to shut down for sixty days and thereby conserve some 0.3 to 0.5 million tons of wheat. Soon afterward, the brewers of beer promised that until February, 1948, they would use no wheat and would limit their use of other grains. This, said the brewers, would save almost one tenth of a ton. The bakers, for their part, undertook to save nearly 0.3 million tons by ending consignment selling of bread and perhaps by reducing the size of bread loaves. The bakers also agreed to make cakes with two layers instead

[19] On reports that Luckman's plan was rejected by his own committee, see *New York Times*, Oct. 3, 1947, p. 1; and "Knee-Deep in Alligators," *Time*, 50:22 (Oct. 13, 1947); press release, address by the President, Oct. 5, 1947, OF 174–F, TP, TL.

[20] "Chicken Fricassee," *Newsweek*, 30:25 (Oct. 27, 1947); for Truman's press conference, *Public Papers of the Presidents: Harry S. Truman, 1947*, p. 466.

of three and pies with one crust instead of two. In ways left unspecified, the wet and dry millers, who manufacture breakfast food, corn starch, and flour, committed their industry to conserve 0.4 to 0.8 million tons. The only difficult negotiation was with the poultry industry. Plagued by small surpluses even before poultryless Tuesdays, the chicken farmer regarded the Government's program as a great burden. After a series of fruitless conferences, Luckman and the industry finally reached an agreement under which the Committee would give up poultryless Tuesdays and in return the poultrymen would save 1.5 million tons of grain by culling flocks and decreasing broiler and turkey production in the next year. Pointing triumphantly to the successful accomplishment of his goal, Luckman resigned on November 20 and turned his campaign over to the Department of Agriculture. Surely now the Government would be able to achieve exports of 15.2 million tons.[21]

As a businessman himself, Luckman should perhaps have had more respect for the guile and enterprise of American industry. The distillers, for instance, took advantage of the three-week delay between the negotiation of their shutdown pledge and the actual stoppage of production to process twice as much grain as in the previous month. After the eight-week suspension was over, the distillers made up for lost time by far exceeding normal grain usage in February, March, and April, though stocks were sufficient to satisfy a year's demand. Congress meanwhile, refused to re-enact legislation giving the Secretary of Agriculture authority to regulate whiskey production. As for the brewers, they process little wheat anyway, and by increasing their use of malt barley, itself a valuable coarse grain, they wiped out what little saving might

[21] For a summary of industrial conservation agreements, Citizens Food Committee, *Final Report*, Dec. 1947, Reports file, Records of Office of Sec. of Ag., Cabinet Food Committee, N.A.; Luckman to the President, Nov. 20, 1947, OF 795, TP, TL.

otherwise have been made. The bakers chose to ignore rather than circumvent their pledge, and consignment selling soon went on as before. The industry steadfastly rebuffed all efforts by the Government to negotiate a new agreement. The wet and dry millers, having undertaken no specific obligation, had the easiest time of all in escaping the burdens of their agreement. Only in the poultry industry could the Citizens Food Committee point to evidence of compliance, for substantial culling of flocks did indeed take place. But, as Anderson had remarked in October, such reductions usually occur "in the last quarter of each year as poultrymen perform their normal culling operations coincident to housing their new crops of pullets." Furthermore, the pledge to cut poultry flocks by 100 million birds fell 28 million short. Throughout the winter and spring of 1948, the Department of Agriculture did its best to negotiate new savings, but, concluded Assistant Secretary Brannan in May, "our efforts to induce distillers, brewers, bakers, and others to eliminate voluntarily the non-essential consumption of grain has not been a success, largely because these industries are unwilling to cooperate with the Government and the public." But the public itself had displayed no disposition to curb its own appetites, and no one ever seriously suggested that meatless, wheatless, and poultryless days ever effected any noteworthy savings. In January, 1948, restaurants ceased observing them on the grounds that they had not been supported by the public. The advertising genius of America, Luckman learned, could not sell everything.[22]

[22] On distillers' use of grain before shutdown, and brewers' use of malt barley, "Luckman's Luck," *Newsweek*, 31:22–23 (Jan. 19, 1948); on excessive use after distillery shutdown and failure of Congress to authorize production curbs, Charles F. Brannan to Forrest C. Donnell, May 7, 1947, Commodities 4 file, Records of Office of Sec. of Ag., Gen'l Cor., N.A.; on bakers, Clinton Anderson to the Attorney General, March 29, 1948, Cooperation 3 file, Records of Office of Sec. of Ag., Gen'l Cor., N.A.; on wet and dry millers, H. K. Baker to Charles Brannan, March 11, 1948, Cooperation 3 file, Records of Office of Sec. of Ag., Gen'l Cor., N.A.; for Anderson's views on poultry pledge,

The Government had undertaken the voluntary conservation campaign only as a substitute for the harsher policies it could not bring itself to recommend, and it never really expected much from the program. Slowly, the Administration began to accept the implications of its own analysis of foreign and domestic conditions. In mid-October Truman blurted out at a press conference that price controls belonged in a police state, but three weeks later the Council of Economic Advisers reluctantly endorsed selective price control. Near the end of October, Truman issued a call for a special session of Congress to convene on November 17, 1947, and at his urging, congressional committees began to take preliminary testimony on the emergency legislation at last deemed indispensable by the Administration.[23]

On November 10, 1947, Secretary Marshall told the Senate Committee on Foreign Affairs, "the problem of overseas payment has become particularly acute in the case of Austria, France, and Italy. It is clear that . . . these countries in the absence of immediate assistance will, during the next few months, begin to suffer from a lack of food and other necessities . . . and the whole economic and social life of the people will be seriously affected." Marshall asked Congress to authorize 597 million dollars to see these countries through the winter. Two weeks later, under the firm hand of its

Anderson to Charles Luckman, Oct. 22, 1947, Senator Anderson's Office, Washington; on partial fulfillment of culling goal, N. E. Dodd to Karl M. LeCompte, Feb. 9, 1948, Poultry Products 6 file, Records of Office of Sec. of Ag., Gen'l Cor., N.A.; for Brannan's harsh indictment of processing industries, Brannan to Frank Pace, May 28, 1948, Organization 2 file, Records of Office of Sec. of Ag., Gen'l Cor., N.A.; on end of restaurant compliance, see New York Times, Jan. 5, 1948, p. 1.

[23] For Truman's remark on price control and the police state, see Public Papers of the Presidents: Harry S. Truman, 1947, p. 468; for Truman's call for a special session, see same volume, pp. 475–476; Council of Economic Advisers to the President, Nov. 5, 1947, Clark Clifford Files, Letters and Memoranda to the President, 1946–47 folder, TL.

great chairman, Arthur H. Vandenberg of Michigan, the Committee unanimously reported out an interim aid bill embodying Marshall's requests. Shortly thereafter, the House Foreign Affairs Committee, after adding China to the list of recipients to pacify the China lobby, sent its own bill to the floor.[24]

Addressing a tense joint session of Congress on November 17, Truman called for passage of the interim aid bill and outlined a ten-point anti-inflation program. Congress, he said, should curb credit, regulate speculators, reimpose controls over exports and transportation, provide for allocation of scarce commodities, "authorize measures which will induce the marketing of livestock and poultry at weights and grades that represent the most efficient utilization of grain," and as the climax of the program, grant the President stand-by authority to impose selective price control and rationing. Confronting as he did a hostile Republican Congress under the leadership of Senator Taft, Truman and his ten points faced a doubtful future.[25]

It did not help Truman's program that it had been conceived only hesitantly and was thereafter defended with reluctance. Clinton Anderson, for instance, went up to the Hill and told Congress that he could not think of any recommendations for implementing the President's request for authority to induce efficient livestock marketing. Of course, price controls could make feeding operations unprofitable, but Anderson was not at all sure that price controls were going to be necessary. Perhaps if the winter wheat crop failed,

[24] For Marshall's testimony, see "Interim Aid for Europe," Hearings before Committee on Foreign Relations, U.S. Senate, 80th Cong., 1st sess., pp. 2–10; on House bill, see "Emergency Foreign Aid," Report No. 1152, *House Miscellaneous Reports*, VI, same session (Dec. 21, 1947).

[25] *Public Papers of the Presidents: Harry S. Truman, 1947*, pp. 492–498; on atmosphere in the House Chamber during Truman's speech, see *New York Times*, Nov. 18, 1947, p. 1.

Congress might have to provide controls, but, he said, "I would be the last to want to see [them] applied." The *New York Times* referred to Anderson after this performance as "the leader of the conservative forces within the Cabinet." In an effort to quell suspicion that he was not behind the President, Anderson soon returned to Congress and made a strong and unequivocal plea for the ten-point program, but he was too late to do the Administration much good. Truman, of course, never did get his controls, but events proved this far less regrettable than appeared in the last bleak months of 1947.[26]

With Vandenberg repulsing all assaults, the Senate approved the interim aid bill on December 1, 1947. But over in the House there was trouble. In that Chamber, talk of "bleeding" the nation and exhausting its resources found a receptive audience among the unconverted isolationists. As Representative Everett Dirksen inelegantly phrased it, its enemies were attempting to "gut this bill" by attaching amendments to curb exports of scarce commodities. But had not the Secretary of Agriculture himself spoken of the need for a reasonable carry-over to protect the nation in case of persisting bad weather? Accordingly, the House approved an amendment, later accepted by the Senate, requiring a four-million-ton wheat carry-over into the next crop year.[27]

[26] For Anderson on authority to induce efficient marketing, see "Anti-Inflation Program as Recommended in the President's Message of November 17, 1947," Hearings before Joint Committee on the Economic Report, 80th Cong., 1st sess., pp. 37-38; for remarks on price control, see "European Interim Aid and Government Relief in Occupied Areas," Hearings before the Committee on Appropriations, U.S. Senate, same session, p. 77; for *Times*'s description of Anderson, see *New York Times*, Nov. 27, 1947, p. 1; for Anderson's strong plea for controls, see "Economic Stabilization Aids," Hearings before Committee on Banking and Currency, U.S. House of Representatives, same session, pp. 89-92.

[27] For Senate passage, see *Congressional Record*, 80th Cong., 1st sess., vol. 93, pt. 9, 10980; for Dirksen's phrase, see p. 11206; for

The failure of voluntary conservation, the improbability of price control legislation, and the new carry-over requirement seemed to presage defeat for the 15.2 million ton goal. But by December, new developments in the market place began to revive hope. As a Department report documented three days later, hogs were coming to market six pounds lighter than last year and twenty pounds lighter than two years ago. Grain prices had climbed so high so fast that feeding operations were growing less profitable. Not until the Department of Agriculture completed the January, 1948, report on wheat disappearance did the full effects of these developments become apparent. Wheat supplies remaining from the first six months of 1947–48 were 21.3 million tons in contrast to 18.2 million in 1946 and 17.2 million in 1947. Thus far a mere 1.8 million tons of wheat had been fed to livestock. But in view of the 4-million-ton carry-over requirement, the Government felt that it still could not raise the export goal from the compromise goal of 13.9 million to 15.2 million tons. Foreign governments should be warned, said the State Department, that shipments at the end of the crop year would probably fall below current rates of export.[28]

The reports on grain supply were not the only hopeful development of January. At this time Argentina began to increase her exports, Australia reported a bumper crop, and

final bill and House vote, see pp. 11405–11412; for Anderson's remarks on need for an adequate wheat carry-over, see "European Interim Aid and Government Relief. . . ." Senate hearings, pp. 6–10, 16–18.

[28] On hog weights and grain prices, "Summary Statement Relating to U.S. Grain Availability in 1947–1948 and 1948–1949," Export wheat and grain file, 12/10/47, Senator Anderson's office, Washington; for report on wheat disappearance, USDA press release, Jan. 25, 1948, Releases 5–2 file, Records of Office of Information, USDA; for reduced feeding of wheat to livestock, Jesse B. Gilmer to the Secretary of Agriculture, Feb. 2, 1948, Grain file, Records of Office of Sec. of Ag., Gen'l Cor., N.A.; proposed dispatch to certain American diplomatic officers, Jan. 22, 1948, Grain file, Records of Office of Sec. of Ag., Gen'l Cor., N.A.

news from the American Southwest told of heavy snows that would rescue the winter wheat crop. The waning of the crisis, of course, did not escape the notice of the speculators, and late in January, grain prices began to slide. On Tuesday morning, February 4, 1948, trading in Chicago started normally, but within one-half hour, heavy selling was underway. By ten o'clock panic seized the grain exchange. By 10:15, brokers were yelling "Keno, Keno," meaning that corn had declined eight cents, the legal limit for one day. By 10:30, wheat and rye had plunged their full limit, and all trading ceased. The same wild selling closed the exchange early every day for the rest of the week, and by Saturday, wheat had fallen fifty-two cents and corn forty cents. This, the sharpest decline ever recorded, persisted for still another week. It had taken the food price index from June, 1947, to January 17, 1948, to rise from 179 to 209. By February 21, it was down to 182.[29]

No one seemed quite sure what to make of this halt in the price spiral. The chairman of the Council of Economic Advisers commented that the time was one for "masterly silence." The Republicans, though more loquacious, shed even less light in attempting to make political capital from the episode. Representative August Andresen, for instance, contended that the Administration had intentionally rigged the price break by withdrawing from the market, and that while wheat farmers were losing 200 million dollars, insiders had made a killing. In truth, the Government had actually bought wheat on the first day of the panic and only decided to withdraw the next day in accord with the usual policy of avoiding unsteady markets. Senator Taft, on the other hand, charged the Administration with trying to reinflate prices.

[29] For panic on grain exchanges, see *New York Times*, Feb. 5, 1948, p. 1; Feb. 6, 1948, p. 1; Feb. 7, 1948, p. 1; Feb. 8, 1948, p. 1; Feb. 9, 1948, p. 29; Feb. 10, 1948, p. 1; Feb. 15, 1948, p. 1E; and memo by Fred Waugh, March 1, 1948, John D. Clark file, TL.

As evidence, he pointed to announcements by the Department of Agriculture on February 6 that the Government would soon resume procurement for export and that in time the export goal might be raised to 15.2 million tons. "The Administration, which talks about bringing prices down," said the Senator, "is afraid that they actually will come down. Of course, they think their only chance of winning the November election is to keep prices up and create an air of false prosperity." Anderson easily proved that the suspect announcements had been prepared before the price break and went on to show that Senator Taft was well aware of the Government's long-time desire to raise the export goal. As for playing politics, Anderson asked Taft, "Are you familiar with the old spiritual, 'It's me, It's me, It's me, O Lord, standing in the need of prayer' ?"[30]

While the debate raged on, the commodity markets regained some stability, and the selling wave came to an end. In the months that followed, most of the decline in food prices was wiped out by the rising cost of meat, the result, of course, of the grain shortage. But the price level did not go much beyond the peak of January, 1948, and by autumn, the inflation was over.

Through February and March, 1948, the Government maintained the compromise grain goal of 13.9 million tons. Though the edge of crisis had grown less sharp, millions in Europe's cities still survived on rations of 1,900 to 2,100 calories per day, which, as one Italian worker said, were not enough to

[30] For Andresen's charges, see *Congressional Record*, 80th Cong., 2nd sess., vol. 94, pt. 1, 1220; on Departmental grain purchases on Feb. 4, see "Commodity Transactions," Hearings before the Select Committee to Investigate Commodity Transactions, same session, p. 97; on Senator Taft's charges, see *New York Times*, Feb. 9, 1948, p. 1; for Anderson's remark on prayer, see Clinton Anderson to Senator Taft, Feb. 9, 1948, Grain file, Records of Office of Sec. of Ag., Gen'l Cor., N.A.; Anderson gives a full account of the Department's role in the grain markets in a letter to Arthur Krock, Feb. 14, 1948, Market break file, Senator Anderson's office, Washington.

live on and not enough to die on. Achievement of the full goal, representing as it did millions of extra loaves of bread for Europe, was still of the highest importance. In April, good harvest prospects for next year induced the Government to set a final goal of 12.9 million tons of wheat and 2.5 million of coarse grain, making a total of 15.4 million tons, slightly above the record exports of the previous year. In part because the inflation in grain prices had discouraged livestock feeding, America had performed another massive rescue operation. In the next year, European food production recovered well, and the Marshall Plan provided funds for continued heavy American exports, needed now not for survival but for good diet. The great European famine was over.[31]

In July, 1948, when the President's Cabinet Food Committee recounted the events of the past twelve months, Anderson was no longer a member. In March, he had announced his intention to resign from the secretaryship to run for the Senate from New Mexico, and in May, he departed from Washington. According to rumor, Anderson, who had retained Truman's confidence until the end, had even been a serious possibility for the vice-presidential nomination of 1948.[32] But the choice of Anderson as Truman's running mate, whether or not ever seriously considered, would have been inappropriate. When he first entered the Cabinet, Anderson fit well into the government that Truman had created. His relief policies, his quarrels with Chester Bowles, and his alienation

[31] On calorie consumption in European cities, Attachment to memo from J. H. Richter to G. H. Gilbertson, March 23, 1948, Food–Food Requirements 5 file, Records of OFAR, Gen'l Cor., N.A.; on crop developments, USDA press releases April 9, 1948, and April 10, 1948, Releases 5–2 file, Records of Office of Sec. of Ag., Gen'l Cor., N.A.; on total exports for the year, Cabinet Food Committee, "Report to the President," July, 1948, OF 174–C, TP, TL.

[32] On Anderson's intention to run for the Senate, see *New York Times*, March 14, 1948, p. 39; on rumors of consideration for the vice-presidency, see *Wallace's Farmer and Iowa Homestead*, April 3, 1948, p. 20.

of the liberals of agriculture were typical of those early years. But by the end of Truman's first term, the Administration was undergoing a transformation. By now confident of his powers, the President had set himself firmly on a liberal course and was surrounding himself with advisers who could speak with the appropriate rhetoric. Anderson's resignation and his replacement by a man with strong liberal connections proved an important step in re-establishing the old Roosevelt coalition by election day, November, 1948. Had Anderson remained, the Administration's successful campaign in the fall to win back the farmers by playing on fears of returning depression would have suffered a serious handicap. Anderson belonged in Truman's first Administration; he might have felt out of place in the second.

8 THE ELECTION OF 1948

🙠 In the spring of 1948 the Democratic party appeared on the verge of dissolution. Lacking the cohesive presence of Roosevelt and weakened by economic prosperity, the coalition of the dispossessed that had fashioned the great victories of the 1930's seemed only a memory. On the leftward fringe of the party, Henry A. Wallace and his Progressives were tempting exasperated liberals with promises of a militant crusade for peace and justice preached in the rhetoric of the New Deal. On the right, angry Southerners were preparing to depart from the party that had abandoned states rights for civil rights. And at the center, approaching the nadir of his popularity, Harry Truman was attempting to suppress a widespread revolt against his candidacy among those factions still loyal to the party. Liberal politicians, labor leaders, and big city bosses hoped in vain to nominate General Dwight Eisenhower and thereby avoid the political rout that all of them now expected. Amid the gloom of the weeks before the Democratic convention, a curious struggle occurred within the Administration on the question of who should succeed Clinton Anderson—curious, of course, because most Administration officeholders were preparing to find employment elsewhere in anticipation of the Republican victory that seemed only months away.[1]

[1] For a readable account of the election of 1948, see Jules Abels, *Out of the Jaws of Victory* (New York: Holt, 1959).

170

Norris Dodd had a strong claim to the office of Secretary. An Oregon farmer, Dodd had risen from county committeeman to become chief of the Agricultural Adjustment Agency in 1943 and then Under Secretary in 1946. But Anderson had fought hard to curb the independence of the AAA and consequently had never been close to its dedicated alumnus. Anderson's own candidate was his "loyal and diligent" subordinate, Assistant Secretary Charles F. Brannan, a man who, Anderson thought, could be counted on to continue his policies.

James Patton, president of the Farmers Union, found himself in rare agreement with the departing Secretary, for he, too, supported Brannan's candidacy. Brannan and Patton had been old friends since the 1930's. In 1935, one year after Patton had become secretary of the Colorado Farmers Union, Brannan left his Denver law practice to become assistant regional attorney in the Resettlement Administration. As allies in the war against rural poverty in the mountain states, the two men began a friendship that was to have significant consequences on subsequent agricultural history. In 1941, Brannan, then only thirty-eight years old, became regional director of the Farm Security Administration (FSA) for Colorado, Wyoming, and Montana. Like the Resettlement Administration before it, FSA devoted its short life to assisting agriculture's disinherited. In the meantime, Patton had become president of the Farmers Union, and in 1944, he used his influence to bring Brannan to Washingtoin to become, first, Assistant Administrator to FSA and then Assistant Secretary of Agriculture. Now in 1948, with the election only months away and Anderson out of the Government, Patton was renewing his allegiance to the Democratic party, an allegiance he had broken in despair two years before. For his part, Truman knew that he had to fight a liberal campaign, and he was quite willing to forgive Patton's earlier defection. Partly because of Anderson's recommendation, partly to secure the support of the Farmers Union, Truman, in May, 1948, made

171

Brannan his Secretary of Agriculture. Dodd's reward for his years of service was the post of Director General of FAO.[2]

Even Brannan's physical appearance was deceiving. Tall, stooped, and balding, Brannan, said one close friend, looked very much like a tired banker. He had moved with little friction upward through the Department, where he had been modest, competent, and even, some said, humble and self-effacing. Brannan's ascension to the secretaryship seemed a fitting prize for a career man who had well performed his bureaucratic chores. For though Brannan had been active in the Democratic party of Colorado and regarded himself as an ardent New Dealer, he had seemed in Washington the model civil servant. The powers and responsibilities of high office would call forth qualities in Charles Brannan that no one could have foretold in May, 1948. Who, indeed, could have known that in succeeding years Brannan would play the game of partisan politics with a ferocity rarely displayed even by the professionals? Who could have perceived his lust for combat, his gift for invective, or the vein of iron that lay beneath his placid surface? Certainly Clinton Anderson had no premonition of what power would do to his former assistant, for later revelations pained him deeply. James Patton, on the other hand, got everything that he bargained for.

While the struggle over the succession was still in doubt, Truman began his campaign to halt the steady exodus of the farm vote from the Democratic party. To underscore his concern with agricultural problems, he sent a sharply phrased special message to Congress in mid-May pleading for enactment of flexible price supports and expansion of existing pro-

[2] For biographical information on Norris Dodd, see *Current Biography*, ed. Anna Roth (New York: H. W. Wilson Company, 1949), pp. 156–159; for Brannan, *Current Biography*, 1948, pp. 57–59; and also press release, "Charles F. Brannan," Biographies file, Records of Office of Sec. of Ag., Gen'l Cor., N.A.; interview with James G. Patton, Aug. 1, 1961.

grams. But the gap between Truman's rhetoric and his actual recommendations was obviously large. Enjoying high income, farmers were not interested in larger appropriations for soil conservation or for subsidized consumption. Moreover, many farmers viewed flexible supports with deep suspicion. Thus the message neither aroused the complacent nor reassured the fearful. Truman, however, was not discouraged, and early in June, a full month before the Democratic convention and two weeks before Congress passed the Agricultural Act of 1948, he made a farm speech in Omaha, Nebraska, calling for enactment of his program. The blame for congressional inaction, he suggested, belonged in part to the Republican presidential candidates who talked loud and often of their love of the farmers but failed to exert influence in their behalf when it really counted.[3]

In the closing hours of the session, the Republican Eightieth Congress answered Truman's demand for a price support law by passing the Hope–Aiken bill. Undaunted by this untimely cooperation, Truman signed the bill and then issued a statement lamenting what the Republicans had left undone. The Congress, he said, had failed to ratify the International Wheat Agreement. It had appropriated inadequate funds for soil conservation and marketing research. It had neglected to legislate a food stamp plan or provide better facilities for rural health and education. Moreover, he continued, an obscure provision in the Commodity Credit Corporation charter passed at the end of the session threatened to cost farmers money. By forbidding the CCC to acquire land or to acquire or lease storage facilities, the charter made it impossible for the Corporation to build new storage bins near farms to hold crops placed under government loan. This meant, the President said, "that the Corporation will have to

[3] *Public Papers of the Presidents: Harry S. Truman, 1948* (Washington: U.S. Government Printing Office, 1964), pp. 256–258, 292–296.

ship grain for livestock feeding . . . from farms to distant points for storage, and then later to ship it back again to farm areas," thus profiting grain dealers at the expense of farmers. This last item in an otherwise unexciting indictment went largely unnoticed at the time. But in the storage provision of the CCC charter resided a seed that would lie dormant for two months and then suddenly sprout into the farm issue that Truman was looking for.[4]

In early July, however, as the Democratic convention assembled in Philadelphia, the quest for the farm vote appeared hopeless. The *Des Moines Register's* poll of Iowa, for instance, gave Truman only 29 percent compared to 56 percent for the Republican nominee, Governor Thomas E. Dewey of New York. Brief, uninspired, and scarcely distinguishable from its Republican counterpart, the party farm plank merely endorsed flexible supports and promised to expand existing programs. The great fight over civil rights, which drove the Dixiecrats into secession, dwarfed all other issues and provoked the only excitement of the convention. Bowing to necessity, the delegates nominated Truman and then dispersed to endure the agony of their party. James Reston of the *New York Times* heard one delegate moan, " 'The Democratic party is breaking up before our eyes.' " Not so, said Reston. "It broke up and scattered long ago."[5]

In his speech accepting nomination, President Truman had told the weary delegates that he would recall the Eightieth Congress to finish its work and to deliver on the promises of the Republican platform. Late in July, therefore, the focus

[4] *Public Papers of the Presidents: Harry S. Truman, 1948*, pp. 399–400.

[5] *Des Moines Sunday Register*, July 11, 1948, p. 9E; for Democratic farm plank, see Kirk Porter and Donald Bruce Johnson, *National Party Platforms, 1840–1960* (Urbana: The University of Illinois Press, 1961) p. 434; for Republican platform, p. 452; for Reston's statements, *New York Times*, July 13, 1948, p. 7.

of politics returned to Washington, where a sterile dialogue between the White House and the Capitol disturbed the midsummer calm. Truman's message to the special session emphasized the menace of inflation, which he still regarded as the major threat to the American economy. In vain he asked enactment of price controls, a public housing measure, federal aid to education, higher minimum wages, expanded social security, and civil rights legislation. For the farmer, only a new plea for approval of the International Wheat Agreement found its way into the message. Peculiarly absent in view of later events was a presidential request for repeal of the provision of the new CCC charter limiting the Government's ability to acquire grain storage.[6]

The lack of attention to farm matters in the President's message not only reflected his failure to find a good farm issue but resulted inevitably from his July campaign strategy. By emphasizing inflation and calling for price controls, the President was appealing to labor and urban consumers at the expense of producer groups, including farmers. But the debate in Washington over inflation went largely unnoticed in the farm belt, for by midsummer, clouds gathering over the grain states were changing the mood of American agriculture. The long awaited price decline had begun. As yet, there was no panic, only watching and waiting and the slow revival of old anxieties.

The descent of grain prices in the summer and autumn of 1948 resulted from the easing of the famine in Europe and record-smashing harvests at home. August crop estimates termed "sensational" by the *New York Times*, predicted a corn crop that would be the largest in history and record production of peanuts, soy beans, and rice. The forecasters expected a wheat crop second only to the bumper year of

[6] *Public Papers of the Presidents: Harry S. Truman, 1948*, pp. 416–421.

175

FARM POLICIES AND POLITICS

1947. With abundant harvests threatening to overwhelm demand for the first time since the 1930's, commodity prices slowly weakened.[7]

For winter wheat farmers, who market their crops in early summer, huge harvests had already meant trouble. On July 26, Secretary Brannan, reporting on marketing conditions for wheat, warned farmers, "country elevators, terminal warehouses, and the transportation system are being overloaded." News reports drifted eastward describing how the huge wheat crop "has glutted rail lines, over-loaded elevators, and spilled onto the streets of small midwestern towns." The situation was particularly alarming in view of the storage provision of the new CCC charter. A month before, Truman had complained to Congress about this provision because it might require farmers to ship grain under price support loans to distant commercial facilities. Now as commercial storage space began to disappear, the provision took on new meaning. If the CCC could not lease land on which to construct new storage bins, and commercial facilities were filled, the CCC might be forced to default on its price support obligations, for only crops adequately stored could receive government loans. Brannan warned farmers that they would have either to build their own storage or face the loss of price support protection. By early August, shortages of grain bins forced wheat farmers in many areas into the commercial market prematurely, and prices fell beneath 90 percent of parity. Fearful that inability to meet price support commitments might result in political injury to the Democratic party, Brannan frantically renewed his pleas to the farmers to begin storage construction.[8]

[7] *New York Times*, Aug. 12, 1948, p. 20.

[8] USDA press release, July 26, 1948, file V B7, WW II Records, ERS, ESA, Ag. Hist. Br., USDA; for quote from the press, see *New York Times*, Aug. 1, 1948, p. 8E; for Brannan's second plea to farmers

In the Corn Belt the harvest would not start until October, but during the late summer of 1948, the problem of storage was already worrying farmers. Sizable decreases in animal numbers in the past three years and the immense corn crop now on the stalk meant that available feed per animal would rise from an average of 0.89 tons during the preceding five years to an estimated 1.6 tons in 1949. Too much corn and too little storage might well send corn prices and eventually hog prices below support levels. The Production and Marketing Administration in Iowa estimated that one third of the 1948 Iowa crop would require storage space, much of it currently nonexistent. PMA officials from Washington went into the field to organize campaigns to instruct farmers in how to build temporary storage. Meanwhile, doubts grew in the Administration that the 90 percent support commitment could be kept. The Gallup Poll of farm voters in August did little to hearten the Administration: Dewey, 48 percent; Truman, 38; Wallace, 2; no opinion, 12.[9]

With its chances seeming only to worsen, the Administration entered September still searching for a farm issue, still hoping somehow to seize the offensive. Then on the second day of the month, Harold E. Stassen, former boy governor of Minnesota and recent unsuccessful aspirant for the Republican nomination, emerged from a strategy conference with Governor Dewey in Albany and gave the Democrats their chance. Continuing the long summer's debate on who was responsible for inflation, Stassen charged that the Administration had deliberately attempted to keep food prices high despite

---

to build their own storage, USDA press release, Aug. 6, 1948, file V B7, WW II Records, ERS, ESA, Ag. Hist. Br., USDA.

[9] For figures comparing feed per ton in 1948 with previous years, see *Des Moines Register,* Aug. 25, 1948, p. 6; for Iowa PMA warnings on storage, *Des Moines Register,* Aug. 20, 1948, p. 8; on doubts that loan rate could be maintained, USDA press release, Aug. 6, 1948, file V B7, WW II Records, ERS, ESA, Ag. Hist. Br., USDA.

bumper crops. To prevent desirable downward adjustments, Stassen said, the Department of Agriculture had made grain purchases for export beyond immediate needs, and Secretary Brannan had actually implied that he would step up procurement. Two hours after Stassen made these remarks, Brannan issued a reply. Stassen's accusation, Brannan said, "is a typically deceptive, inaccurate, political statement. This is in essence an attack on the price support system. I demand that Mr. Stassen or Mr. Dewey name the specific commodity which they had in mind." Stassen, of course, had said nothing at all about price supports. In the absence of real issues, Brannan decided to invent some of his own.

The next day Brannan called a press conference to elaborate on his charges. First, he repeated that Dewey, through Stassen, had attacked price supports "by falsely attributing to that legislation the exorbitantly high prices on certain foods." Turning then from Republican words to Republican deeds, Brannan struck out in a new direction. After a whole summer of worrying about the lack of grain storage and fuming helplessly against the CCC charter for tying his hands, Brannan finally saw the political opportunity that had been his all along. After all, a Republican Congress had enacted the charter. On behalf of grain traders, Brannan told the press, the Republicans had deliberately crippled the price support system by passing the storage provision, and on Republicans rested the blame for the faltering behavior of the price support mechanism. Brannan's accusation was a brilliant stroke that at once relieved the Administration of responsibility for low prices and threw the Republicans on the defensive.[10]

[10] For Stassen's accusations, see *New York Times,* Sept. 3, 1948, p. 1; for Brannan's first statement attacking Stassen, press release, Sept. 2, 1948, McCune files, 1948 folder, FUL; for his second statement in which he makes CCC charter a campaign issue, statement by Secretary of Agriculture, Sept. 3, 1948, PPF 97, TP, TL.

The charge against the Eightieth Congress had some substance. It had indeed been at the insistence of the grain trade that the offending provision found its way into the charter. Commercial grain dealers had asked Congress to impose some inhibition on the Government's power to acquire potentially competitive storage. The fears of the traders were largely imaginary, for the Government's storage consisted of bins on or near farms that did not interfere with commercial trading. Though at one time during the war, the Government owned farm storage holding 300,000,000 bushels, deterioration had led the Government to sell most of what it owned. Nevertheless, the traders induced Congress to add a clumsily worded proviso to the CCC charter that said, "The Corporation shall not have power to acquire or lease any [storage or servicing] plant or facility or lease real property." What Brannan failed to tell farm audiences during the next two months was that no Democrat in Congress ever protested inclusion of the amendment. Only Republican H. Carl Andresen raised a question about the provision, but he too voted for the new charter. Neither Congress, nor for that matter the grain trade, had intended to hamper price support operations. Designed to appease the grain trade, the offending provision became the primary weapon of a Democratic campaign to convince farmers that Republicans meant to sabotage price supports.[11]

Brannan's inventive and energetic response to Stassen's statement ended the long months of groping for a farm issue. Taking a cue from the Secretary, National Chairman Howard McGrath was soon accusing the Eightieth Congress of "double-

[11] For example of opposition of grain trade to power of CCC to acquire its own storage, see "Commodity Credit Corporation Charter," Hearings before Committee on Agriculture and Forestry, U.S. Senate, 80th Cong., 2nd sess., pp. 122–123; for the text of the charter, see *Congressional Record*, 80th Cong., 2nd sess., vol. 94, pt. 7, 8866–8868; for Andresen's remarks, p. 8872.

crossing" farmers by extending price supports without providing storage space for CCC crops. President Truman began quoting a *Wall Street Journal* editorial commending Stassen for his supposed attack on the support system. Meanwhile, evidence of farm unrest began slowly to accumulate. The *Des Moines Register* reported in early September that farmers, while willing to accept the sliding scale, "are frightened by talk of getting rid of price supports." Elsewhere in the same edition, the *Register* told its readers, "Building suitable cribs in which to put this year's corn crop is one of the most serious situations confronting [farmers] . . . since the depression of the 30's." By mid-September, the growing intensity of the Democratic campaign forced Governor Dewey to issue a special statement assuring farmers that he subscribed fully to the principle of price supports. As for the charge that the Republicans planned to end such supports, it was, said Dewey, "created out of thin air. It was an intentional fabrication designed to deceive the producers of America's food." If Dewey thought his endorsement of supports would end further deceptions, he was wrong. Within the hour, Brannan dismissed Dewey's statement as mere "lip service," claiming that Stassen's trial balloon attacking supports had burst, thereby forcing Dewey's retreat. "It is significant," said Brannan, "that he does not disclaim the Stassen statement that price supports are responsible for the high cost of living, although this statement is an obvious falsehood."[12]

[12] For McGrath's attack, see *New York Times,* Sept. 13, 1948, p. 7; on Truman's use of *Wall Street Journal,* summary of controversy between Secretary Brannan and Harold Stassen, prepared by Wesley McCune, October, 1948, McCune files, 1948 campaign folder, FUL; for quotation on fears caused by talk of ending price supports, see *Des Moines Register,* Sept. 5, 1948, p. 39H; for quotation on most serious situation, see *Des Moines Register,* Sept. 5, 1948, p. 8H; for Dewey's special statement endorsing price supports, see *New York Times,* Sept. 18, 1948, p. 1; for Brannan's remarks on Dewey's statement,

The day after this exchange, Truman inaugurated his whistle-stop tour of the West by delivering a major address at the National Plowing Contest in Dexter, Iowa, where a farm audience of 80,000 gathered to enjoy a day at the fair and listen to the President of the United States. The acres of shiny new automobiles and the rows of private aircraft testified to the current prosperity of his listeners, but Truman did not talk of good times or even of the inflation that had worried him a few months before. In words ill-suited to the holiday atmosphere, Truman sought to revive fading memories of the Depression and tell again how the Democratic party had routed despair and restored prosperity. In language described by one liberal commentator, Thomas Stokes, as "raw, harsh, and demagogic," Truman warned of a new depression that awaited the farmer if he returned Wall Street to power. "I think," the President said, "that Wall Street expects its money to elect a Republican Administration that will listen to the gluttons of privilege first and to the people not at all . . . The Republican gluttons of privilege are cold men. They are cunning men . . . They want a return of the Wall Street economic dictatorship." Shifting targets, Truman returned to the Republican Eightieth Congress, which, he said, "had already stuck a pitchfork in the farmer's back." The pitchfork was, of course, the CCC charter, itself merely the prelude to overthrow of the whole price support system. Lack of storage is a "man-made disaster bearing the Republican trade mark," the President went on. "For 16 years the Democrats have been working on a crop of prosperity for the farmer . . . The question is: Are you going to let another Republican blight wipe out that prosperity?"

The attack on Wall Street, the charges of conspiracy, the desperate rhetoric on behalf of an oppressed people were

"Excerpts of Secretary Brannan's Reply to Governor Dewey," Sept. 17, 1948, McCune files, 1948 campaign folder, FUL.

hauntingly familiar. Here was the ghost of William Jennings Bryan—only this was a Bryan without eloquence, without magnetism, without even a depression. The crowd listened politely, but there were few cheers, and most reporters concluded that the speech was a failure. Only one correspondent, Stokes, reported crowd reaction somewhat differently. Truman had, said Stokes, "confirmed the farmers' own secret doubts, born of past experience, about the permanence of the present very high level of prosperity . . . For now as the President spoke, wheat and corn and hogs were down considerably below their summits of the war years. The President had touched a sensitive nerve of memory." But even Stokes thought that Truman's appeal to the fears of his audience was "an error in human psychology."[13]

Truman's demagogic appeal for the farm vote did not disturb the Republicans. Two days after the President's departure, Dewey came to Iowa to deliver a major address. Reciting platitudes on the necessity of restoring faith in American ideas and virtues, he said not a word about the farm problem. Earl Warren, Dewey's running mate, declared that he was shocked by Truman's charges of Republican treachery against the farmers and demanded removal of agricultural issues from the campaign. Meanwhile, the public opinion polls seemed to support growing Republican confidence. Well into October, both the Gallup Poll and the poll of the *Des Moines Register* gave Dewey 53–54 percent of the Iowa vote to 38 percent for Truman. The prediction of a landslide still stood.[14]

During October, as the price of corn continued its steady

[13] *Public Papers of the Presidents: Harry S. Truman, 1948,* pp. 503–508; for a description of the crowd and its reactions to the speech, see *Des Moines Register,* Sept. 19, 1948, p. 1; for Stokes's comments, see "Mood of America, Election Time, 1948," *New York Times Magazine* (Oct. 17, 1948), pp. 11, 70, 71, 73.

[14] For Dewey's Iowa address, see *New York Times,* Sept. 21, 1948, pp. 1 and 20; for Warren's remarks, see *New York Times,* Sept. 22, 1948, p. 19; for the polls, see *Des Moines Register,* Oct. 10, 1948, p. 1.

decline, the Democrats intensified their attack. By far the most active campaigner in a defeatist Cabinet, Brannan gave scores of speeches throughout the farm belt, speeches in which he charged Republicans with intending to destroy supports and played with skill on growing fears of farm depression. At the start of his tour, Brannan read drily from a loose-leaf notebook stuffed with fact sheets, but as he gained confidence, he began speaking with only occasional references to his notes, and by the end of the campaign, he had adopted the extemporaneous and informal style of the President. As one reporter commented, "Brannan the politician had arrived." Truman himself delivered countless whistle-stop speeches that were simply variations of his address at Dexter. Time and again, in major appearances and beside corn fields, he conjured up for his listeners an imaginary Republican ogre who was plotting the end of their prosperity. By mid-October, Democratic workers were deep in what one reporter called a "whispering campaign" to convince farm voters that Dewey intended to end the agricultural programs of the New Deal.[15]

"I wish," said Truman in Springfield, Illinois, "the Wall Street crowd would let their candidate stamp his 'Me Too' on the agricultural policy that my party and my Administration stand for." Dewey and his party, of course, had no objection to Truman's mild program: flexible supports, expansion of soil conservation programs, and consumer subsidies. But for the most part, the Republicans had remained curiously silent. Finally, on October 15, Dewey decided that the time

[15] For a description of Brannan as a campaigner, see Jay Walz, "The Battling Author of the Brannan Plan," New York Times Magazine, Aug. 28, 1949, pp. 10, 47, and 48; for a typical speech, "Recording by Secretary Brannan for the Democratic National Committee," Oct. 8, 1948, Public Addresses of Charles F. Brannan, II (privately owned by Mr. Brannan); for an example of Truman's rhetoric, see Public Papers of the Presidents: Harry S. Truman, 1948, p. 935; on whispering campaign, see Des Moines Register, Oct. 17, 1948, p. 1.

had come to make his first major farm address. Said the
Governor in St. Paul, Minnesota, "I am wholeheartedly and
unequivocally for the [Hope—Aiken bill] and don't let any-
body tell you anything different." In the remaining weeks of
the campaign, Dewey repeated this endorsement whenever
he had the chance.[16]

Had Truman gained any ground with his "give 'em hell"
tactics? The nation's press thought not. James Reston of the
New York Times admitted that Truman had tried hard, but
"he is not . . . the warrior type . . . He says he is mad at
everybody but he doesn't really look as if he's mad at any-
body." His campaign, in short, had fallen flat. In the *New
Yorker* Richard Rovere wrote that people "would be willing
to give [Truman] just about anything he wants except the
presidency." According to Walter Lippman, Truman's extended absence from Washington accomplished only one
thing. It proved "how small a part Mr. Truman actually plays
in the great office which he holds. Nothing . . . that it would
have been seemly for [Mr. Dewey] to say could have demonstrated as has this campaign tour how negligible is Mr.
Truman's role in the great crisis of our times." On the eve
of the election, Arthur Krock commented, "If the event shows
Mr. Truman has surmounted the heavy odds against him . . .
he will rank as the miracle man in the history of American
politics." In common with every other reporter in America,
Arthur Krock foresaw no miracle. A game try, they agreed,
but a prosperous America had no ears for Truman's message.
Until the last day, however, the President repeated with
fervor his warnings of returning depression.[17]

[16] *Public Papers of the Presidents: Harry S. Truman, 1948*, p. 764;
for Dewey address, see *New York Times*, Oct. 16, 1948, p. 7.

[17] *New York Times*, Oct. 27, 1948, p. 15; Richard Rovere, "Letter
from a Campaign Train," *New Yorker*, 24:69–79 (Oct. 9, 1948);
Lippmann's column can be found in *Des Moines Register*, Sept. 27,
1948, p. 8; for Krock's comments, *New York Times*, Oct. 31, 1948, p. 3E.

The best poll taker of all, it happened, was Harry S. Truman. When the long and dramatic night of November 2 finally ended, he was still President of the United States. "Labor did it," the President reportedly said when word of his victory finally arrived. Others, then and later, gave the credit to the farmers. But no one could dispute that the biggest upset of the election occurred in the Middle West.[18]

In the industrial East, Dewey ran much better in 1948 than he had in 1944, this time carrying Pennsylvania, New York, New Jersey, Connecticut, and Delaware. Had he swept the Middle West as all experts forecast, he would have won the presidency. Truman, however, not only held on to Minnesota, Missouri, and Illinois, which Roosevelt carried in 1944; he actually won Iowa, Wisconsin, and Ohio, which Roosevelt had lost. Only Michigan switched from Democratic in 1944 to Republican in 1948. Republicans in the wheat belt states of Kansas, Nebraska, and North and South Dakota averted defeat but suffered sharp declines in the heavy majorities that they had piled up four years before. The 101 electoral votes that Truman won in the Middle West secured him the election.[19]

Since the farm population in every one of Truman's midwestern states was less than 30 percent, farmers obviously could have won no battles alone. In fact, in Illinois, the story of the election is best told in Cook County, where labor

[18] For the quotation from Truman, see *New York Times,* Nov. 4, 1948, p. 7; for extreme claims of farmer contributions to Truman's election, see Wesley McCune, "Farmers in Politics," *Annals of the American Academy of Political and Social Science,* 319:41–51 (Sept. 1958); and Louis Bean, "Forecasting the 1950 Election," *Harpers,* 200: 36–40 (April 1950); for a discussion of crucial importance of the urban vote, see Samuel J. Eldersveld, "The Influence of Metropolitan Party Pluralities in Presidential Elections since 1920: A Study of Twelve Key Cities," *The American Political Science Review,* 43:1189–1206 (Dec. 1949).

[19] For election returns by state and county, see *World Almanac for 1949.*

185

and the Democratic machine obtained a 125,000 vote plurality for Truman and so won him the state. In Missouri, Truman did very well in rural districts, but, more important, he carried Kansas City and St. Louis by bigger majorities even than had Roosevelt. In Ohio, Iowa, and Wisconsin, however, victory was the fruit of a temporary repair in the farmer-labor alliance of the 1930's. In these states, sizable urban support was not enough. Had not farmers in large numbers switched back to the Democrats, the 47 electoral votes of these three states would have been lost, and the election would have been thrown into the House of Representatives.[20]

In Ohio, Truman ran behind the 1944 Democratic pace in the big cities, but carried the state because of sizable gains in the rural vote. Ten agricultural or semiagricultural counties shifted from Republican in 1944 to Democratic in 1948, while Republican majorities in other Ohio farm counties declined. The 12,000 vote majority for the Republicans in 1944 became a 7,000 majority for the Democrats in 1948. In Wisconsin a strong shift in rural areas again overcame faltering Democratic performances in the cities. While Truman ran behind Roosevelt in Milwaukee, the Democrats nevertheless converted a 27,000 vote deficit in 1944 into a 57,000 vote majority in 1948.[21]

To the pollsters, the results in Iowa were the most shocking of all. Its traditional Republicanism having reasserted itself after 1936, Iowa was supposed to cast its eleven votes resoundingly for Dewey. But as the nation's leading corn state with a particularly serious storage problem, Iowa lent a ready

[20] On Illinois and Missouri, see "Rural Vote's Decisive Role," *U.S. News and World Report*, 25:19–22 (Nov. 19, 1948); and *The Almanac*, 1949, pp. 67, 75–76.

[21] On Ohio, see careful survey in *New York Times*, Nov. 29, 1948, p. 5; and "Rural Vote," *U.S. News;* also *The Almanac*, 1949, p. 81; on Wisconsin, see "Rural Vote," *U.S. News;* and *The Almanac*, 1949, pp. 89–90.

ear to Truman's campaign warnings. While counties dominated by metropolitan areas increased their Democratic majority only slightly (from 13,000 to 20,000), farm areas switched dramatically. In the thirteen counties of Iowa with no urban population and half of the population living on farms, Truman won 5 percent more of the vote than had Roosevelt. In the *Future of American Politics*, Samuel Lubell argues that this switch among midwestern farmers in general and Iowa farmers in particular is accountable in part to the return of the German–Americans to the Democratic party from which they supposedly had fled over foreign policy issues in 1940. While no consistent pattern emerges from statistical analysis of Lubell's contention, heavily German–American counties did tend to switch more spectacularly than counties with few German–Americans. The switch in the farm vote to the Democrats, however, was not a phenomenon restricted to German–American counties. When all the ballots were counted, the 40,000 vote Republican majority in 1944 was transformed into a 28,000 bulge for Truman in 1948. Though Truman could not have carried even Iowa without labor support in the cities, it was the farmers who made possible his upset.[22]

In the 1930's, farmers marched with other dispossessed groups behind the banner of the New Deal. Though the first to desert the liberal army, they were nonetheless pleased with the mechanism that Roosevelt had devised to give them security. When, therefore, the threat of depression reappeared in 1948, farmers returned in large numbers to the

[22] For returns of metropolitan counties, see *Almanac*, 1949, p. 69; to establish counties with no urban population and more than half of inhabitants living on farms, Bureau of Census, *Census of the Population*, II, pt. 15 (1950), 100–105, 127–138; for election returns, see State of Iowa, *Official Register*, 1945–1946 (41st no.), and 1949–1950 (43rd no.); to establish the predominantly German counties, Bureau of Census, *Fifteenth Census of the United States: Population*, III, Pt. 1 (1930), 787–788; Samuel Lubell, *The Future of American Politics* (New York: Harper and Brothers, 1952), pp. 132–134, 159–160.

party that had proved itself their protector in bad times. As pollster Lubell has said, farmers in a way were merely acting with customary conservatism. To them Dewey and the Republicans were just too risky to trust in times of depression. One result of falling prices was the behavior of the PMA committees. As corn fell from $1.78 a bushel in September to $1.38 in mid-October, and far below support levels to $1.00 in some markets on election day, the PMA committees, created by the Depression and seasoned in its wars, felt a revival of the passions of the 1930's. Led by a Secretary of Agriculture who spoke their language as Clinton Anderson never could, committeemen in the Middle West forgot the fight over the reorganization of 1946 and gave the Administration full support. Apparently detecting no impropriety in using part of the federal bureaucracy for partisan purposes, the chairman of the Iowa State Committee, H. E. Hazen, wrote to President Truman after his victory, "PMA, through its leaders in Iowa, was a very important factor, if not the most important, in putting Iowa in the Truman column . . . PMA carried up-to-date economic facts not available over the radio or in the newspapers out to our local leaders, who, in turn, passed them on to farmers." To the PMA, 1948 was 1936 all over again.[23]

The campaign of 1948 did not end with the election. As if to compensate for their languid response to Truman's farm speeches before November, Republicans spent the next four years in vigorous if futile refutation. Leader in the belated counterattack was Delaware's Senator John R. Williams, who had spent a good part of his life in the grain business. In the spring of 1949, supported by farm state Republicans, Williams claimed that the storage issue was a hoax and that a politically desperate Administration had rigged the price

[23] For Lubell's argument that farmers had behaved conservatively, see *Future of American Politics*, pp. 160–168; on corn prices, see USDA, *Agricultural Situation* (Nov. 1948), p. 14; H. E. Hazen to the President, Nov. 12, 1948, OF 1y misc. file, TP, TL.

decline of the previous autumn. Republicans pointed out that in 1949 the Department managed to find authority for making loans to farmers to help them build their own storage bins. Since this authority existed in 1948 but had gone unused, the Democrats, it was charged, must have sought to prevent solution of the storage problem. Furthermore, to keep prices down, the Administration had delayed purchases for export until after election. Years later Senator Aiken of Vermont claimed that Democratic manipulations had cost farmers one billion dollars.[24]

The Republicans were correct in asserting that the Administration had not employed all available means to combat the grain bin shortage. This, however, was the result of oversight rather than an Administration plot. Republicans, too, had failed to suggest the use of loans during the crisis. Actually the Democrats had first feared that the scarcity of storage would injure them and stumbled almost by accident onto its political value. As for allegations that the Administration had put its export program to political use, heavy government purchases during the last week of the campaign were sufficient refutation. Shrewd as the President's campaign was, neither he nor his advisers could have foreseen that low prices in the farm belt would help elect the Democratic ticket. The Democrats did not create farmer anxieties, but they exploited them skillfully.[25]

"Brannan Sees Debt Owed to Farm Voters," headlined the *Des Moines Register*, a week after the election. The Secretary

[24] For Williams' charges, see *Congressional Record*, 81st Cong., 1st sess., vol. 95, pt. 4, 4939–4949; for a full statement of the Republican case, see Glenn D. Everett, "Wow! Did Truman Ever Fool the Farmers," *Saturday Evening Post*, 225:30, 83–84 (Aug. 16, 1952); for Aiken's claim, see "Investigation of Storage and Processing Activities of the Commodity Credit Corporation," Hearings before Committee on Agriculture and Forestry, U.S. Senate, 82nd Cong., 2nd sess., p. 1887.
[25] On heavy government purchases during the last week of the campaign, see *Des Moines Register*, Nov. 2, 1948, p. 16.

let it be known that it was a debt he and Harry Truman intended to pay. No one, least of all Brannan, knew how accounts would be settled. Doubtless, however, the Farmers Union and the PMA would have a large voice in the final reckoning. Thus the victory of the Democrats reopened all the old questions on matters of farm policy and initiated a new search for answers. The result would be the famous Brannan Plan, which in a way was merely a postscript to the election.[26]

[26] *Des Moines Register*, Nov. 10, 1948, p. 1.

9 THE BRANNAN PLAN

During the campaign of 1948 Truman had denounced the Republicans for their neglect of soil conservation, their indifference to rural electrification, and their subversion of the price support program through the CCC charter. But in his campaign speeches, Truman remained steadfast in his endorsement of flexible price supports, the major farm contribution of the Republican Eightieth Congress. Curiously, however, some analysts pondering the election returns attributed the President's upset victory in the Middle West to widespread fear of the sliding scale. *U.S. News and World Report*, for instance, told its readers that the farm state shift to Truman occurred only in the last two weeks of the campaign, when farmers suddenly comprehended the threat of 60 percent of parity. It is true that in some states Democratic candidates did campaign for 90 percent, and according to rumor, PMA committees had spread reports among farmers that Truman's victory would mean welcome destruction of flexible supports. Little evidence exists, however, to substantiate the view that the sliding scale was an important factor in the campaign. What is beyond dispute is that Truman's triumph ignited a drive among his chief adherents in the world of agriculture for 90 or even 100 percent of parity.[1]

"Some farmers have blood in their eye," *Wallace's Farmer*

[1] "Why Farmers Swung to Truman," *U.S. News and World Report*, 25:23–24 (Nov. 19, 1948).

reported. " 'We won the election,' they say. 'Now give us what we want.' " The two farm groups that had worked hardest for Harry Truman were the Farmers Union and the PMA committees in the Middle West. In the spring of 1948, Farmers Union President James Patton had testified that flexible supports seemed sensible to him, and as recently as July, the *National Union Farmer*, official publication of the organization, called the Hope–Aiken Act "about the only constructive piece of legislation to come out of the 80th Congress." But after the election, Patton recalls, "when I went to report to the boys, I got worked over for compromising." Electrified by Truman's triumph, the Farmers Union was undergoing a rebirth of militancy, and militancy in the last days of 1948 meant high price supports. The meeting of Farmers Union leaders at St. Paul in mid-November that rebuked Patton also called the Hope–Aiken Act "a sneak attack on farm prices" and drafted a new legislative program asking for 100 percent of parity. Secretary Brannan journeyed to St. Paul to join the discussion, and while he had no public comment on the meetings, the *National Union Farmer* was not so reticent. According to its boast, Brannan had "indicated his policies would closely parallel the program of the Farmers Union." Specifically, he would demand "revision of the Hope–Aiken farm bill to provide a more rigid high level price support system that will offer greater protection to small farmers and less to the corporation-type operator."[2]

In December, 1948, PMA officials meeting in St. Louis endorsed straight 90 percent supports. According to the *Des Moines Register*, state PMA leaders "are said to be urging this kind of program on the grounds that the election proved

[2] *Wallace's Farmer and Iowa Homestead*, Jan. 1, 1949, p. 6; *National Union Farmer*, July, 1948, p. 1; for Patton's quotation, interview with James G. Patton, Aug. 1, 1961; for a report of the November meeting of Farmers Union leaders and of Brannan's alleged views, see *National Union Farmer*, Dec. 1948, pp. 1 and 2.

farmers wanted it." The *Register* editorialized, "We hope Secretary of Agriculture Brannan will not fall into the 'mandate' trap being laid for him by Southerners and others who are lobbying for rigid price supports."[3]

Southern farmers, of course, had given Truman considerable support in the election. At the Farm Bureau Federation convention in December, 1948, Southerners staged their second annual rebellion on behalf of 90 percent. Opposing them again were the midwestern farm bureaus and Allan B. Kline, who threatened to resign the presidency if the cotton and tobacco interests prevailed. The convention tried to mend the Federation's internal division by endorsing flexible supports and then requesting the board of directors to study a recommendation that the "price support for any basic commodity be at 90% of parity whenever marketing quotas are in effect on any such commodity." (The range of support in the Hope–Aiken Act for commodities under production controls after 1949 was 72 to 90 percent of parity.) In January, 1949, the Board of Directors of the Federation declined to recommend revision of the price features of the Hope–Aiken Act, and so Southerners suffered another defeat.[4]

Almost everyone had had his say except the Secretary of Agriculture. Only the Farmers Union felt that it had divined his intentions. To others, his cautious, even cryptic, comments after the election, seemed to offer few clues. What did he mean, for example, when he told the Farm Bureau that he had never regarded the Hope–Aiken Act as "really firm"? Though in November Brannan used his new authority to lower potato supports to 60 percent of parity, he did so only reluctantly and announced that his action would not neces-

---

[3] *Des Moines Register,* Dec. 20, 1948, p. 8.

[4] On Kline's threat to resign, see *New York Times,* Dec. 14, 1948, p. 40; for compromise resolution, see *American Farm Bureau Official Newsletter,* Dec. 22, 1948, p. 8; for decision of Board of Directors against raising support levels, see *Farm Bureau Newsletter,* Feb. 2, 1949, p. 1.

sarily set any precedents. Once, when reminded that the PMA had come out for 90 percent, Brannan merely replied, "But I didn't." The impression was nonetheless spreading that the Administration intended to reverse itself and recommend high, rigid supports. On December 18, 1948, Allan Kline wrote to President Truman to warn him against such folly. Kline said, "there are those who construe the fact that Ohio, Illinois, Iowa, and California voted for you as meaning that farmers had deserted the principles of the long-range farm bill . . . This is not the case . . . They are for the long-range farm bill with its flexible price supports of 60% to 90% of parity." But Kline, a Republican, had reportedly been one of Dewey's choices for Secretary of Agriculture and could, of course, exert little influence at the White House. While the Agricultural Committee for the President's Inaugural Program contained many high-ranking Farmers Union officials, the Farm Bureau found itself virtually ignored.[5]

From the Farm Bureau's viewpoint the year 1949 opened auspiciously. In the third annual report of the President's Council of Economic Advisers, flexible supports received a full endorsement. But in truth, not even Charles Brannan really knew what the Administration's farm policy would be. Early in January, Brannan asked O. V. Wells, chief of the Bureau of Agricultural Economics, to organize seminars on national agricultural policy to define problems and give Department members a chance to express themselves on issues. Some twenty departmental officers, joined occasionally by

[5] For Brannan's remark about whether Hope-Aiken Act was "really firm," USDA press release, Dec. 15, 1948, Releases 5–2 file, Records of Office of Information, USDA, N.A.; for Brannan's comments on lowering potato price supports, USDA press release, Nov. 18, 1948, same file; *New York Times*, Feb. 20, 1949, p. 35; Allan Kline to President Truman, Dec. 18, 1948, OF 524, TP, TL; on Agricultural Committee for the President's Inaugural, see Reo M. Christenson, *The Brannan Plan: Farm Politics and Policy* (Ann Arbor: University of Michigan Press, 1959), p. 53.

specialists on various problems, met with the Secretary in eight long sessions between January 26 and March 3 to debate price supports, compensatory payments, food stamp plans, and other important policy questions. Exploratory in nature, these discussions sought no conclusions. Only once and then not until the sixth meeting did Brannan give any indication of his slowly developing ideas. On March 3rd the Secretary ended the seminars and formed a smaller group of five men to work with him on the final formulation of departmental policy. On April 6, 1949, one day before he went to the Capitol to present his proposals, Brannan met with President Truman, explained those portions of his testimony that might arouse political opposition, and received assurances of presidential support.[6]

On April 7, 1949, Brannan presented his long-awaited recommendations to a joint hearing of the House and Senate Committees on Agriculture. Across from him as he spoke were some of the most famous veterans of the agricultural wars, all of whom would play leading roles in the great struggle that was soon to unfold—Cooley, Pace, Aiken, Elmer Thomas, and a newcomer to the Senate Committee named Clinton Anderson. Brannan told the congressmen that his proposals were "not likely to startle anyone; I have no revolutionary ideas to present to you." But what Brannan had to say would provoke a great national debate over the farm problem, create deep political antagonisms, and catapult the Secretary of Agriculture into highest prominence both in the Administration and in the Democratic party. From then on Brannan's very name was a political issue.[7]

[6] For Bureau's report of Council's views, see *Farm Bureau Newsletter*, Jan. 19, 1949, p. 1; on Brannan's seminars and the smaller group, see Christenson, *The Brannan Plan*, pp. 26–33; also interview with Wesley McCune, July 29, 1961; on Truman's promise of support, interview with Charles F. Brannan, July 29, 1961.

[7] For Brannan's quotation, see "General Farm Program," Hearings

The Brannan Plan was an ingenious effort to wed the concept of abundance to the demands of the Administration's farmer constituency—an attempt to give consumers more food and farmers higher income.[8] First, Brannan tried to divorce farm policy from the antiquated notion of parity prices still lingering on in the modernized parity formula of the Hope–Aiken Act. Indeed, the heart of the Brannan Plan was the Income Support Standard, which sought to shift the focus of policy away from farm prices to farm income. The Support Standard attempted to establish a minimum income goal for agriculture equal in any one year to the average annual purchasing power of farmers in the first ten of the last twelve years. Thus the income goal for 1950 would be the average yearly farm cash receipts for 1939–1948 ($18.2 billion) adjusted for altered value of the dollar. If the prices of things farmers buy were 1.44 times higher in 1950 than during the ten-year average, $18.2 billion would be multiplied by 1.44 to get the income goal for 1950 of $26.2 billion. At this point Brannan was forced to translate the income goal into individual farm prices, so that in the end, his new formula merely substituted one set of support prices for another. For 1950, and all succeeding years, a moving base period of the preceding ten years would be used to calculate individual support prices. Since the income goal for 1950 ($26.2 billion) was 1.25 times the average annual cash receipts of 1940–1949, the average market price of individual commodities during the base period would be multiplied by 1.25 to arrive at final support prices for 1950. This complicated formula achieved two of Brannan's purposes. Since the base period for the next several years would include the

before the Committee on Agriculture, U.S. House of Representatives, 81st Cong., 1st sess., p. 139.

[8] The following summary of the Brannan Plan is based on Brannan's testimony in "General Farm Program," House hearings, pp. 137–156.

Comparison of support prices under different support standards

Commodity	Unit	Income support standard	90% current parity	60% Aiken	90% Aiken
Wheat	bu.	1.88	1.95	1.24	1.85
Corn	bu.	1.46	1.42	0.90	1.35
Cotton	pd.	0.2799	0.2745	.1739	0.2608
Butterfat	pd.	.669	.582	—a	.2608
Milk	cwt.	4.22	3.55	—	3.70
Hogs	cwt.	19.00	16.10	—	16.60
Eggs	doz.	0.458	0.476	—	0.453
Chickens	pd.	.290	.252	—	.252
Potatoes	bu.	1.59	1.62	—	1.74
Beef cattle	cwt.	16.90	12.00	—	14.80
Lambs	cwt.	18.40	13.00	—	16.00

Source: "General Farm Program," Hearings before Committee on Agriculture, U.S. House of Representatives, 81st Cong., 1st sess., p. 156.
a In Aiken Act, nonbasic commodities had no mandatory minimum support level.

exceedingly prosperous war and postwar periods, supports on all commodities would be at high levels for a long time to come. Also, by using a moving average based on recent history, Brannan improved on the old formula by substantially raising support prices for meat and dairy products in relation to other commodities, thus encouraging farmers to shift production from surplus crops like wheat and cotton to feed grains, grasses, and meat animals. Increased meat production would lower meat prices, increase meat consumption, and raise the nation's nutritional standard. To this extent Brannan was remaining true to the agricultural liberalism of the early postwar years. That his still generous supports for wheat and cotton might impede the shift in resources to meat production did not disturb the Secretary. Rather than vary according to supply or suffer reduction to some arbitrary percentage, Brannan's supports would be 100 percent

197

and would be inflexible. The Farmers Union could have asked nothing more.

Brannan next proposed expansion and revision of the list of so-called basic commodities for which price supports would be mandatory. Under the Hope–Aiken Act, these were corn, cotton, wheat, peanuts, tobacco, and rice. Brannan instead suggested a group of ten commodities "of prime importance, both from the standpoint of their contribution to farm income and their importance to the American consumer family"—corn, cotton, wheat, tobacco, whole milk, eggs, farm chickens, hogs, beef cattle, and lambs. Nonbasic commodities would receive support only at the discretion of the Secretary according to available funds.

The most notable feature of this revised list was the inclusion of perishable commodities—milk, eggs, chickens, and meat animals. The Steagall period had already demonstrated the hazards of supporting perishables at high, rigid support levels. Brannan's solution was a device that proved politically explosive. Rather than attempt to store and perhaps waste perishables, he proposed that a free market set prices, with direct government payments ("production payments") making up the difference between actual and support prices. When paid on commodities like meats and milk, which consumers buy in larger quantities when the price decreases, direct payments would mean higher farm income, lower consumer prices, more meat and milk consumption, and improved nutrition. Like high supports on livestock, therefore, production payments would keep Brannan's program faithful to the concept of abundance and give the Brannan Plan appeal beyond the farm. To protect the Department from too great an expansion of production and consequently huge expenditures for production payments, Brannan requested authority to impose production controls on all basic commodities whenever necessary. In supporting storable farm products, the Department would mainly rely, as before, on storage programs, with production payments serving only as a supplementary method.

And finally the Brannan plan proposed certain conditions and restrictions on the receipt of its benefits. To protect what he called "the family-sized farm," Brannan suggested that farmers receive no supports on production beyond a certain quantity, thus discouraging "development of extremely large-scale industrial farming." The basic unit in Brannan's limitation formula was ten bushels of corn, which at 1949 prices was worth $14.50. That amount of cotton, wheat, or any other commodity equal to the value of ten bushels of corn would be the basic unit for that crop (8 bushels of wheat, 155 pounds of cotton, each worth about $14.50). No farmer would receive price supports on more than 1800 units of his production, that is, approximately $26,100 worth of his crop. Questioned later about this part of his program, Brannan conceded that any farmer complying with production controls should receive supports on all he produced beyond 1800 units, thus robbing the formula of most of its significance. And while he always defended it, Brannan was obviously less fond of this proposal than any of his others, and he implied on occasion that he would not object if Congress dropped the idea.[9]

The issues raised by the Brannan Plan proved exceedingly complex and technical, but many Democratic politicians embraced it as the instrument that would perpetuate their supremacy in national politics for years to come. Though Republicans, the press, professional economists, and the Farm Bureau expressed immediate and violent opposition, Brannan found enough party support to tell a departmental staff meeting, "I say frankly that I am quite optimistic about the

[9] For Brannan's retreat from the limitation formula, see "General Farm Program," House hearings, p. 337.

reception the program is getting and is going to get." What Democrats like National Chairman Howard McGrath saw in the Brannan Plan was an opportunity to cement the tentative alliance of farmers and laborers that elected Truman in 1948. Indeed, the CIO convention of December, 1948, had gone on record in favor of production payments as the best method to preserve farm prosperity and at the same time lower prices for urban workers. A month after Brannan offered his Plan, its political appeal seemed so irresistible that rumors naming Brannan as the 1952 Democratic nominee for president began to circulate. To mobilize their forces on behalf of the Brannan Plan, midwestern Democrats planned a June conference in Des Moines that soon grew into a major political event attended by the Vice-President, leading congressional Democrats, and some of the nation's prominent labor leaders. At the meeting Democrats boasted that with the Brannan Plan as an issue in 1950, they would pick up twenty seats in the House and four in the Senate. That the Plan might not pass in the current session of Congress did not disturb them, for many in the party hoped to save the issue for an election year anyway. The conference adjourned after resolving to "accept the challenge of the Republican leadership to make the farm programs offered by the two parties the major campaign issue."[10]

The Republicans feared that the Democrats might be right in their assessment of the Brannan Plan's political appeal. "That the Republicans will fight it is already evident," reported the New York Times, "because as one observer said,

[10] For Brannan's statement to the staff meeting, see Transcript of Staff Meeting of April 19, 1949, Meetings 6 file, Records of Office of Sec. of Ag., Gen'l Cor., N.A.; for McGrath's views, see New York Times, April 11, 1949, p. 2; for a report of farm views of CIO, see Wallace's Farmer, p. 20; on rumors that Truman would select Brannan as the Democratic nominee in 1952, see Des Moines Register, May 8, 1949, p. 5X; for reports on the conference in Des Moines, see New York Times, June 12, 1949, pp. 1, 43; June 14, 1949, p. 3.

'if the Democrats get it through, they are in for life.'" Before April had passed away, Republican National Chairman Hugh Scott announced that recapture of the farm vote must be the first objective of his party. The Republican National Committee began holding strategy meetings on the farm vote and took steps to create a special subcommittee on agriculture. Actually the main outlines of the Republican attack on the Brannan Plan emerged the same day it was unveiled. What would the Plan cost? asked Representative August Andresen of Secretary Brannan. Brannan replied that he did not know, any more "than the people who came up with the first price-support program involving loans were able to make the estimate for you then." Soon Republicans were predicting that the Brannan Plan might cost $5 to $8 billion annually. That afternoon, addressing the upper house, Senator Aiken developed the second major Republican objection. The Plan, said Aiken, would place wheat, cotton, tobacco, and corn "under complete and continuing controls," presumably because the high support levels would encourage overproduction. "After the program had been in effect a short time," he continued, "controls would have to be extended to hogs, chickens, beef, lamb, pork, and dairy products. It would be a controlled economy with a vengeance." Brandishing the prospect of immense expenditures and regimentation, the Republicans were ready for war.[11]

The general response of the nation's newspapers and magazines was almost as hostile as that of the Republicans. The *New York Times* called the Brannan Plan politically inspired, a bit of legerdemain that created the illusion of lower prices

[11] *New York Times,* April 24, 1949, p. E9; on Scott's views, see *New York Times,* April 26, 1949, p. 21; on Republican strategy meetings, see *New York Times,* April 29, 1949, p. 13; for the exchange between Andresen and Brannan, see "General Farm Program," House hearings, p. 164; for partisan cost estimates of Brannan Plan, see *New York Times,* April 11, 1949, p. 2; for Aiken's remarks, see *Congressional Record,* 81st Cong., 1st sess., vol. 95, pt. 3, 4031–4032.

by subsidizing a privileged group from the public treasury. *Times* columnist Arthur Krock described the Plan as "one of the most elaborate devices for a regulated national economy that has been sponsored by the Executive Department of a nonautocratic Government in the present age." *Time* magazine was predictably unfriendly. *Life* forecast that the Brannan Plan "would make the farmer the doer of the Agriculture Department's will in exchange for a guaranteed living." Knowledgeable in farm matters, moderate papers in the Middle West were less severe but still critical. Long an advocate of production payments, the *Des Moines Register* nevertheless had to oppose the Brannan Plan for attempting to guarantee "boom period incomes to farmers." *Wallace's Farmer*, another supporter of production payments, believed that the high level of supports in the Brannan Plan would create huge surpluses for storable crops. Even in some liberal quarters, the Plan met resistance. The *Nation* feared that the Income Support Standard would overinflate farm income and so induce too many people to stay in agriculture. *Commonweal* said that the plan would increase controls and augment the size of the bureaucracy. If the Democrats were to sell the Brannan Plan to the public, they would have to do it without much assistance from the press.[12]

Neither would help be forthcoming from academic circles. "In common with almost all agricultural economists with whom I am acquainted," wrote Walter W. Wilcox, "I have doubts about the desirability and feasibility of Secretary Brannan's proposal . . ." John D. Black, the most respected of the professionals, formulated his case primarily against the

[12] For its editorial on the Brannan Plan, see *New York Times*, April 8, 1949, p. 24; for Krock's column, see *New York Times*, April 26, 1949, p. 21; "Farmers," *Time*, 53:23–27 (June 19, 1950); "Brannan's Plan," *Life*, 26:32 (April 25, 1949); *Des Moines Register*, April 18, 1949, p. 6; *Wallace's Farmer*, May 7, 1949, p. 6; "New Farm Plan Needed," *Nation*, 168:649–650 (June 11, 1949); "New Farm Program," *Commonweal*, 50:29–30 (April 23, 1949).

high level of Brannan's supports and their rigidity. Still arguing that the sliding scale was the best way to induce shifts from surplus crops to livestock, Black feared that Brannan's generous supports would actually encourage surplus production of cotton and wheat. To avert this misfortune, Brannan would have to resort to production controls, an ineffective and discredited solution. As for direct subsidies, "Secretary Brannan can say that his production payments will keep down prices to consumers and expand consumption, but I shall have to say: Not without larger expenditures or production payments than Congress will ever provide." With only limited funds at his disposal, the Secretary could not permit market prices to fall very far, consumption would not increase very much, and production controls would have to be extended to perishables. Furthermore the social value of production payments had been overrated. "The general effect," said Black, "will be to reduce prices to middle and upper income groups whose demand for food is relatively inelastic, as well as to the lower income groups where most elasticity is found." A million dollars spent on lowering food costs to the nation's poor, he said, "will expand food consumption probably twice as much as if spent on lowering prices for all food consumers."[13]

Theodore Schultz agreed that Brannan's supports would be altogether too high. "It will be necessary," he said, "to correct the unwarranted optimism of policy makers regarding the value of farm products . . . Farm products simply are not worth 90% of parity or as much as the Brannan Plan would specify." Even when production payments were in use, Bran-

[13] Walter W. Wilcox, "Comments on Agricultural Policy," *Journal of Farm Economics*, 31:806–813 (Nov. 1949); for Black's views, lecture by John D. Black to USDA Graduate School, Dec. 5, 1949, file IV A2, WW II Records, ERS, ESA, Ag. Hist. Br., USDA; see also his testimony in "Agricultural Adjustment Act of 1949," Hearings before a subcommittee of the Committee on Agriculture and Forestry, U.S. Senate, 81st Cong., 1st sess., pp. 143–171.

nan's overinflated prices would force a retreat to production controls. Production payments, in Schultz's view, are only defensible in times of depression and then should be used for both perishable and storable commodities. The free market in times of full employment should determine price.[14]

All the economists regretted that the Brannan Plan left untouched the plight of the rural poor. D. Gale Johnson made a statistical study to demonstrate how the Brannan Plan's benefits would aggravate income inequality within agriculture. In Iowa commercial farmers grossing $8,000 to $20,000 a year would receive twelve times more of the Plan's benefits than farmers producing $200–$3,000 worth of farm products. According to W. H. Hendrix, almost 80 percent of the 1.5 million cotton farmers in the South grew less than eight bales of cotton apiece. For them the Brannan Plan would do almost nothing. It was indeed a great shame that a man of Brannan's liberal instincts chose to employ his considerable talents on behalf of rural America's least needy.[15]

No group opposing Brannan proved more potent than the Farm Bureau. On the day before he went to Congress with his recommendations, Brannan met with Allan Kline to explain his Plan. Years later Kline still had a clear recollection of that memorable encounter. After hearing Brannan's presentation, "I said to him," Kline recalls, "that farmers simply were not philosophically prepared for stringent controls over their operations which would be made necessary by the level of prices which he proposed to guarantee. [Brannan] re-

[14] Theodore W. Schultz, "The Brannan Plan v. the Agricultural Act of 1949," a paper delivered to Annual Conference, Agricultural Extension Service, University of Missouri, Dec. 9, 1949 (in Library of Department of Agriculture.)

[15] D. Gale Johnson, "High Level Support Prices and Corn Belt Agriculture," *Journal of Farm Economics*, 31:509–519 (Aug. 1949); W. E. Hendrix, "The Brannan Plan and Farm Adjustment Opportunities in the Cotton South," *Journal of Farm Economics*, same issue, pp. 487–496.

sponded that after all I full well knew that one did not talk philosophy to farmers; you talked price to farmers. My response was to suggest that if he cared to go out and appear with me before a farm audience where he talked what he called price and I talked what he called philosophy, I was sure I could improve his understanding of the point." Kline also objected to the 1800 unit cutoff formula. "I pointed out to the Secretary," Kline remembers, "that farming was a high expense business and that many of what must be called family farmers had more than $25,000 gross sales and very modest net incomes indeed." Kline returned to see Brannan the next day, and the dialogue continued. According to Kline, Brannan justified his proposals as a necessary protection against approaching farm depression. Brannan "said to me," in the words of Kline, "that when you had pneumonia and the doctor prescribed penicillin, you did not argue with the doctor but took the penicillin. I commented that there were a couple of things awry about his analysis. I didn't have pneumonia and he didn't have penicillin." In the future, exchanges between Brannan and Kline would contain less wit and more heat. Soon Kline was telling Congress that the Brannan Plan "means Government-administered farm prices and farm income, with Government control of all land and livestock production." And, of course, "the cost of implementing the proposal would be staggering." Like Brannan, Kline avoided an over-all cost estimate, but he claimed that if milk, for instance, fell to 15 cents a quart, a price Brannan thought desirable, the Government would have to spend 2.4 billion dollars a year on milk alone. Flexible supports, said Kline, were the best way to bring desirable production shifts and keep American agriculture free.[16]

[16] For Kline's recollection of his meetings with Brannan, letter to the author, July 20, 1964; for his other remarks on the Brannan Plan, see "General Farm Program," House Hearings, pp. 431-442.

The avalanche of criticism did not dismay Brannan. Rejoicing at the prospect of battle, he answered his enemies vigorously and with skill. For purposes of debate, Brannan was most vulnerable for his sponsorship of high rigid supports. For as Representative Charles B. Hoeven asked him, "is it not a fact that . . . you . . . proposed flexible price supports on a permanent basis at the time the Aiken bill was enacted?" Brannan lamely denied this charge, claiming that the meaning of the word "flexibility" as he and the Department had always used it was "elasticity in means, methods, and devices for providing price support," rather than the levels of such support. Brannan was here defending his consistency but would have been wiser merely to admit the charge. At any rate, to vindicate his new position, the Secretary marshaled historical evidence to prove that lower farm prices did not discourage production and that therefore flexible supports were misconceived. Between 1925 and 1928, he noted, potato prices fell from $1.70 to $0.52 a bushel, but potato acreage steadily increased until 1929. While the price of wheat fell from 1925 to 1929, wheat acreage actually grew. In the case of cotton, "farmers have harvested as many or more acres after receiving prices of less than 10 cents as in years after they received 30 and 35 cents." Faced by declining prices, Brannan contended, farmers actually increase output, for they are more interested in their individual incomes than in aggregate production.[17]

Professor Black rightly disputed Brannan's examples. They were, he said, chosen from abnormal periods. Statistically valid studies proved falling prices led farmers to shift production. Only in depression when prices of all crops are unattrac-

[17] For Brannan's exchange with Hoeven, see "General Farm Program," House Hearings, pp. 184–185; for Brannan's definition of "flexibility," Brannan to Elmer Thomas, Oct. 7, 1949, Mr. Brannan's private files, Denver; for historical evidence against the sliding scale, see "Agricultural Adjustment Act of 1949," Senate hearings, pp. 50–51.

tive would flexible supports fail to work.[18] What Black did not foresee was that in a few years aggregate overproduction would depress most farm prices and, of course, render his sliding scale impotent. But the technological revolution would probably have been as unkind in the 1950's to the Brannan Plan as it was to Black's flexible supports, for in order to keep from being overwhelmed by rising crop yields, Brannan's program would have required Congress to raid the treasury with unaccustomed abandon or to decree the kind of stringent controls that politicians have always resisted.

In meeting charges that his production payments would necessitate vast expenditures, Brannan avoided a comprehensive cost estimate and instead offered estimates for individual commodities. At 90 percent of old parity, hog supports would be at $16.50 per hundred weight. If the Government entered the market and bought one billion pounds, the cost would be $230 million. If the same amount of money were used for production payments instead of storage, hog prices could fall by $1.10 "before it would cost this Government one cent more money than it would be obligated to pay under the purchase method." Brannan concluded, "if a 7 percent reduction could be carried all the way through to the retail level, it would be possible to reduce the consumer's price of pork by about 7 percent and at the same time give him access to the finished product of one billion pounds of live hogs." For milk, Brannan estimated that for every cent per quart decrease in price, Government expenditures would total $150 million a year. As for potatoes, if the $225 million spent in 1948 to support potatoes had been used for production payments, consumers would have paid $1.00 a bushel instead of $1.75. (Since potato demand is inelastic, Brannan admitted that strict production controls would still be neces-

[18] "Agricultural Adjustment Act of 1949," Senate hearings, pp. 158–161.

sary under his support system.) Brannan's cost analyses compared price supports achieved through storage operations with his production payment scheme, assuming in both cases support levels of 90 percent of current parity. But since Brannan's Income Support Standard was generally higher than 90 percent and would have cost considerably more, his examples were partly misleading.[19]

Replying to the regimentation charge, Brannan asserted that his Plan would use only those controls already provided in the Hope–Aiken Act—acreage allotments and marketing quotas. Furthermore by encouraging increased consumption, his Plan might ultimately prove less restrictive. But Brannan could not deny that by extending the list of basic commodities, he was placing many more products under potential control, and that by establishing high supports for wheat and cotton, he would be inviting a return to the restrictionist policies of the 1930s'. Brannan could reply that farmers had always given overwhelming approval to production control and obviously worried less about regimentation than did politicians. Without the support of politicians, however, there could be no Brannan Plan.[20]

Until the June rally of Democrats in Des Moines, Congressman Pace's House subcommittee on agricultural policy intended to report a unanimous recommendation for one year's extension of 90 percent supports. But the increasing political momentum of the Brannan Plan changed the mind of the Democratic leadership. Pace accordingly drafted a bill that would enact Brannan's Income Support Standard, give the Secretary authority to hold a trial run for production payments on three perishable commodities of his own choosing, and provide 100 percent supports on corn, cotton, wheat,

[19] "General Farm Program," House hearings, pp. 213–215.
[20] For Brannan's defense of his program on these points, see "General Farm Program," House hearings, pp. 216–217.

tobacco, rice, peanuts, hogs, milk, butterfat, and shorn wool. (Beef producers preferred to do business without supports.) On June 28, 1949, the full House Committee on Agriculture approved the Pace Bill 17–9, with Northern and Southern Democrats uniting behind the Administration's program. One reason why Pace, a Georgian, had been selected to sponsor the modified Brannan Plan was the high regard in which he was held in farm circles generally and among Southerners particularly. If the Democrats could stay united, the Brannan Plan had a chance.[21]

But on July 13 Representative Albert Gore of Tennessee served notice of a Southern revolt. Gore introduced a bill to continue for one more year the present program of 90 percent of parity for the basic storables and 60–90 percent for the old Steagall commodities. Mounting pressure from farm bureaus back home, hostility among large, established cotton planters to the Plan's apparent bias on behalf of small producers, and suspicion of any proposal with strong labor support, led many Southern congressmen to join the swelling ranks of Brannan's opponents. Though most Republicans and the Farm Bureau leadership had no love for 90 percent supports, they saw the Gore Bill as the best instrument to destroy the hated Brannan Plan and so swung behind the South.[22]

On the eve of the House debate on the Brannan Plan, Administration leaders sought to avert impending defeat by

[21] On relationship between the Pace bill and the Des Moines meeting, see *Congressional Record*, 81st Cong., 1st sess., vol. 95, pt. 7, 9852; for content of the Pace bill, see House Report 998, "Agricultural Act of 1949," *House Miscellaneous Reports*, V, same sess.; on House committee vote, see *New York Times*, June 29, 1949, p. 5.

[22] On introduction of Gore bill, see *Congressional Record*, 81st Cong., 1st sess., vol. 95, pt. 7, 9417; for text of Gore bill, see *Congressional Record*, same sess., pp. 9932–9933; on reasons why Southern congressmen opposed the Pace bill, see Congressional Quarterly, *U.S. Agricultural Policy in the Postwar Years* (Washington, 1963) pp. 26–27; on American Farm Bureau support of the Gore bill, see *Wallace's Farmer*, Aug. 6, 1949, p. 26.

making a strategic concession. Instead of permitting Brannan to select the three commodities on which production payments could be made, the House bill would now authorize such payments only for shorn wool, potatoes, and eggs. The point of this concession was to end any chance for a trial run on hogs. A few months before, when hog prices were sagging toward support levels, many congressmen thought hogs would be the best commodity for an experimental program. But hog prices had since recovered, and cattle producers, fearful that low subsidized hog prices would drag down beef, too, were lobbying intensively against the Brannan Plan. Relatively unimportant, the three commodities now chosen would hopefully create little disturbance for the House managers. If half the Southern congressmen could be kept in line, the Administration still might win at least a portion of the Brannan Plan.[23]

For two days late in July, the House listened to wild charges of regimentation and national bankruptcy if the Pace bill were permitted to become the opening wedge of the Administration's farm program. One Republican critic charged that the real authors of the Brannan Plan were Henry Wallace, Rexford Tugwell, and Alger Hiss. In an effort to stay the rising flood of opposition, Speaker Rayburn rose to warn fellow Democrats, "I found out a long time ago that in this House the people who get along the best go along the most." But not even Rayburn could save the Administration. With 73 of the 113 Southerners in the House voting for the Gore bill, it won an easy victory, 239–170. So far as the House was concerned, the Brannan Plan was dead.[24]

[23] For revised Pace bill, see *Congressional Record*, 81st Cong., 1st sess., vol. 95, pt. 8, 9934–9935.

[24] For "real authors" of the Brannan Plan, see *Congressional Record*, 81st Cong., 1st sess., vol. 95, pt. 7, 9839; for Rayburn's remark, *Congressional Record*, same sess., p. 9955; for the vote, see pp. 9962–9963.

The House, at least, had shared Brannan's belief in high rigid supports. In the Senate, where the sliding scale had won a decisive victory only a year before, the Brannan Plan never had a chance. In June, a Senate subcommittee began hearings on the possibility of a trial run on hogs, and though the chairman, Guy Gillette of Iowa, owed his election to Truman's capture of the farm vote in 1948, he and his committee turned down the proposal.[25] On July 7 another subcommittee, this one chaired by freshman Senator Clinton P. Anderson, opened hearings on the full Brannan Plan. Though no chance of favorable Senate consideration existed, Truman asked Anderson to hold hearings to save the face of the Administration. A little more than a year before, Anderson had been a powerful member of the Administration, an intimate friend of the President, and sponsor of Brannan's promotion to the secretaryship. Try as he might, however, he could not support the Brannan Plan.

On the day Brannan explained his proposals to Congress, Anderson's silence was so conspicuous and widely reported that party loyalty prompted him to issue a statement that was a masterpiece of equivocation. "On second reading of Secretary Brannan's program," he said, "I am struck by the fact that the more it is studied the better it looks." Some of its objectives were indeed laudable, and Brannan could hopefully bring cost estimates to Congress "to allay the fears of some of the members." Anderson concluded, "I have not endorsed Secretary Brannan's program as yet because I think Congress should study it first. That does not mean that I do not endorse his goal of decent standards of farm income, because I do. I particularly support his emphasis on using

[25] For hearings of Gillette's subcommittee, see "Price Support for Hogs," Hearings before a subcommittee of the Committee on Agriculture and Forestry, U.S. Senate, 81st Cong., 1st sess.; on rejection of production payments by Gillette's committee, see *Wallace's Farmer,* Aug. 6, 1949, p. 26.

what our farms produce. Best of all, he not only seeks to improve the lot of our farm population but he counts consumers in as beneficiaries of a farm program. I believe his suggestions will grow in favor as they become more thoroughly understood."

But Anderson could not remain poised forever between party loyalty and loyalty to the principles he had supported as secretary. Shortly before he began hearings on the Brannan Plan, Anderson wrote a letter to Elmer Thomas, chairman of the full Senate Committee on Agriculture to outline his policy views. While he would postpone any consideration of the 1800 unit limitation, Anderson was willing to grant Brannan's request for a trial run on hogs (not yet voted down by the Gillette committee.) "If we had a chance to experiment," he wrote cautiously, "on hogs a little bit this fall, we might be in a position to try a couple of other commodities during 1950 and then slowly and carefully feel our way until our experience teaches us a safe basis on which we can expand." As for Brannan's Income Support Standard, Anderson found it inferior to the parity formula in the Aiken Act. And finally, Anderson reaffirmed his commitment to the sliding scale, though Anderson preferred a range of 75–90 percent to 60–90 percent. Anderson sent a copy of this letter to Brannan for his comments. Relations between the two men had already begun to cool, and Brannan's reply left no doubt that complete estrangement was inevitable. "I guess you were right," Brannan wrote, "in saying that I would not like it. But more importantly, I don't understand it or the purpose for which it was written. It seems to me to suggest an almost one hundred percent rejection by the Senate Committee of the Administration's proposals before the Committee has had an opportunity to hear witnesses or critically to examine our proposals . . . I would respectfully say to you that your letter seems to me to coincide with the Allan Kline [point of view]."[26]

A few days later Anderson objected on personal grounds to an unimportant appointment that Brannan had recently made. Brannan's reply was a clear expression of the antagonism he now felt toward his old chief. "Taking an arbitrary stand of this character with respect to the membership of a relatively unimportant committee gives me some concern," a concern that was somehow related to the debate over the Brannan Plan. Had not Allan Kline been waging a "personal, punitive attack upon me," and had not Brannan forborne to remove him from his numerous committee posts within the government? "Incidentally," Brannan added, "he [Kline] and his people maintain that this attack is being carried on with your tacit acquiescence." Anderson, of course, regarded these evidences of hostility as completely without justification. Indignantly (but in private) he accused the Administration of ingratitude for failing to appreciate his long silence on the Brannan Plan. "I left the Brannan Plan entirely alone for months and never said a word against it, but did say some words quite favorable to its full consideration prior to the time the House overwhelmingly rejected it . . . How anyone can truthfully say that I got Congress to sidetrack it is more than I can imagine." Later, Anderson's relations with the Administration had deteriorated so badly that he wrote a note to his old friend, the President. "I know that some people may have left the impression that my votes on Administration issues could not be counted upon but I had the feeling that I was doing a good job. I know that you keep a little record of your own, which you should, and I am, therefore, sending you my memorandum analyzing my voting record in the first session

[26] Statement by Clinton Anderson, April 9, 1949, McCune files, FUL; Anderson to Elmer Thomas, June 29, 1949, Mr. Brannan's personal files, Denver; Brannan to Anderson, June 30, 1949, same files.

of the 81st Congress. Will you check it with your record and see if I haven't been right almost all the time?" Though Anderson and Brannan were to maintain a formally correct relationship, in reality they were becoming bitter and irreconcilable enemies.[27]

In mid-July, after Anderson's subcommittee completed its hearings, the full Senate committee voted unanimously to kill the Brannan Plan for that session. Even Chairman Thomas, an Administration stalwart, abandoned it. "The time is too short," he said, "and the country is not ready to take up the Brannan bill to get it through this session . . . We don't think we would be justified in spending more time on that question." The committee then instructed Anderson's subcommittee to write a bill of its own.[28]

By August 12, 1949, Anderson completed a draft bill, which, on first reading, seemed like a victory for the sliding scale. For corn, cotton, wheat, rice, and peanuts, supports were to range from 75 to 90 percent, according to supply. (Once more, to appease the Senators from Kentucky and North Carolina, tobacco was to receive 90 percent as long as marketing quotas were in effect.) Price supports at 60–90 percent would be mandatory for a list of nonbasics including shorn wool, tung nuts, mohair, and Irish potatoes. Though defined as a nonbasic, milk was to receive mandatory supports at 75–90 percent. Hidden in the Anderson bill were provisions that made a mockery of the sliding scale. First of all, if production controls on a basic commodity became effective following a year in which there had been no controls, supports were to be at 90 percent. Thus in 1950, when controls

---

[27] Brannan to Anderson, July 13, 1949, Committees file, Records of Office of Sec. of Ag., Gen'l Cor., N.A.; for Anderson's private indignation, Anderson to Tris Coffin, Oct. 10, 1949, senatorial files, Senator Anderson's office, Washington; Anderson to the President, April 3, 1950, PPF 2614, TP, TL.

[28] *New York Times,* July 28, p. 2.

on basic commodities would most likely be needed for the first time in a decade, support levels would remain at 90 percent of parity. Also, Anderson worded his bill so that the sliding scale was merely a suggestion to the Secretary, who was empowered to set supports on basics wherever he wished within the 75–90 percent range. When asked how he would use this discretionary authority, Brannan replied, "I am on the high side of the price support controversy." Another bonus for advocates of high guaranteed prices was revision of the parity formula of the Aiken bill so that it included the cost of hired labor, incidentally raising the parity price on all commodities by 6 percent. To quiet the fears of the hysterical opponents of the Brannan Plan, Anderson ended the Secretary's authority, granted in the Aiken Act, to make limited use of production payments.

Anderson regretted that he had not been able to remain more faithful to the principle of flexibility, but, he wrote, "we had the practical question of getting a bill which could pass the Senate and to which the House might agree." Brannan, who spent a whole afternoon working on the bill with Anderson's committee, recognized that between the Gore bill and the Anderson bill, he had little to choose, and at first he disclosed no preference. But in spite of their similarity, these bills became symbols in the great price support struggle dividing agriculture, a struggle between the champions of 90 percent, who rallied behind the Gore bill, and the defenders of flexibility, who would accept only the Anderson bill.[29]

[29] For text of the Anderson bill, see "Farm Price Support Program," Hearings before Committee on Agriculture and Forestry, U.S. Senate, 81st Cong., 1st sess., pp. 1–6; for Brannan's remark, see same hearings, p. 18; on Anderson's regret that his bill compromised the principle of flexibility, Anderson to Arthur Hays Sulzberger, Aug. 1, 1949, senatorial files, Senator Anderson's office, Washington; for Brannan's view of the Anderson bill, Brannan to Anderson, Aug. 12, 1949, McCune files, FUL.

FARM POLICIES AND POLITICS

Without leadership from the Executive on the farm question, Senate Democrats fell to warring among themselves. Elmer Thomas, chairman of the Senate Committee on Agriculture and Forestry and long an advocate of 90 percent, took a dim view of Anderson's handiwork and refused to report the bill from his committee. Majority Leader Scott W. Lucas, a champion of the sliding scale, then told Truman that it was the Anderson bill or no bill at all. Merely in the interest of getting some legislation that session, Truman persuaded Thomas to report the Anderson bill. When it arrived on the Senate floor, Southern and Western Democrats moved to replace it with a permanent program of 90 percent supports for the basic commodities, but heeding Anderson's plea for salvation of the sliding scale, the Senate voted 38–37 against 90 percent. Even before the voting was finished, however, Representative Gore entered the chamber and warned Kentucky's Senator Garrett L. Withers, who had voted with Anderson, that unless the Senate voted for straight 90 percent, the House would kill special privileges for tobacco. Minutes later Withers moved for reconsideration of the defeated motion. This time the Senate divided 37 to 37, and all eyes turned to Vice-President Alben W. Barkley. "The position of the Chair," he said, "heretofore has been in favor of 90 percent. In every speech he made last year he declared the same position. He cannot now repudiate it and therefore votes 'Yea.'" Said Majority Leader Lucas of the Vice-President, "that was the god-damnedest performance I've ever seen. Barkley doesn't know a thing about farming." But Lucas managed temporarily to recommit the Anderson bill to committee, where Anderson shrewdly tinkered with its provisions to win needed votes for his original proposals. Plucked wool (a by-product of lamb slaughtering) would now join shorn wool on the list of nonbasics receiving mandatory supports. Immediately three Republican wool Senators

216

changed their minds and announced for the Anderson bill.[30]

Committed to the Brannan Plan and reluctant to break openly with Clinton Anderson, the Administration had kept out of the argument. But the appearance of the strengthened Anderson bill finally provoked Brannan and Truman to exert leadership. Brannan wrote a public letter to make clear his opposition to flexible supports, and by implication, the Anderson bill. (Anderson told the press that the Administration is as "anxious as it can be" to defeat this bill, "because if it doesn't there won't be such a case for the Brannan Plan.") For his part, Truman summoned party leaders to the White House to plead for 90 percent to keep farmers loyal to the Democratic party, but his intervention came too late. On October 12, 1949, the Anderson bill passed the Senate, and the battle now moved into conference.[31]

The House opened the conference by demanding a straight five-year extension of 90 percent supports. The ensuing deadlock seemed hopeless, but inevitably the conferees reached a compromise. The Gore–Anderson bill would unequivocally extend 90 percent supports for basic commodities through 1950. Minimum supports for 1951 would then fall to 80

[30] On lack of agreement among Democrats in the Senate, see *Wallace's Farmer*, Sept. 3, 1949, p. 14; on role of Truman, see *New York Times*, Aug. 29, 1949, p. 1; for debate on proposal for 90%, see *Congressional Record*, 81st Cong., 1st sess., vol. 95, pt. 10, 13742–13759; for Gore's warning to Withers, see "King Farmer," *Newsweek*, 34:29–30 (Oct. 17, 1949); for Barkley's comment and his vote, see *Congressional Record*, same sess., p. 13774; for the Majority Leader's remark on the Vice-President, "King Farmer," *Newsweek;* for the revised version of Anderson's bill, see Senate Report No. 1129, "Stabilization of Agricultural Prices," Oct. 6, 1949, *Senate Miscellaneous Reports*, IV, same sess.

[31] For Brannan's implied rejection of the Anderson bill, Brannan to Elmer Thomas, Oct. 7, 1949, Brannan's personal files, Denver; for Anderson's remarks to the press, *New York Times*, Oct. 8, 1949, p. 2; on Truman's plea to Senate leaders for 90%, see *New York Times*, Oct. 12, 1949, p. 1; for Senate passage of the Anderson bill, see *Congressional Record*, 81st Cong., 1st sess., vol. 95, pt. 11, 14324.

percent, and not until 1952 would the range be 75–90 percent. After perfunctory debate, both houses accepted the conference report, and the months of wrangling ended. Though Truman signed the bill, the Administration clearly had no intention of conceding its permanence.[32]

Defeat in Congress did not diminish the Administration's ardor for the Brannan Plan. Truman devoted Labor Day to praising the Plan and emphasizing the essential unity of farmers and laborers. Toward the end of the congressional session, Senator Thomas served notice that in 1951 he would sponsor the Administration's farm program. Brannan, meanwhile, maintained his heavy speaking schedule and continued to skirmish with his enemies. When Kline pointedly refused to invite him to the Farm Bureau's annual December convention, Brannan sent Kline a letter sincerely regretting "that members of the American Farm Bureau Federation will not have the opportunity to hear more than one point of view." ("We're sorry he feels hurt," Kline told the press.) At the National Farmers Institute at Des Moines a few months later, Brannan ignored the etiquette governing such occasions to denounce the leadership of the Farm Bureau for distorting his Plan and opposing improvements in current price programs. According to the Bureau's *Newsletter*, the audience of 4000 roundly booed the Secretary's oratory.[33]

But through it all, Brannan felt certain that he would have the last word in the debate. By the beginning of 1950, a

[32] For conference bill, see *Congressional Record*, 81st Cong., 1st sess., vol. 95, pt. 11, 15055–15060.

[33] For Truman's Labor Day speech, see *Public Papers of the Presidents: Harry S. Truman, 1949* (Washington, 1964), pp. 464–469; for Thomas' intentions to reintroduce the Brannan Plan, see *Congressional Record*, 81st Cong., 1st sess., vol. 95, pt. 11, 14309; Brannan to Kline, Dec. 10, 1949, file IX B2 d(1), ERS, ESA, Ag. Hist. Br., USDA; for Kline's retort, see *New York Times*, Dec. 13, 1949, p. 37; for Farm Bureau's account of Brannan's Des Moines speech, see *American Farm Bureau Newsletter*, Feb. 27, 1950, p. 1.

great disquiet was permeating American agriculture. Net farm income, which had been a record $17.3 billion in 1947, had declined to $13.7 billion in 1949 and was expected to fall to $12 billion in 1950. To support farm prices in 1949, the CCC had nearly exhausted its $4.7 billion borrowing capacity, forcing the Administration to request an additional $2 billion for 1950. The largest corn carry-over in all history threatened hard times in the Middle West, and the nearly 300 million bushels of wheat under government loan would no doubt be augmented by new surpluses in the coming season. Potatoes were still a national scandal, soon to be joined by eggs, butter, and other perishable commodities benefiting from mandatory supports. Faced by the prospect of overproduction in 1950, the government decreed acreage allotments for all basic commodities, thus inaugurating a new era of restrictionism. The gloom generated by the obvious inadequacy of current farm policies was Brannan's best hope. "From this atmosphere of frustration and desperation," one reporter wrote, "the Brannan Plan, so far given short shrift by Congress, appears to be drawing a little nourishment."[34]

In 1950 Brannan confined his legislative efforts to potatoes. Senator Thomas dutifully introduced a bill to provide production payments, along with marketing quotas, on the 1951 crop. When the Senate refused to grant even this small concession to the Administration's program, discussion of the Brannan Plan virtually ended for the rest of the session. Meanwhile Representative Harold Cooley, chairman of the House Committee on Agriculture and once a supporter of the Brannan Plan, announced that he was withdrawing support from the Administration's proposals and would henceforth

[34] For description of agriculture's situation at beginning of 1950, see testimony of Secretary Brannan, "Borrowing Power of Commodity Credit Corporation," Hearings before Committee on Agriculture and Forestry, U.S. Senate, 81st Cong., 2nd sess., pp. 2–28; for reporter's statement, see *New York Times*, March 19, 1950, p. E7.

work to make existing programs a success. Still worse, Representative Pace decided to retire from Congress at the conclusion of the Eighty-first Congress, leaving Rayburn without a single lieutenant to direct the Administration's farm policies. Among influential farm Democrats in the Senate, only Elmer Thomas had been willing to link his name to the Brannan Plan, and he, too, was serving his last year in Congress.[35]

Truman would still not give up. As signs of favorable grass roots support for the Brannan Plan began to appear, the Administration hoped for vindication at the November elections. Early in June the Administration's program scored its first political success, when Albert Loveland, Brannan's Under Secretary, won the Democratic nomination for United States Senator in the Iowa primary on a pro-Brannan Plan platform. But in the last week of June 1950, the North Korean armies snuffed out Brannan's last bit of hope. Suddenly the surpluses of yesterday became essential material for fighting the Korean War. Even the potato problem, Brannan's invaluable bad example, passed into history. Farm prices surged upward, full production became a military necessity, and new problems, for which the Brannan Plan was no solution, appeared overnight.[36]

Another war casualty was the farmer-labor alliance that Truman had hoped to cement with the Brannan Plan. Vote your pocketbook, he told audiences in the 1950 congressional campaign. Vote Democrat. But the rhetoric of 1948 no longer spoke to the deepest fears of the nation. As in 1946, inflation anxieties hurt the Democrats in farm areas, but more important were frustration over the fall of China, doubt about the

[35] For Senator Thomas' bill, see "Marketing Quotas for Irish Potatoes," Hearings before Committee on Agriculture and Forestry, U.S. Senate, 81st Cong., 2nd sess., pp. 1–6; on loss of key farm leaders in Congress, see *New York Times*, April 6, 1950, p. 22.

[36] On Loveland's primary victory, see *New York Times*, June 7, 1950, p. 23.

THE BRANNAN PLAN

conduct of the war, memories of Alger Hiss, evidence of Democratic corruption in the big cities, and belief that the answer to betrayal from within was McCarthyism. The Republicans hardly scored a rout, but they won twenty-eight seats in the House and five in the Senate. Significantly, the Republicans wiped out midwestern gains that Democrats had made in 1948. Republican senatorial candidates in Ohio, Illinois, Iowa, and Wisconsin scored landslide victories. In Iowa, loser Loveland, who had planned in June to fight his campaign on the Brannan Plan, faced such changed conditions in the autumn that he hardly mentioned the issue at all. Elsewhere other farm Democrats tried to ignore the Administration's farm program but went down to defeat nevertheless. "The Brannan Plan," said *U.S. News and World Report*, ". . . with little chance before the voting, had virtually none after the votes were counted." Thus farmers returned to the Republican party, the alliance with labor became only a fond memory, and the Brannan Plan suffered premature oblivion.[37]

[37] On Truman's appeal for votes according to pocketbook, see "After the Deluge," *New Republic*, 123:6–7 (Nov. 20, 1950); for a good discussion of the issues of the 1950 campaign and the quotation declaring end of Brannan Plan's chances, see "Trouble Ahead for Truman," *U.S. News and World Report*, 29:14–16 (Nov. 17, 1950).

10   THE KOREAN WAR

𝕫𝕡 During the unhappy years of the Korean War, Americans who tried to make sense of the contemporary scene were baffled. Korea was war, and yet it was not. The nation was rearming, but only partially. United Nations troops knew both victory and defeat, but ultimately were denied either. Amid unparalleled prosperity, citizens at home suffered uneasiness and discontent without quite knowing why. In their confusion men turned often to history, hoping by analogy to understand the present and to devise policies able to cope with it. For American agriculture in this period, absorbed first in the problems of inflation and then with presidential politics, the past proved a poor guide. As the country began to turn plowshares back into swords, the inflationary pressures that created OPA in an earlier war seemed to reappear, but only slowly did policy-makers learn that 1951 was not 1942. In the 1952 campaign for the presidency, the memory of the past also misled politicians unable to escape obsession with the farmers' revolt of 1948. It became clear only at the end of the War that the inflation and politics of the Korean period had a distinctive character all their own.

In the first months of the Korean War Americans had one chief domestic anxiety—inflation. On June 23, 1950, as the nation enjoyed a last few hours of peace, the wholesale commodity index stood at 264. During the first week of fighting, it leaped to 269 and by the end of July, it was 303.1. Wholesale food prices, up 13 percent in five weeks, led the advance. Lagging behind as usual, the consumers' price index nevertheless rose menacingly from 170.2 in June to 172.5 in July. In the first months, of course, scare buying rather than any genuine shortages were inflating prices. Memories of World War II tripled sugar sales in New York and increased purchases of tires by 700 percent in Fort Worth. On July 13, 1950, President Truman attempted to allay the nation's worst fear: "There is no prospect of any food shortages in this country at any time," he said.[1]

A week later, in his special message to Congress on Korea, the President asked for a ten-billion-dollar additional appropriation for defense and an end to limitation of military manpower. To assist him in mobilizing the economy, Truman asked for authority to allocate scarce materials, power to restrain credit, and money for loans to help defense industries. Heavy taxes would be needed to finance the war and curb inflation. Significantly, Truman made no mention of price and wage controls. That evening, looking grim and aroused, the President went on television to denounce hoarding. "If I had thought that we were actually threatened by shortages of essential consumer goods," he said, "I should have recommended that price and wage control and rationing be immediately instituted . . . If prices rise unduly because of excessive buying or speculation . . . I will not hesitate to recommend rationing and price control."[2]

[1] On movements of wholesale commodity index, see *New York Times*, Aug. 13, 1950, p. 2E; on consumers' price index, see U.S. Dept. of Labor, *Monthly Labor Review*, 73:118 (July 1951); on scare buying, see *New York Times*, July 23, 1950, p. 2E; for Truman's assurances on food supply, Transcript of press conference, July 13, 1950, Records of White House Reporter, TP, TL.

[2] For Truman's special message, see *Congressional Record*, 81st Cong., 2nd sess., vol. 96, pt. 8, 10626–10630; for his radio speech to the nation, see *Vital Speeches*, 16:610–612 (Aug. 1, 1950).

Though many congressmen regretted Truman's failure to ask for full control authority, the House and Senate were on the verge of passing the Defense Production Act of 1950 in substantially the form requested by the President, when, on July 26, Bernard Baruch, the eighty-year-old sage, offered his testimony to the Senate Banking and Currency Committee. Baruch had been the successful head of the War Industries Board in World War I and an adviser to the Office of War Mobilization in World War II. "The bill," Baruch told the respectful Senators, "is an invitation to inflation . . . A system of priorities [for scarce materials] without price control is a foundation built on shifting sand." If defense agencies took large quantities of materials in short supply, a free market would bid up what was left to dangerous heights. When Illinois's Senator Paul Douglas pointed out that the President's request for ten billion dollars more for defense was only 4 percent of the national income, hardly enough to justify blanket price control, Baruch made it clear that in his view, the President's policy of partial mobilization was inadequate. According to columnist Arthur Krock, Baruch had "electrified Congress by the voltage of an idea." Republicans as well as Democrats began to clamor for price controls. As Administration stalwarts swayed before the pressure, Truman let it be known that he would approve stand-by price and wage controls if Congress insisted on putting them in the bill. Passed in September, 1950, the Defense Production Act included stand-by authority to curb prices and wages. A provision exempting from price control those farm products selling below parity prices assured farmers their usual special treatment.[3]

[3] For Baruch's testimony, see "Defense Production Act of 1950," Hearings before the Committee on Banking and Currency, U.S. Senate, 81st Cong., 2nd sess., pp. 97–108; for Krock's comment, see *New York Times*, July 30, 1950, p. 3E; for Truman's reluctant acceptance of price control authority, Truman to Bruce Spence, Aug. 1, 1950, file

In the months that followed, the price level rose and fell according to the fortunes of war. From the beginning, many economists (including Senator Douglas), argued that direct controls over all prices and wages were too severe a remedy for current conditions and that indirect controls, principally higher taxes to drain off excess buying power, would probably suffice. And, indeed, as the North Koreans were halted in August and then routed in September, scare buying slackened and price rises slowed down. It seemed for a time that Truman would never have to resort to price control. But Chinese intervention in November, 1950, initiated a new buying wave, and the upward trend resumed. From June, 1950, to January, 1951, the consumers' price index showed retail prices in general up 6.6 percent and retail food prices up 9.3. Under heavy pressure from anxious workers, nearly every major manufacturing industry had granted wage increases, causing average hourly earnings to rise 7 percent in the last six months of 1950. The inflationary spiral, it appeared, was well launched.[4]

On September 9, 1950, Truman named as his Economic Stabilizer, Alan Valentine, an educator with little experience either in business or politics. Not until November 30 did Valentine appoint Michael V. DiSalle, former mayor of Toledo, Ohio, to head the Office of Price Stabilization (OPS), and only in early January did Valentine delegate any real powers to DiSalle. Valentine hoped that appeals to the public spirit

---

IV A 1a, ERS, ESA, Ag. Hist. Br., USDA; for text of the Act, see *Congressional Record,* same sess., vol. 96, pt. 10, 14120–14128.

[4] For views of Senator Douglas, see the "Separate Statement" appended to Report No. 2250, *Senate Miscellaneous Reports,* V, 81st Cong., 2nd sess.; for views of a professional economist, see H. Gordon Hayes, "How to Control Prices," *Nation,* 172:106–108 (Feb. 3, 1951); on consumers' price index, see U.S. Department of Labor, BLS, *Consumers' Price Index and Retail Food Prices,* Jan. 15, 1951, issued March 2, 1951; on wage increase, see U.S. Dept. of Labor, *Monthly Labor Review,* 73:117 (July 1951).

of the business community would hold prices down, but by mid-December, voluntary methods had obviously failed. On December 16, 1950, amid what seemed a deteriorating military and economic situation, President Truman declared a national emergency and appointed Charles E. Wilson of General Electric (not to be confused with Charles E. Wilson of General Motors) to the post of Defense Mobilizer with vast powers over the economy and authority over Valentine. Valentine, in truth, distrusted controls on principle and had, according to his critics, deliberately failed to recruit a staff in order to avoid exercising real power. In January, 1951, when DiSalle received authority to halt the price spiral, he challenged Valentine's policies. Droll and good humored, DiSalle would also reveal in the months ahead remarkable strength and shrewdness. He now proposed an immediate thirty-day freeze of all prices and wages but was turned down by Valentine. Wilson, however, intervened on behalf of DiSalle's proposal, and Valentine resigned. By January 25, 1951, the Administration was ready to act.[5]

"Government stabilizers announced their price-wage freeze tonight," reported the *New York Times*, "at a rough and tumble news conference that outdid Hollywood's wildest conceptions of newspapering." With one hundred shouting newspapermen and photographers jammed into the ornate room usually reserved for the President's own press conferences, DiSalle attempted to explain his freeze order. Contrary to expectation, he did not roll back prices to December 1,

---

[5] On Valentine, see Willard Shelton, "The Warm Freeze," *Nation*, 17:689–691 (Dec. 30, 1950); for Truman's proclamation of a national emergency, see Proclamation 2914 (Dec. 16, 1950), *Code of Federal Regulations*, III, 1949–1953 Compilation, 99–100; for Truman's announcement of creation of Office of Defense Mobilization, see text of his address to the nation on Dec. 16, 1951, *Congressional Record*, 81st Cong., vol. 96, pt. 18, A7839–7841; on DiSalle's proposed freeze and Valentine's resignation, see "The Shape of Things," *Nation*, 172:69 (Jan. 27, 1951).

1950, but allowed businessmen to charge the highest price they had asked between December 19, 1950, and January 25, 1951. Except, of course, for food, the freeze applied to all levels—production, wholesaling, and retailing—and would last until OPS issued specific price regulations for each industry.[6]

The long series of political headaches that price and wage controls brought the Administration began immediately. Businessmen were relieved because OPS did not roll back prices, but consumer groups and organized labor complained bitterly. When DiSalle and Wilson began to remove inequities from the freeze order and to issue specific regulations, labor winced at the generous treatment accorded business. Convinced in the late winter of 1951 that the only real controls were on wages, labor temporarily boycotted the whole mobilization program. "In the broader picture," said the *New York Times,* "there is likely to be a bitter struggle between labor and farmers." Since labor wanted lower food prices, it campaigned for deletion of the parity provisions from the Defense Production Act. On the other hand, farmers opposed the whole concept of OPS and freely threatened to sell in black markets. Echoing the rhetoric of 1946, Allan Kline of the Farm Bureau said that controls "contradict the fundamental principle of initiative and reward under our system. Price control is not the American way."[7]

The tragedy of it all was that price controls proved unnecessary. The Administration made a great mistake in 1951 —a mistake caused by a fundamental misconception and by unexpected short-term developments. Bernard Baruch had

[6] *New York Times,* Jan. 27, 1951, p. 4; for DiSalle's freeze order, see *Federal Register,* 16:808–816 (Jan. 30, 1951).

[7] For a report on labor and consumer protest over the freeze order and business approval, see *New York Times,* Jan. 28, 1951, p. 1E; on labor's boycott of stabilization program, see *New York Times,* March 1, 1951, p. 2E; for prediction of farmer-labor conflict, see *New York Times,* Jan. 29, 1951, p. 1E; for Kline's remarks, see *New York Times,* Jan. 28, 1951, p. 48.

called for price controls to accompany an all-out war mobilization, but the nation had embarked only on partial
mobilization. The rise in defense spending from $38.3 billion
in 1950 to $56.8 billion in 1951 was insufficient fuel to main-
tain a rampant inflation, especially since other factors emerged
after the general freeze order to curtail inflationary pressures.
Neither Truman nor DiSalle could be blamed, of course, for
failing to foresee that stalemate between Chinese and United
Nations troops would soon occur; that consequently, panic
buying would cease; that retail merchants, holding heavy
inventories, would then cut back their orders; that the public
would fool all forecasters by saving an amazing 9 percent of
its income in the last three quarters of 1951 (compared to
4 percent in 1950); and that the federal deficit would not
reach the dangerous level forecast in the beginning of the
year. As wholesale prices declined, consumer price rises
slowed down, so that by the end of 1951, the consumers'
price index was only 2.6 percent above January—a happy
circumstance having little to do with the efforts of OPS.
Compounding its errors in prophecy, the Administration continued to insist after inflationary pressure abated that the
economy was in a temporary lull and would soon be threatened again. But inflation never did return. (The consumers'
price index rose only 1.3 percent in 1952.) The Administration,
however, kept up a constant vigil on behalf of a generally
ungrateful country.[8]

While the true direction of the economy was still obscure,
OPS launched a gallant struggle against the nonexistent inflation. Regarding rising food prices as its main problem,

---

[8] For reasons why no serious inflation developed in 1951, see Council
of Economic Advisers, *The Economic Report of the President* (Washington: Government Printing Office, 1952), transmitted to Congress,
Jan., 1952, pp. 46–47, 55–63, 73–74, 88–89; for price stability in 1952,
see *Economic Report of the President* (1953), transmitted Jan. 1953,
pp. 35–37, 39–41.

OPS faced three particularly vexing puzzles: what to do about parity, cotton, and cattle. As even casual newspaper readers knew, farmers whose products were selling below parity were free of price control. Moreover, processors and distributors of these commodities could raise their own prices whenever higher farm prices added to their costs. To labor and the urban press, the parity loophole was the great weakness in the price control program. At first it seemed that the Administration itself would lead the fight to purge price control authority of the offending provision. If the parity concept interfered "with efforts to secure economic stability," said DiSalle, "we shall have no other recourse than to recommend its modification." According to its more extreme critics, the parity provision might keep most food prices permanently controlled. As farm prices rose, they would add costs to other industries, which would have to raise their prices, thus lifting the parity index higher and permitting farm prices to keep rising. Only a freeze of the parity index could halt the cycle. Speaking within the Administration on behalf of the farmer, Secretary Brannan took a different view. Since the government had decided to allow cost of living increases for labor and higher profits for business, equity required that farmers have an escalator too. Only if wages and prices were really frozen, said Brannan, would he support a freeze of parity. In the end the Administration merely proposed that parity prices be calculated once a year instead of once a month, so that rising farm costs would not immediately be reflected in higher parity prices. Though the *New York Times* thought this an "empty gesture," Congress refused to tamper with the sacred parity principle even to this small extent.[9]

[9] For a critique of the parity provision, see Louis J. Walinsky, "Price Control: A Critical Review," *New Republic*, 124:141 (May 28, 1951); DiSalle's remarks on parity provision are quoted in Keith Hutchison, "DiSalle's Worst Headache," *Nation*, 172:206 (March 3,

Farm products selling above parity in 1951 (cattle, sheep, hogs, cotton, wool, rice, and prunes) proved an even tougher problem than those selling below. Though DiSalle could legally have frozen the prices of these commodities at the farm, he chose not to do so for "reasons of administrative impracticality." Instead he froze prices at the processor and distributor level, so that, for instance, if cattle prices rose, meat slaughterers would have to absorb the increased costs rather than pass them on in the form of higher processor prices. OPS hoped that economic necessity would force processors to refrain from entering into competitive bidding against each other for supplies and so keep down prices on the farm. But in the case of cotton and cattle, scarcity of supply seemed certain to wreck OPS hopes and drive up prices at the farm level, even though processors would be caught in a squeeze between their own frozen prices and rising costs.[10]

A bumper crop in 1949 had yielded over 16 million bales of cotton and left the nation a 6.8-million-bale carry-over. But in 1950 bad weather and other factors resulted in a crop of slightly less than 10 million bales. After the Korean War began, domestic and foreign demand for cotton became heavy, much heavier than 1950 supplies could meet. Prices shot up to peaks unknown since the Civil War—from 26.5 cents per pound in January, 1950, to 45 cents in January, 1951. In September, 1950, Brannan tried to assure adequate domestic supplies and keep prices down by imposing strict export restrictions on cotton, an action that so angered the cotton bloc in Congress that Brannan soon found it politic to ease restrictions in response to Southern demands. A few

1951); for Brannan's position on a freeze of parity, Brannan to Charles E. Wilson, Feb. 15, 1951, Prices 1 file, Records of Office of Sec. of Ag., Gen'l Cor., N.A.; for *Times's* phrase on suggested change of parity calculation, see *New York Times,* April 27, 1951, p. 22.

[10] See DiSalle's freeze order, *Federal Register* 16:808–816 (Jan. 30, 1951).

months later DiSalle's general freeze played havoc with the complexities of cotton trading, and the nation's cotton exchanges closed down to await clarifying instructions from Washington.

DiSalle believed that if raw cotton prices kept rising, textile manufacturers, operating under frozen prices, would be driven out of business. After the end of World War II, OPA, too, had faced a cotton shortage. Bowles had then contemplated ceilings on raw cotton, but retreated in the face of congressional opposition. Convinced that cotton prices might now go beyond 50 cents a pound, DiSalle decided to attempt what even Chester Bowles had feared to do. Though angry Southern congressmen beseiged the White House and Brannan strongly disapproved, DiSalle defied them all and, on March 8, forbade any seller of cotton futures to ask more than 45.39 cents per pound—in effect placing a ceiling on raw cotton. The cotton exchanges grumbled but opened their doors. Cotton congressmen proved less tractable. Warning that it meant "the socialization of agriculture," Senator Burnet R. Maybank of South Carolina, chairman of the Banking and Currency Committee, threatened "something drastic" unless the order were revoked. Mississippi's Representative John E. Rankin denounced "the communistic mistreatment that the cotton growers are now receiving at the hands of the Federal Government." Claiming that controls were unworkable and would discourage production, cotton congressmen girded themselves for war. DiSalle, to his credit, never flinched. But before the battle really began, cotton prices began to sag, and the congressmen lost interest. In a few months, estimates of a huge 1951 crop led to a break in the market, and cotton prices never again threatened to press against the ceiling. In May, 1952, OPS suspended controls on raw cotton. Thus events in the market place rendered DiSalle's heroism unnecessary. He had earned the enmity of powerful cotton interests on behalf of a cotton order that was never needed.[11]

Swollen demand, rather than shrunken supply, provoked the inflation of cattle prices. Beef supplies per capita in 1950 were little different from 1949, but expanding consumer income, decreasing unemployment and the boom psychology led consumers to demand more steaks and roasts. To a public highly sensitive to meat prices—the housewife's personal inflation barometer—the 15 percent jump in beef at retail during the first eight months of the Korean War was a real crisis. Beef-eaters were not satisfied with the freeze of January, 1951; they demanded a rollback of beef prices at retail. Price stabilizers, however, soon became more worried about slaughterers and packers than about consumers. Operating under frozen price ceilings, processors suffered real hardships as uncontrolled live cattle prices climbed from $27.00 per hundred pounds in January, 1951, to $30.20 in April. The danger was that slaughterers would be forced to charge black market prices to their customers, incidentally obtaining

[11] For cotton production and carry-over figures, USDA, "Facts about the Cotton Situation," Dec., 1950, Records of Office of Sec. of Ag., Gen'l Cor., N.A.; on cotton prices, C. J. McCormick to Lindley Beckworth, Jan. 11, 1951, cotton file, Records of Office of Sec. of Ag., Gen'l Cor., N.A.; on Brannan's attempt to place curbs on cotton exports and his retreat in the face of congressional opposition, see "Cotton Prices Zooming," Newsweek, 36:69 (Dec. 4, 1950); on shutdown of cotton exchanges, see New York Times, Feb. 11, 1951, p. 1F; on DiSalle's fears that cotton prices might go above fifty cents, see "Defense Production Act: Progress Report No. 5," Hearings before Joint Committee on Defense Production, 82nd Congress, 1st sess., p. 159; for Brannan's opposition to DiSalle's cotton order, see Brannan to DiSalle, Feb. 24, 1951, Cotton file, Records of Office of Sec. of Ag., Gen'l Cor., N.A.; for DiSalle's cotton orders, see Federal Register, 16:2060–2063, 2150–2151 (March 6 and March 8, 1951); for Senator Maybank's remarks, see New York Times, March 5, 1951, p. 16; for Rankin's comment, see Congressional Record, 82nd Cong., 1st sess., vol. 97, pt. 2, 1945; on large 1951 crop and price decline, see New York Times, Aug. 12, 1951, p. 1F; for suspension of the cotton order, see "Ceiling Price Regulation 8, Amendment 1," OPS, May 20, 1952, cotton file, Records of OPS, N.A.

sufficient funds to bid up live cattle even higher. OPS sought to eliminate black market operations by refusing to license new (and presumably dishonest) slaughterers and by decreeing slaughtering quotas so that black market operators could not obtain more than their usual share of cattle. By late February, 1951, New York slaughterers informed OPS that they could not pay the going price for live cattle and stay in business. As some slaughterers curtailed production, the big cities began to complain of meat shortages. DiSalle knew that the public would ultimately judge OPS on its meat performance. He knew, too, of the treacherous pitfalls that had brought ruin to the OPA. Heedless of the special interests that he might antagonize, DiSalle moved with customary boldness to solve the problem.[12]

Late in April, 1951, DiSalle announced that on May 21, he was putting ceilings on live cattle. On that day he would roll back cattle prices 10 percent to assure processors reasonable profit margins. Had DiSalle stopped there, he might have escaped without much damage. But despite doubts within his own agency, DiSalle went on to announce two more rollbacks on live cattle, each of 4½ percent, to take place August 1 and October 1—these rollbacks to be reflected in lower consumer prices. Within hours, telegrams from all segments of the meat industry deluged Congress to protest DiSalle's cattle order. The House Committee on Agriculture met hurriedly to approve a motion demanding repeal "without delay." In a matter of days, industry spokesmen arrived in Washington. ("I'm Chris Finkbeiner of the Little Rock Pack-

---

[12] For explanation of and supporting statistics on inflation of beef prices, see Secretary Brannan's testimony in "Beef Ceiling Price Regulations," Hearings before Committee on Agriculture, U.S. House of Representatives, 82nd Cong., 1st sess., pp. 153–172; for a discussion of OPS's slaughtering control regulation, see "Controls are Trying to Check This Rise," *Business Week* (Feb. 24, 1951), p. 26; on complaint of New York slaughterers, see *New York Times*, March 1, 1951, p. 1; for a report of meat shortages, *New York Times*, April 26, 1951, p. 1.

ing Co.," one lobbyist greeted a reporter. "We're up here to get controls off the meat industry.") Early in May, nineteen farm organizations rented the dining room of the National Press Club for a lavish cocktail and dinner party at which one hundred members of Congress and one hundred reporters gathered to learn about hardship down on the farm. Though in Washington the meat industry's crude lobbying met with only mixed success, cattlemen back home expressed their wrath more effectively. With the Defense Production Act due to expire on June 30, 1951, and Congress still debating its fate, cattlemen declared a producers' strike to win concessions or even to kill OPS.[13]

On May 21, 1951, when the first rollback took place, cattle marketings in Chicago were the smallest in the history of the stockyards for a Monday in May. Soon acres of pens stood empty, and Chicago slaughtering plunged to 42 percent of normal. When the Army requested sixteen million pounds of beef for delivery on June 6, packers offered to sell only six million. (Industry representatives told military people that if the Army would exert pressure for withdrawal of the beef rollbacks, Army orders would be filled the next day.) By June 7, however, having received assurances that Washington would heed their pleas, lobbyists returned home to spread the good news. By the time Truman went on the radio (June 14) to warn cattlemen that their tactics would not intimidate him, the strike was over. At no time did shortages reach the alarming dimensions of 1946. As the cattlemen expected, when Congress passed an emergency one-month

[13] For DiSalle's order, see *Federal Register,* 16:3696–3701 (May 1, 1951); on doubts within OPS about the second and third rollback orders, "History of Ceiling Price Regulation 24, Beef at Wholesale, 1951–1953," Operational History Papers, OPS (June 1953), Decentralized file of Various Directors, Records of OPS, N.A.; on demand of the House Agriculture Committee, see *New York Times,* May 3, 1951, p. 1; on activities of lobbyists, see *New York Times,* May 13, 1951, p. 10 E.

extension of the Defense Production Act, it tacked on an amendment forbidding any rollbacks during July. Farmers, it was clear, were going to defeat the stabilizers once again.[14]

In the month that followed, Congress debated the Defense Production Act, and as expected killed all but the first beef rollback. The legislators, however, wrought far worse damage. DiSalle's challenge to agricultural interests and the subsequent storms of protest had placed OPS on the defensive. "Lobbies did extraordinarily effective work against controls," the New York Times reported. "Representatives of cattlemen, farmers and various business groups consulted each other and supported each other's pet proposals. There were so many lobbyists milling around and buttonholing members in the corridors outside the House chambers last week that it was hard to walk through." "Beyond question," said the Times, "the single greatest force on Capitol Hill now is the farm bloc. It . . . can claim credit for knocking out many of the key props in the stabilization program."[15]

Late in July, with price controls due to expire in a matter of hours, Congress passed the Defense Production Act Amendments of 1951 and sent them to the President. Denouncing the bill as "the worst I ever had to sign," Truman approved it to save what little remained of price controls. Three provisions struck Truman as especially dangerous. First was the

[14] On cattle marketings on first day of the rollback, see New York Times, May 22, 1951, p. 26; on acres of empty pens, see New York Times, June 10, 1951, p. 2E; on volume of slaughtering in Chicago, "Beef Cattle Situation" (unsigned report), Files of J. W. Tapp, Records of OPS, N.A.; on the attempt of packers to apply pressure through the Army, McClanahan to DiSalle, June 13, 1951, Meat–Information file, Records of OPS, N.A.; on departure of the lobbyists, see New York Times, June 7, 1951, p. 1; on return of cattle to market, see New York Times, June 13, 1951, p. 1; for Truman's speech, see Vital Speeches, 17:549–552 (July 1, 1951); for passage of one-month extension of Defense Production Act, see Congressional Record, 82nd Cong., 1st sess., vol. 97, pt. 6, 7471–7475.

[15] New York Times, July 15, 1951, pp. 2E and 10E.

Capehart amendment which permitted producers to pass on in the form of higher prices all cost increases that had occurred in the thirteen months since Korea, whether or not the producer needed such relief. This amendment, said the President, "is like a bulldozer, crashing aimlessly through existing pricing formulas, leaving havoc in its wake." Next was the Herlong amendment, which guaranteed pre-Korean percentage mark-ups to wholesalers and retailers, thus inviting "America's two million distributors to become commission salesmen for inflation." But worst of all was the Butler–Hope amendment, ending slaughtering quotas on live animals.[16]

Those who spoke for the Butler–Hope amendment in Congress argued that quotas discouraged production because cattle feeders were always afraid that quotas would be filled before they were ready to go to market. In reply defenders of OPS noted how easily the government could and did adjust quotas upward whenever supply increased. Clinton Anderson reminded the Senate that experience during the days of OPA proved that quotas were indispensable in channeling meat to legitimate slaughterers. Opponents of slaughtering quotas likewise realized their importance to price control, and for that very reason struck quotas down.[17]

By mid-August, 1951, shady slaughterers, now free of quotas, began to bid up cattle prices and take more than their fair share of supply. By the end of the month, legitimate companies were flooding OPS with complaints about the

[16] For text of Defense Production Act amendments, see *Congressional Record*, 82nd Cong., 1st sess., pt. 7, 9141–9147; for Truman's remark that the bill was the "worst," see *New York Times*, Aug. 1, 1951, p. 12; for his description of the Capehart amendment, see Truman's statement on signing the bill in *Congressional Record*, same sess., pp. 9357–9358; for Truman's description of Herlong amendment, see his message to Congress explaining why he signed the bill, Senate Document No. 61, *Senate Miscellaneous Documents*, same Congress.

[17] For Senate debate on Butler–Hope amendment, see *Congressional Record*, 82nd Cong., 1st sess., pts. 5 and 6, 7245–7249, 7895–7913.

dearth of cattle at ceiling prices. On September 5, DiSalle took the extraordinary step of suspending price ceilings for the rest of the month for processors who, because they had obeyed OPS regulations, had been unable to buy 50 percent or more of their usual supply. At the end of September DiSalle began a massive enforcement drive to halt black markets. In one day DiSalle's agents invaded 500 slaughtering houses in 125 cities, catching 222 violators. The industry, said Di-Salle, was guilty of widespread "chiseling and sharp practices." The American Meat Institute replied that such statements were "the irresponsible ranting of a frustrated individual." When the Army could not find meat at ceiling prices, OPS announced its intention to requisition beef for the military from slaughterers killing more than their usual number of cattle. The Government even toyed with a scheme that would make it the sole buyer of live cattle. In the meantime, DiSalle kept pressure on Congress for re-enactment of slaughtering quotas.[18]

Then, overnight, the crisis ended. By November cattle came flooding into markets, and prices dropped of their own accord. Assured that rollbacks were over, cattle feeders had bought heavily during the summer and were ready for market by November. Ironically, the demands of the cattle industry in 1951 contributed to its near ruin by late 1952. By forcing abandonment of DiSalle's last two beef rollbacks, cattle growers prevented adjustment of beef prices to more reason-

[18] On appearance of black marketeers, OPS press release, Aug. 17, 1951, file V A 1b, ERS, ESA, Ag. Hist. Br., USDA; on suspension of price ceilings for legitimate slaughterers, OPS press release, Sept. 5, 1951, Livestock file, Records of Office of OPS, N.A.; for enforcement drive and DiSalle's criticism of the industry, see *New York Times*, Sept. 27, 1951, p. 1; for retort of the American Meat Institute, see "Why Price Control is Failing," *Newsweek*, 38:171 (Oct. 8, 1951); for announcement of intended requisitioning of beef, see *Federal Register*, 16:11958–11961 (Nov. 28, 1951); on consideration of Government as sole buyer, see *New York Times*, Oct. 25, 1951, p. 1.

able relationship with other livestock prices and encouraged overexpansion of cattle numbers. "There is no doubt," concludes the official summary of OPS cattle operations, "that ceilings . . . were accepted by cattle producers and feeders as some assurance that the high market levels would continue." By the end of 1952, live cattle were at record numbers, and prices, which had been 150 percent of parity in January, 1951, fell to 85 percent of parity in February, 1953.[19]

By late 1951 DiSalle's struggle with the meat industry was over. In a few months he would go back to running for office in Ohio. His energy and courage would have found little scope in an agency whose only function in 1952 was quiet vigilance and gradual decontrol of the economy.

As price control lost its importance, American agriculture turned to the great national game of presidential politics. For Secretary Brannan, the Korean period had so far been a gloomy one. The issues touching American farmers had been shaped by other men in departments other than his own. Occasionally he emerged from obscurity to issue a partisan appeal, hover around the edges of policy, or denounce his enemies as of old, but his audience dwindled and his headlines were few. With the defense effort largely in the hands of big businessmen, Brannan's counsel no longer carried authority at the White House. When, for instance, he tried to get defense funds for loans to help expand food production, Truman turned him down. Even in his own department the Secretary faced a revolt against his authority in the Production and Marketing Administration, a revolt quelled only when Brannan fired two top PMA officials. To compound Brannan's troubles, private warehouses storing government grain chiseled the CCC out of a few million dollars and

[19] "History of Ceiling Price Regulation 24, Beef at Wholesale 1951–1953," Operational History Paper, OPS (June 1953), Decentralized file of various directors, Records of OPS, N.A.

inspired gleeful Republicans to charge the Secretary with lax administration. Frustrated by these setbacks and anxious to resume his place in the first ranks of the political wars, Brannan sought to improve his fortunes through the Farm Family Policy Review.[20]

In January, 1951, Brannan created a committee to review all the programs of the Department in light of their contribution to the family farm. Participating in the work of the committee were members of every agency in the Department and representatives of many nongovernmental organizations such as the National Council of Churches, the National Catholic Rural Life Conference, the Association of Land Grant Colleges, the Grange, Farmers Union, and the Farm Bureau. After five months work, the committee completed a 121-page report (entitled *Farm Family Policy Review*) describing current departmental programs and tentatively suggesting some new ones. Sending the *Review*, on July 15, 1951, to employees in the states and counties, Brannan instructed them to conduct discussions on the document among grassroots farmers and then to report back on farmer reaction by September 15. The Secretary hoped to make the grassroots meetings into a crusade on behalf of that politically attractive symbol, the family farm—a crusade which he no doubt hoped would redound to the benefit of the Democratic party on the eve of an election year. But as one of Brannan's own bureau chiefs noted, the Department itself claimed that 98 percent of all American farms were family farms. "It is my conviction," said this critic, "that the whole project will flop

---

[20] For Brannan's request for defense funds, Brannan to the President, April 23, 1951, Farm Programs 7 file, Records of Office of Sec. of Ag., Gen'l Cor., N.A.; for Truman's rejection of the request, the President to Brannan, June 19, 1951, OF 212, TP, TL; on revolt within PMA, see *American Farm Bureau Newsletter*, April 9, 1951, p. 2; on warehouse scandal, USDA press release, "A Brief Factual Statement about So-Called 'Grain Conversion Cases,'" Feb. 28, 1952, OF 1, TP, TL.

as a crusade unless issues of the family farm are sharpened."²¹

Lack of precise purpose was the least of the *Review's* problems. In May, shortly before Brannan's special committee finished the *Farm Family Policy Review,* the Farm Bureau withdrew from participation and assailed the whole project. As long as the survey confined itself to Washington, the Farm Bureau had no objection, but any departmental excursion into the grassroots seemed a threat to the Bureau's claim that it alone knew what farmers really wanted. The *Review,* Allan Kline told the Department, "is fraught with danger. We have fundamental reservations with regard to a procedure whereby an administrative agency of the Government takes an active role in the developing of grass-roots support for public policy recommendations . . . It would appear to us to be difficult, probably impossible, for the Department to present a set of recommendations to local people all over the country without getting into a position where it would be . . . charged with trying to develop support for its own recommendations, on a political basis." Calculated to enrage the Farm Bureau and give substance to its charge of political intent was an underlined passage in the *Review* describing the advantages of production payments over conventional support operations. Production payments were, of course, a principal feature of the Brannan Plan.²²

By mid-summer, 1951, the Farm Bureau was deep in an energetic campaign to discredit the survey. On August 30, Roger Fleming, the Bureau's Washington representative, told an audience of county farm bureau presidents in Indianapolis,

²¹ See USDA, *Family Farm Policy Review* (Washington, 1951); for criticism of the project, C. C. Taylor to Sherman Johnson, Committees file, Records of BAE, N.A.

²² For a copy of Kline's letter, see "Reorganization of the Department of Agriculture," Hearings before Committee on Expenditures in Executive Departments, U.S. Senate, 82nd Cong., 1st sess., pp. 424–425; for discussion of production payments, *Family Farm Policy Review,* p. 45.

"Alger Hiss is one of the parents of the new farm program which Secretary of Agriculture Brannan is trying to impress on the nation's farmers through the *Family Farm Policy Review*." Congressmen began to report a rising volume of complaints against the project. But it was too late for Brannan to back down, and in August and September, 1951, small groups of farmers gathered throughout rural America in response to the Department's invitation.[23]

Supplied with too few copies of the *Review*, discouraged by its excessive bulk, and given only sixty days to report back to Washington, the grassroots meetings did little constructive work and were, in fact, politically harmful to the Administration. As the press duly reported, some of the meetings displayed open hostility both to the survey and to the programs of the Department. *Time* magazine enjoyed telling its readers about Bad Axe, Michigan, where two hundred farmers denounced Government soil conservation payments as socialism and voted unanimously to throw the *Review* out of the meeting. In Lee County, Arkansas, farmers opposed making the federal government into a "godfather of every farmer." In Mills County, Iowa, a meeting went on record against departmental attempts to initiate new policies, especially policies like the Brannan Plan. By a vote of 82–33, farmers in Rock County, Wisconsin, voted against soil conservation payments "for doing those things which are good farm practices anyway." In Rappahannock County, Virginia, fear of mounting Government debt led farmers to vote for abolition of all price supports. According to the Richmond *Times-Dispatch*, farmers throughout Virginia "have minced no words in expressing their rejection of this attempt to pull

[23] Fleming is quoted in Jean Begemen, "The Farm Bureau's Big Smear," *New Republic*, 125:11 (Oct. 15, 1951); for example of Congressional report of rising volume of criticism, see "Reorganization of Department of Agriculture," Senate hearings, 82nd Cong., 1st sess., p. 427.

the wool over their eyes and lead them to the slaughter in 1952." Attracting far less attention, hundreds of other meetings in the nation raised no protest against the survey or the Department's programs; but their reports proved a "hodge-podge," yielding no insights into the grassroots mind. Nevertheless Brannan announced that the survey was "highly successful" and that he might even call for more of them later. But no matter how brave his front, Brannan could not hide the fact of failure. The Farm Bureau had again proved too formidable a foe. Instead of entering 1952 leading a crusade on behalf of family farmers, Brannan found himself once more dodging brickbats tossed by Allan Kline.[24]

As 1952 began, Truman himself raised the issue that all sides believed would be politically crucial: the level of price supports. In his January message on the economy, Truman said, "the sliding scale in existing price support legislation has aroused concern in the minds of many farmers." Actually the Anderson–Gore Act of 1949 granted the Secretary of Agriculture considerable discretion in fixing support levels, and as long as Brannan ran the Department, supports would generally remain at 90 percent of parity. But some other secretary in another Administration might use the same authority to reduce price supports to a low of 75 percent. In June, 1952, Congress attached an amendment to the Defense Production Act requiring supports for basic commodities at

[24] "Farmers," *Time*, 58:25–26 (Sept. 17, 1951); for views of farmers in Lee County, see letter from committee on the *Review* to H. B. Piper in *Congressional Record*, 82nd Cong., 1st sess., vol. 97, pt. 15, A6087–6089; for minutes of Mills county meeting, see *Congressional Record*, same sess., pp. A5833–5836; on farmers of Rock County, see editorial from *Janesville Gazette* in *Congressional Record*, same sess., p. A5744; for committee report on Rappahannock farmers, see *Congressional Record*, same sess., pt. 14, pp. A5627–5628; for the editorial from *Richmond Times-Dispatch*, see *Congressional Record*, same sess., pp. A5528–5529; on description of the reports as a "hodge-podge," see *New York Times*, Oct. 14, 1951, p. 26; on Brannan's opinion that the survey was successful, see *New York Times*, Nov. 18, 1951, p. 64.

90 percent during the life of the Act. Since the Act was to expire in April of 1953, the protection would be merely for one year.[25]

On the eve of the national conventions, the House Committee on Agriculture decided that the moment for stronger legislation had arrived. First, the Committee proposed that the modernized parity formula, suspended by the Gore–Anderson Act, would continue in abeyance until 1956 for those basic commodities (corn, cotton, wheat) doing better under the old parity formula than they would under new parity. And second, the bill would make price supports at 90 percent of parity mandatory for all basic commodities through 1955. The House Committee claimed that its bill was a war measure, designed to encourage full production during the current emergency. Though the Farm Bureau and the Grange actively opposed the bill, the House renewed its allegiance to high supports 207–121. While Republicans from farm districts voted for the bill, Republicans as a whole voted against it 85 to 74. In the Senate, where a majority had long favored flexible supports, champions of 90 percent could do no better than win an extension of the delay of the new parity formula. In conference, the House conferees shrewdly altered their demands and proposed that 90 percent supports be continued only through 1954 instead of 1955 as originally provided. Since the Defense Production Act now assured farmers of 90 percent in 1953, the House was merely proposing to extend high supports for one additional year. After 1954, the Gore–Anderson Act, with its flexible support provisions, would finally become effective. The Senate conferees acquiesced, and on July 5, after only desultory opposition, the conference report won approval in the Senate

[25] For text of Truman's message on the economy, see *New York Times*, Jan. 17, 1952, p. 16; for text of the amendment requiring supports at 90%, see *Congressional Record*, 82nd Cong., 2nd sess., vol. 98, pt. 7, 8523.

without a record vote. Truman, of course, signed the bill into law. In an election year, no one was particularly anxious to stir up the farmers.[26]

"In November," said *Time*, "the farm vote probably will be crucial." Both parties agreed with this analysis. The 1948 farmers' revolt had left deep scars on the memory of the Republican party and Republicans determined to spare no efforts in making amends. In March Republican leaders from twenty-one midwestern and Rocky Mountain states met to organize a drive to bring out the farm vote. In May, Thomas E. Dewey, who understood better than most the importance of aggressive pursuit of farm voters, placed the Republicans on the offensive by charging Truman with having rigged farm prices in 1948. Untrue though it was, Republican orators were to repeat this charge endlessly in the coming months. The party, of course, found attack more congenial than formulating policy. At the Republican National Convention at Chicago, the platform committee found itself split on the question of high supports versus the sliding scale. The delegates decided not to write specific price support figures into the platform and instead devised a farm plank containing an evasion that was a masterpiece of its kind. Said the platform, "We favor a farm program aimed at full parity prices for all farm products in the market place . . . Our program should include commodity loans on all nonperishable products supported at the level necessary to maintain a balanced production. We do not believe in restrictions on the American farmer's ability to produce." If this means anything at all, a doubtful supposition, it is endorsement of the sliding scale. Less confusing was the platform's indictment of Administra-

[26] For views of House Committee on Agriculture, see Report No. 2188, *House Miscellaneous Reports*, III, 82nd Cong., 2nd sess.; for House vote, see *Congressional Record*, same sess., vol. 98, pt. 7, 8655–8656; for Senate debate and passage, see pp. 9513–9521; for text of conference committee report, see pp. 9653–9654.

tion policies. "We charge the present Administration with seeking to destroy the farmers' freedom . . . We condemn the Brannan Plan which aims to control the farmer and to socialize agriculture. We brand as unscrupulous the Administration's manipulation of grain markets in the 1948 election campaign." The convention's nominee, General Dwight Eisenhower, freely admitted his ignorance on farm matters and was expected, as a matter of course, to run on the platform.[27]

The task of the Democrats was much easier. In 1948 the party plank had endorsed flexible price supports, but Democrats had since become identified with high, rigid support levels. "The Democrats appeared to have a popular position here," observed the *New York Times*. The platform accordingly affirmed 90 percent supports. On the Brannan Plan, however, the farm plank kept silent, though Democrats pledged to "continue to advocate practical methods for extending price supports to other storables and to the producers of perishable commodities." The party's nominee, Governor Adlai E. Stevenson of Illinois, came from a leading corn state, but his views on agriculture were as little known as his opponent's. He could be expected, however, to accept the plank in his platform that seemed most likely to win him votes.[28]

The battle between Eisenhower and Stevenson for the farm vote began, and in a sense ended, on September 6, 1952, at Kasson, Minnesota, where the National Plowing Con-

[27] "The Powerful Paradox," *Time*, 60:15 (Aug. 11, 1952); on March meeting of farm Republicans see *New York Times*, March 9, 1952, p. 43; on Dewey's charge, see *New York Times*, May 16, 1952, p. 1; for party's platform, see Kirk H. Porter and Donald Bruce Johnson, *National Party Platforms, 1840–1960* (Urbana: University of Illinois Press, 1961), pp. 501–502; for Eisenhower's admission of ignorance on farm matters, see *New York Times*, June 17, 1952, p. 20.

[28] For quotation from the *Times*, see *New York Times*, July 15, 1952, p. 13; for Democratic platform, see Porter and Johnson, *National Party Platforms*, pp. 479–480; on the fact that Stevenson's views were little known, see *New York Times*, Aug. 17, 1952, p. 10E.

test attracted 100,000 attentive but undemonstrative farmers to hear the candidates. Eisenhower spoke first. Beginning like a good Republican, he sneered at the "agricrats" in Washington, who have grown "cynical and arrogant." They had intentionally spread panic by driving down grain prices in 1948, he said, and they are trying to scare farmers again by telling them that the Republicans will pull the rug from under the farmer. "Puro bunk," said Eisenhower. "Here and now," he went on, "without any 'ifs' or 'buts,' I say to you that I stand behind—and the Republican party stands behind —the price supports now on the books. This includes the amendment . . . to continue through 1954 the price supports on basic commodities at 90% of parity." With these few sentences Eisenhower upset the plans of his opponents and robbed them of their best farm issue. The General chose to ignore the equivocation framed at Chicago and end whatever embarrassment the platform might have caused him. Those like the leaders of the Farm Bureau who liked Ike in part because they expected him to endorse flexible supports were, however, acutely embarrassed. But they finally found a way to bend Eisenhower's Kasson speech in their own direction. By supporting the laws on the books, they said, Eisenhower was really supporting the Agricultural Act of 1949 and its flexible support provisions. But to the public and to farmers, Ike's pronouncement at Kasson had only one meaning: he, too, was for 90 percent.[29]

Addressing the same crowd a few hours later, Stevenson was at his eloquent best. While skywriters overhead spelled out the word "Ike," Stevenson told his audience, "I am not going to waste your time telling you in the political tradition all about how I, myself, am a farmer." Neither was he going

[29] For text of Eisenhower's speech, see *New York Times*, p. 70; for Farm Bureau's views, see *American Farm Bureau Newsletter*, Sept. 15, 1952, p. 1; and *Annual Report of the Secretary-Treasurer*, American Farm Bureau Federation, 1955.

to run, as Democrats had run for so long, against Herbert Hoover. He stood simply on the Democratic farm plank and its promise of 90 percent of parity. Stevenson tried hard to cope with the surprise that Eisenhower had sprung a few hours before. "I observed here this morning," he said, "that my distinguished opponent . . . evidently concluded to plow under the Republican platform altogether." But none of Stevenson's rhetoric could disguise the damage that Eisenhower had done him. A week later, when the *New York Times* regional correspondents reported from farm areas, they noted that price supports stood low on the list of issues that were troubling farmers.[30]

The Democrats had no intention of giving up the farm vote without a fight. If they could not run against Eisenhower, they could run against the platform, against the Republican record in Congress, and even against Herbert Hoover. At Fort Dodge, Iowa, on October 4, Stevenson told his audience how a majority of House Republicans had voted against 90 percent a few short months ago. Moreover, Stevenson reminded the crowd, Senator Taft "believes that General Eisenhower . . . will be for flexible farm support after the present two year agreement of 90% of parity is over . . . Senator Taft has, as you know, established himself as the greatest living authority on what General Eisenhower really thinks; and if he says that the General's honeymoon with the Democratic platform is going to be a short one, the rest of us can believe it." In the cliché of that day, while Stevenson was taking the high road, President Truman rode his campaign train on the low road. "Are you a farmer?" Truman asked at Fargo, North Dakota. "Then you'd better 'look out neighbor.' The men who are going to write the farm ticket for the Republican candi-

[30] For Stevenson at Kasson, see *New York Times*, Sept. 7, 1952, p. 1; for text of Stevenson's speech, p. 71; for views of regional correspondents, see *New York Times*, Sept. 14, 1952, p. E7.

date are no friends of yours. Do you own your own farm? Then you'd better 'look out neighbor.' The last time you had a Republican Administration, farm mortgages were being foreclosed so fast you couldn't count them." Meanwhile Democratic campaign managers throughout the farm belt beseiged national headquarters for more speakers to intensify the assault.[31]

Secretary Brannan spent sixty days touring fourteen states to boast of his party's achievements. Like all Democratic speakers, he hoped that in the end, people would vote their pocketbooks, and so he recited often the tale of how the Democrats had saved farmers in the Depression and were sponsoring their prosperity in the present. In addition he took pot shots at Eisenhower whenever the General criticized the Democrats on farm matters: "Your attempt [Brannan told the General publicly on October 16] . . . to keep your audience at Waco, Texas, in stitches by reading them excerpts from a Department of Agriculture bulletin on dishwashing shows a complete disregard for the millions of housewives who have not had the privilege of housekeepers or orderlies to do their chores and displays your customary eagerness to tell only a small part of the story." Eisenhower had also ridiculed a pamphlet entitled, "How to Choose and Use Dried Prunes." Brannan noted that this one "was published in cooperation with Land Grant Colleges and has been distributed to the public only through the colleges. As you probably know, your brother Milton is President of the Association of Land Grant Colleges." When Eisenhower criticized the PMA for political activity, Brannan retorted, "The fact that you are ignorant of what these patriotic and hardworking men are actually doing is no excuse for any form of slander."

[31] For text of Stevenson's speech at Fort Dodge, see *New York Times*, Oct. 5, 1952, p. 81; for text of Truman's speech at Fargo, see *New York Times*, Sept. 30, 1952, p. 28; on requests for more speakers in the farm belt, see *New York Times*, Oct. 5, 1952, p. 57.

Clumsy and humorless, these sallies largely went unnoticed.[32]

For his part, Eisenhower continued to make gains in his quest for the farm vote. On October 15, at Memphis, Tennessee, Ed O'Neal, a lifelong Democrat and the past president of the Farm Bureau Federation, introduced Eisenhower to a Southern farm audience. I am for him, O'Neal said, because "he is the best candidate for the good people of the South." A week later O'Neal issued an open letter to American farmers explaining in more detail his desertion of the Democrats. It was, he thought, time for a change in Washington. As for farm policy, it had been the work of both parties in Congress and had no place in the campaign. O'Neal then proceeded to flay the "infamous Brannan Plan."[33]

Two days before the election, the Republicans tried to strike the last blow. Like so much of this curious campaign, the last-minute accusations were actually inspired by the distant events of 1948. Senator Aiken of Vermont, a usually responsible Republican, telegraphed Eisenhower, "reports have reached me which indicate that the Administration has broken the price of corn by dumping an excessive amount of corn owned by the CCC in the market in recent months." Aiken also charged the Administration with having "organized a whispering campaign . . . falsely charging that a Republican Administration would not support farm prices. This is a shocking situation and looks like a twist to the 1948 election." Brannan replied that the price of corn had declined only seasonally. "The Government has little if any stocks of corn," he said, "and the sale thereof could not materially affect the

[32] USDA press release, letter from Brannan to Eisenhower, Oct. 16, 1952, McCune Master file, FUL; for Brannan's defense of PMA, USDA press release, letter from Brannan to Eisenhower, Oct. 29, 1952, same file.

[33] For a report on O'Neal's introduction of Eisenhower, see *New York Times*, Oct. 16, 1952, p. 22; O'Neal quotes from his remarks at Memphis and discusses his position in greater detail in "An Open Letter to American Farms from Ed O'Neal," Oct.. 23, 1952, David N. Lloyd files, TL.

market price of corn even if we were selling it, which we are not." But by November, no charge or countercharge could affect the Republican tide. Eisenhower swept the nation, and as the *New York Times* noted, "The farm vote was not a decisive factor in yesterday's general election."[34]

By depending on bread and butter issues to win the farm vote, Democrats were the victims of a serious miscalculation of the national mood. For months reporters from the grass-roots found that Korea was the great issue. "The Korean conflict," said one dispatch, "epitomizes all the searchings uppermost in rural voters' minds." James Reston reported a few days before the election that Eisenhower "has gained great strength among the farmers . . . and it is generally agreed that the main reason for this has been that Korea has demonstrated the Republican slogan that it's time for a change." Korea, however, was a symbol as well as an issue. The spy scare, the fall of China, the explosion of the Russian A-bomb, the rise of Senator McCarthy, the seeming prevalence of crime and corruption created a national malaise, a mood of self-doubt and frustration already evident in 1950 and now focusing on the war. Interest group politics rooted in the New Deal, so important in the first Truman Administration, no longer gave expression to the nation's deepest anxieties. Thus the campaign waged by both parties for the farm vote spoke to fears long since departed in words no longer relevant.[35]

Shortly after his party's defeat, Brannan sent a questionnaire to men in farm states whose "judgment in the past have made them reliable political observers." Brannan wanted to know why the Democrats had lost in 1952. Among the twenty replies was one from H. E. Hazen, state chairman of the

[34] For Aiken's charge and Brannan's reply, see *New York Times*, Nov. 3, 1952, pp. 1 and 12; for the quotation from the *Times*, see *New York Times*, Nov. 6, 1952, p. 35.

[35] For quotations from the reporters, see *New York Times*, Nov. 2, 1952, pp. 58 and 3E.

Iowa PMA, who had written jubilantly to President Truman four years before to tell how his organization had helped carry Iowa for the Democrats. Hazen sounded the themes of most of the other respondents: "The strongest Republican issues," he wrote, "were Korea, corruption, and change." These issues made farmers and laborers forget the gains they had made under the Democrats. "We would say," he continued, "that none of the [farm] speeches had any great effect on the popular vote other than Eisenhower's at Kasson. The majority of Iowa farmers and laboring men seemed to take his assurances that no good thing would be lost and that he could and would do a better job in promoting the worthwhile things for the common man. The election most assuredly turned on non-farm issues."[36]

Amid the melancholy that is the companion of defeat, Truman returned to the rural peace of Independence, and Brannan went back to Denver to become an attorney for the Farmers Union. Behind them were eight of the most eventful and prosperous years in the history of American agriculture. Never had the productive genius of the American farmer been better rewarded nor made a more valuable instrument of national policy. Not the least of the achievements of that era was its fertility in the creation of new issues and arguments concerning the great American farm problem. The mid-1960's have seen a revival of some of the ideas formulated or popularized in the Truman Era. As the gap widens in developing countries between population growth and agricultural productivity, the abundance of American agriculture seems again a blessing rather than a curse. Reminiscent of the earlier period too are the current emphasis on parity income rather than parity price and the

[36] On sending the questionnaire to political observers in farm states, see unsigned note, 1952 election folder, McCune files, Denver; H. E. Hazen to Brannan, Jan. 6, 1953, 1952 election folder, same file.

adoption by Congress of the production payments so much maligned when Brannan first proposed them. As the liberals of the early postwar period once forecast, full production and farm prosperity may yet be reconciled. Indeed, with the approach of a world food crisis whose potential gravity recalls the famine years after World War II, the experience of policy-makers in the Truman years assumes an unwelcome relevance.

INDEX

INDEX

HARVARD HISTORICAL STUDIES

22. *Howard Levi Gray.* English Field Systems. 1959.

23. *Robert Howard Lord.* The Second Partition of Poland: A Study in Diplomatic History. 1915.

32. *Lawrence D. Steefel.* The Schleswig-Holstein Question. 1932.

33. *Lewis George Vander Velde.* The Presbyterian Churches and the Federal Union, 1861–1869. 1932.

34. *Howard Levi Gray.* The Influence of the Commons on Early Legislation. 1932.

37. *Roland Dennis Hussey.* The Caracas Company, 1728–1784: A Study in the History of Spanish Monopolistic Trade. 1934.

38. *Dwight Erwin Lee.* Great Britain and the Cyprus Convention Policy of 1878. 1934.

39. *Paul Rice Doolin.* The Fronde. 1935.

40. *Arthur McCandless Wilson.* French Foreign Policy during the Administration of Cardinal Fleury, 1726–1743. 1936.

41. *Harold Charles Deutsch.* The Genesis of Napoleonic Imperialism. 1938.

48. *Jack H. Hexter.* The Reign of King Pym. 1941.

60. *Robert G. L. Waite.* Vanguard of Nazism: The Free Corps Movement in Postwar Germany, 1918–1923. 1952.

62, 63. *John King Fairbank.* Trade and Diplomacy on the China Coast: The Opening of the Treaty Ports, 1842–1854. One-volume edition. 1964.

64. *Franklin L. Ford.* Robe and Sword: The Regrouping of the French Aristocracy after Louis XIV. 1953.

66. *Wallace Evan Davies.* Patriotism on Parade: The Story of Veterans' and Hereditary Organizations in America, 1783–1900. 1955.

67. *Harold Schwartz.* Samuel Gridley Howe: Social Reformer, 1801–1876. 1956.

68. *Bryce D. Lyon.* From Fief to Indenture: The Transition from Feudal to Non-Feudal Contract in Western Europe. 1957.

69. *Stanley J. Stein.* Vassouras: A Brazilian Coffee County, 1850–1900. 1957.

70. *Thomas F. McGann.* Argentina, the United States, and the Inter-American System, 1880–1914. 1957.

71. *Ernest R. May.* The World War and American Isolation, 1914–1917. 1959.

72. *John B. Blake.* Public Health in the Town of Boston, 1630–1822. 1959.

73. *Benjamin W. Labaree.* Patriots and Partisans: The Merchants of Newburyport, 1764–1815. 1962.

74. *Alexander Sedgwick.* The Ralliement in French Politics, 1890–1898. 1965.

75. *E. Ann Pottinger.* Napoleon III and the German Crisis, 1865–1866. 1966.

76. *Walter Goffart.* The Le Mans Forgeries: A Chapter from the History of Church Property in the Ninth Century. 1966.

77. *Daniel P. Resnick.* The White Terror and the Political Reaction after Waterloo. 1966.

78. *Giles Constable.* The Letters of Peter the Venerable. 1967.

79. *Lloyd E. Eastman.* Throne and Mandarins: China's Search for a Policy during the Sino-French Controversy, 1880–1865. 1967.

80. *Allen J. Matusow.* Farm Policies and Politics in the Truman Years. 1967.